THE

PSYCHOLOGICAL

MYSTIQUE

RETHINKING THEORY

GENERAL EDITOR

Gary Saul Morson

CONSULTING EDITORS

Robert Alter
Frederick Crews
John M. Ellis
Caryl Emerson

THE
PSYCHOLOGICAL

MYSTIQUE

STEWART JUSTMAN

NORTHWESTERN UNIVERSITY PRESS
EVANSTON, ILLINOIS

Northwestern University Press
Evanston, Illinois 60208-4210

Copyright © 1998 by Northwestern University Press.
Published 1998. All rights reserved.

A shorter version of chapter 2 appeared in
Social Research 61 (1994): 457–76.

Printed in the United States of America.

ISBN 0-8101-1601-4

Library of Congress Cataloging-in-Publication Data

Justman, Stewart.
    The psychological mystique / Stewart Justman.
       p.   cm.—(Rethinking theory)
    Includes bibliographical references and index.
    ISBN 0-8101-1601-4 (alk. paper)
    1. Psychology—Philosophy.   2. Ethnopsychology.   I. Title.
II. Series.
  BF38.J87 1998
  150'.1—dc21   98-29522
                                              CIP

To my son

Contents

Introduction

As novel as the popularity and cultural stature of therapy are, the idea of therapy traces back, like so much else, to Plato. According to Plato, philosophy itself is the corrective or cure — the *therapeia* — of human ignorance and confusion. As a therapy, philosophy "begins with diagnosis, and only thereafter supplies its distinctive method of release and transformation,"[1] which is also to say that it doesn't so much add to the number of things I know as change me, the knower, and bring me to a recognition of what I know obscurely already. The recovery of buried knowledge, the working-through of perplexity, the clearing of consciousness, even the overcoming of resistance to therapy itself: all of these now familiar elements of therapy have their beginnings in the wry method of Socrates, that physician of the soul.

Through Boethius's *Consolation of Philosophy* (A.D. 524) the idea of medicine for the mind exerted broad influence over the Christian culture of the Middle Ages. Condemned like Socrates on political charges and awaiting execution, the author is visited by the figure of Philosophy who works to cure his attachment to false goods like prosperity and fame. Again and again in the *Consolation* the medical analogy is used. Philosophy offers "medicine," acts as "physician," shows the despondent Boethius the causes of his "diseased condition," all to the end of freeing his mind from error's grip. One measure of the influence of this work is the stature of its translators: into French the brilliant poet Jean de Meun, into English Alfred the Great, Chaucer, Elizabeth I. And yet within the *Consolation* itself is a limitation on its influence. With its prescription for settling one's own confusions and mastering one's own desires, the *Consolation* inspires withdrawal into the fortress of self rather than the construction of a therapeutic program for others. Not until the "positive liberty" of self-mastery encountered more modern conceptions of freedom (and a number named in this study are concerned in that story) did efforts to extend therapy to the multitudes begin in earnest.[2]

1

The concept of therapy is nothing new. New are its popularization and the endeavor to mass-produce its benefits through the media, the schools, and the helping literature. This study argues that modern psychology, with its roots in Locke — a physician in fact — belongs to the technological paradigm that sponsored mass production in the first place; and it traces a technological expansion of Locke's project of curing vice and producing virtue. Secondarily it argues that those modern ideologies that, like Plato, call for "the revolutionizing of the entire mind" are breakaways from the Locke tradition and employ its techniques of production for other ends, and on a still higher scale.[3]

In one of his films Charlie Chaplin plays a glass fitter who makes work for himself by employing a waif to break windows. The glass shattered, the glazier is on hand to repair it. An alliance also exists, I believe, between the therapists who work to repair damage to the self and the society that provides their business. Far from being a temporary convenience though, the alliance has both depth and duration, for as a matter of history the introduction of psychological categories and the practice of medicine on the mind accompany the formation of modern commercial society. The aim of curing delusion and revealing the ways of the mind, as well as of forming the mind of the young in the first place, is written into the work of Locke. Not that he was the first to search the self. The Puritans made a practice of it. "Puritanism would make every man an expert psychologist," able to expose the deceits of his own mind.[4] If the Protestant ethic reflects Puritan practices of discipline as many believe, at the heart of those practices was self-examination, a kind of methodical worry about the self. It is when psychology is used to manage and mold others, as in the pedagogy of Locke — himself of Puritan descent — that its power as a technique really comes into play. And just as technique enables increases in the efficacy, scope, and scale of work, so the psychology that begins in self-discipline extends among Locke's successors to schemes for disciplining others by the thousands; while in our own seemingly far-from-puritanical culture, psychology is so tied in with the mass production of ideas and images that it has become a virtual consumer good in its own right.[5]

So it is that the psychology market has its own fashions and crazes.[6] Who today remembers the once popular *Psychological Care of Infant and Child* by John B. Watson, with its advice that mothers shake hands with their children instead of loving them to death? Or for that matter the once notorious fancies of B. F. Skinner, also a behaviorist? As with consumer goods per se, the passing of this or that psychological style in no way cools the enthusiasm for psychology itself. Never, though, has it had the popular standing it does today, enjoying at once the market of a beverage and the repute of a moral good. Such is the vogue of therapy that psychological counsel now pours out over the airwaves, as though any line between the public and intimate realms were a thing of the past. There are even television series *about* psychologists, comedies as it happens. Grown men and women clutching teddy bears flock to John Bradshaw to discover their inner child. A football team loses a big game and commentators talk about the wound to its psyche. The Dow Jones average crossing 6000 is acclaimed a psychological breakthrough. A professed sex addict turns psychologist in order to help others similarly afflicted. One of the O. J. Simpson trial jurors proposes group therapy to speed the jury's recovery from its ordeal. Someone goes amok with a gun and grief specialists show up to help with the healing process. A psychiatrist collects a fortune from Blue Cross for conducting group therapy sessions among a patient's 120 personalities, one of which is a duck.[7] A documentary on cats quotes experts on the psychology of cat ownership. Tobacco companies use psychology to get people smoking,[8] and smokers get help to stop. Students specialize in something called music therapy — it seems aroma therapy hasn't yet been accredited — while others have their false consciousness cured or their emotional injuries tended under the guise of academic work. Literature is taught in high school in order to "release [the student] from fears and obsessions."[9] The classroom is a clinic. People are locked up on the strength of the "recovered memories" of their accusers, and therapists press fabulous diagnoses, even of "satanic ritual abuse," on reluctant patients.[10] Their mainstream colleagues appear as experts in court, testifying on either side of the question, as if they really possessed the key to the mind. Television shows compete to name new psychological debilities, "compulsive shopping disorder" for one. Psychology is as much a part of the hustle of American life as sports psychology is of the crassness of professional sports. Were it not a clinical term itself, one might say America was addicted to psychology. With the mass circulation of its clichés, psychology undermines the very benefits that might have been expected of it, such as a lively sense of the poverty of mere formulas and a feeling for the responsibility we bear as individuals, the correlate and price of our uniqueness.

Considered by many the final arbiter of human questions (already there is talk that candidates for assisted suicide will have to get psychiatric clearance), psychology agrees only too well with the reductive tendencies of our culture. Perhaps there is no better evidence of belief in a psychological last word than the use of psychology as a trump card in argument. Opponents are not just wrong but ill. Those offended by homosexuality are diagnosed with a sickness called homophobia — poetic justice, perhaps, considering that not long ago homosexuality itself was deemed a disease, a neurosis. The deep reading of others has become an intellectual art, one practiced even in the face of witch-hunts that illustrate the dangers of fascination with a hidden truth. In a play that made a sensation in the days of McCarthy (and veiled a homosexual subtext) a woman demands of her husband, "Did it ever occur to you that you persecute in Tom . . . the thing you fear in yourself?" A stage direction reads, "She has hit close to the truth he has never let himself be conscious of."[11] Sign of an enlightened mind, the mildly psychoanalytic view contained in this remark has been further popularized in high school English classes where students explore the human psyche, a guiding theory being that literature exposes the fears that imprison us and make us into conformists and bigots. We project onto others what we shudder to confront in ourselves. So widely did this doctrine circulate in American society that Charles Manson, on trial for murder, was able to taunt the court with it. "I think that it is high time that you all start looking at yourselves, and judging the lie that you live in," he declared. "You can project it back at me . . . but I am only what lives inside each and every one of you."[12] A generation later, the "Unabomber," too, peered deep into the psyche, discoursing in his manifesto on the "demoralization, low self-esteem, inferiority feelings, defeatism, depression, anxiety, guilt, frustration, hostility" induced by the industrial order.[13] Just as his hatred of technology led him to make bombs, his challenge to the technological society was framed in its own favored jargon of psychology. With its pretension to medical status, psychology has in fact managed to trade on the repute of science as such. When Marxists treat incorrect thought like a medical problem or make to psychoanalyze the masses in order to expose what blinds them to their true interests, Americans see through their sham, as we do the "psychistic fallacy" that declares everything possible for Maoists of pure faith,[14] yet none of this seems to have shaken faith in our own therapeutic model or put in question the notion that psychology is the "open sesame" of human life.

The exorbitant influence of psychology stands in ironic contrast to the modesty of the author of the psychological paradigm itself. Locke believed the essence or constitution of physical things unknowable, and so I believe we should regard the core of a human being, for reasons both philosophical and moral. Respecting the unknowable, however, is contrary to the knowing tone of the mass media as well as the interests of the psychological culture.

What I find offensive in the psychological culture isn't just the painful banality of its clichés ("But how do you *feel* about it?") so much as the blaring of those clichés night and day — the violence done to the privacy of the self. With us the most private is public. It is the argument of Jürgen Habermas, however, that from the turn of the eighteenth century the modern public realm was a construction of private men. Again and again the reader of *The Structural Transformation of the Public Sphere* gets caught in seemingly impossible entanglements of the words "public" and "private."[15] But in discussing a culture where the ordeal of Clarissa Harlowe became a kind of public event, there may be no undoing such knots. Today's society, eager for tales of abuse, carries on the tradition of the readers of *Clarissa,* that psychological novel, savoring the violation of innocence with pretended horror. From Joseph Addison's deft work in building up the reading public and spreading Lockean views, to the publicity tactics of Freud's nephew Edward Bernays, psychology in any case has entered into the very framework of the public sphere. It is because I am concerned with the public credit enjoyed by psychology — its use as coin of the realm — that a chapter of this study is given to such a popularizer and middleman of ideas as Bernays.

Some may benefit from psychological or psychiatric treatment. What interests me is the propagation of psychological clichés and the cultural dominance of psychology itself, a stature out of proportion to its parenthetical place in medicine. Whence the inordinate influence of psychology? As inquiry into the genesis of our ideas placed psychology at the foundation of the human sciences, so mechanistic philosophy inspired the search for the "springs of action." Says Voltaire, "The passions are the wheels" making the machine of progress go.[16] In tracing the status of psychology back to Locke and the intellectual movement over which his name presided, my purpose isn't to vilify either. Locke's intellectual humility in particular seems to me highly admirable, and the Enlightenment spirit of inquiry indispensable to freedom itself. Neither Locke nor his successors intended the sort of psychological culture we now have, one where the personal responsibility that he and they insisted on[17] fades out like an archaism in its own right.

Indeed, a claim of this study is that around the same time the doctrine of unintended consequences was taking shape, Locke's own thought was being put to work on a scale he never imagined or intended. And it may have been the application, or projected application, of psychology by reformers in the humanitarian tradition that first magnified its role, raised it from a kind of obscure art to the master key to human existence. Only with the help of psychology would it be possible to cure children, the criminal, the multitude of undesirable habits and create a good and happy society. (This study, accordingly, looks into some attempts to activate Lockean psychology rather than into the vast perplex of eighteenth-century psychomedical theory.) Locke intends education for a few; James Mill dreams of educating humankind. "In psychology," writes his son and pupil John Stuart Mill, "his fundamental doctrine was the formation of all human character by circumstances, through the universal Principle of Association, and the consequent unlimited possibility of improving the moral and intellectual condition of mankind by education."[18] A physician like Locke cures some; the legislator, according to Jeremy Bentham, cures "millions at a time" — cures their minds.[19] Bentham's thought, moreover, great in its influence, became for some a creed. The social psychology of Auguste Comte was the annunciation of a new religion. That of Gabriel Tarde was "widely popularised" like a gospel in its own right.[20] Psychology in each case is more than just a body of theory or knowledge: it is something like the answer to the riddle of existence.

The notion that *technology* is the answer to all things of course receives great play just now, but as shown by the eighteenth-century concern with balancing one passion against another by a kind of engineering, psychology itself has roots in the technological paradigm. The argument that the desire for wealth could counteract the more dangerous passions of our nature was critical in raising the repute of commerce and establishing the commercial society. A "curative connotation" was bestowed on the pursuit of wealth.[21] Today psychology speaks of managing stress rather than setting a balance, of tapping potential rather than harnessing passion, but the line of descent seems clear enough. And being part of the technological model, psychology partakes of the popular success of the model itself and the production it underwrites. Those whose answer to everything, including the failure of therapy, is "more therapy" espouse, in fact, something like the logic of more and more that drives the production of consumer goods. In any event psychology goes hand in hand with the popularization of goods. The emergence of a literature designed to shape children's minds — and this in the spirit of Locke's theory of education, if on a new scale — reflected the vastly increased market for consumer goods in the early Industrial Revolution.[22] The new literature championed virtues like "industry" and was a consumer good itself. It was to play on the mind of the buying public that one of the great industrialists, Josiah Wedgwood, created the very elements of modern marketing. It was with the creation of a national market for consumer goods that Americans first discovered a kind of national appetite for psychology. The founder of behaviorism, John B. Watson, became a vice president at the J. Walter Thompson advertising agency. It was as a consultant to the Fortune 500 of his day that Bernays, the architect of public relations, worked his psychological magic. From the investigation of "the psychology of envy, competition, desire, and imaginary wants" by economic theorists at the time of Locke[23] to the rising demand for psychology itself in the affluent society, psychology has provided the very jargon of the consumer economy.

Possessing at once the potency of myth and the prestige of science (despite the fact that therapy takes place in secret, with results hard to determine, much less reproduce), psychology is thought capable of everything from recovering lost memories to helping pitchers regain their edge. As a sort of universal tool, it answers a technological society's fascination with solutions. It even decodes works of literature. Significantly, the birth of what some call the "literary criticism industry" coincided with the introduction of psychological methods into literary study in the 1950s; with the aid of this machinery it was possible to grind out readings of works in quantity, by analogy with the production of clever things by industry itself. As we read of "the use of psychological tools" in literary study, the terms themselves place us in the technological paradigm.[24] The atom had been split: so had the psychological atom, the self. But it bears remembering that the weapon dropped on Japan in 1945 in such a way as "to make a profound psychological impression on as many inhabitants as possible" was the result of the largest industrial project ever to that point undertaken.[25]

Psychology belongs to the technological paradigm: the same wish to get hold of the secrets of Nature that inspired Bacon's vision of scientific discovery and invention also inspires the probing of inner nature — the self. Even now pop psychology speaks of unlocking the "potential deep within you," by analogy with the secret of the universe unlocked, as it was said, by the atomic bomb. Through American society in general, indeed, runs a loose notion that the psychological atom has yielded up its secrets and an infinite potential now lies in our hands. As with the infinite promise of the atom per se, the uses of the new cosmic force turn out to be less than advertised. Presumed to be in touch with the workings of our own nature — what used to be called the springs of action — psychology becomes a tactic of influence. A political party, looking to market its program, takes a reading of the public mind. Slogans are tried out on test groups to see if they make them feel good or bad, and when it is discovered that people get nervous at talk of changing Medicare, a strategy team urges the phrase "preserving Medicare" instead.[26] (A stroke of subtlety in the tradition of Bernays, who pointed out that criticism of evacuation hospitals in World War I ceased when their name was changed to "evacuation posts.") The party can then go about changing Medicare under the banner of preserving it, a hoax equal in cynicism to the kind of manipulations practiced in societies where they don't worry much about pleasing the electorate. Like the use of psychological warfare in Vietnam — a subject to be taken up later — this exercise, so degrading, so crass, is no less an expression of the psychological ethos than the most caring psychotherapy; indeed, psychology and the theory and practice of human engineering grew up together.

Whether or not they succeed for a time, gambits like the use of "preserve" surely add to disgust with the entire public realm in the long run. And both parties play the psychology game, which might be likened to a race for a secret weapon that doesn't exist. Reporters are psychologists too. On National Public Radio tracts of news time are given to analyzing the public mind and foretelling the way people are going to react to this or that, a hollow exercise if only because the predictions are never followed up. By the time they were disproved they would be old news. Under the influence of the psychological model politicians stage their shams and reporters present their soundings of the public mind in place of events themselves. In either case real events recede.

A master manipulator of public perception and contributor to the psychologization of American life is, once again, Edward Bernays, whose rise to influence corresponded with big business's shift from indifference to public opinion to courtship of public favor. Nephew of Freud, Bernays had psychology in his blood and, in a 1928 article entitled "Manipulating Public Opinion," cited "the findings of introspective psychology" as the source of his insight into the public mind. I've said that the popularization of therapy reflects the rise of corporate power. This link is borne out in the story of Bernays contracting his services to General Electric, Bank of America, and countless other corporate powers even while playing on the psychological mystique and promoting, as he believed, the health of the nation. Bernays belongs to that moment when the unconscious was the talk of the town and reticence about sex came under attack as an unhealthy conspiracy of silence. Nevertheless (as I'll argue) in a deeper sense he belongs to the tradition that seeks to manage people by regulating their "impressions" — the Locke tradition. If Bernays promoted the health of an industrial society, a number of Locke's followers at the time of the Industrial Revolution, some of them physicians like himself, believed in the therapeutic effects of industrial discipline. Like Bernays they envisioned themselves men of benevolence manipulating others for their own good and advancing the cause of public health. As it happens, one of them also invented many of the tactics of modern salesmanship, including Bernays's favorite, the endorsement. Bernays was a modernist, but so were innovators like Josiah Wedgwood in their time — and they too were men of psychology, mechanistic psychology in this case. They too dreamed of forming the opinions of others, just as Bernays shared their ambition of "engineering . . . a good and happy life."[27] They and Bernays belong to different phases of a tradition concerned both with the rationalization of production and the cure of minds.

In Locke's theory of education these aims are one. That is, his educational method is designed both to generate an end product (or, as the author says, to make a gentleman) and to cure bad attitudes. "Cure" is his word. This study goes back to Locke because he did much to establish the therapeutic ideal that has since extended its reign over our culture. In the Lockean belief that "rational control can extend to the re-creation of our habits, and hence of ourselves,"[28] we discover the inspiration of all those therapies that call for the reconstruction of our very selves or, for that matter, promise "a new you." As the pop psychologists say, people "can change almost anything about themselves if they really want to."[29] More immediately, though, Locke's method of forming and reforming the habits of the child carried over into efforts to reform workers, criminals, and the poor, inside and out. And with the adaptation of his pedagogy on a larger scale in ways he never imagined or intended (such as in schemes to subject workers or paupers to a like kind of therapeutic conditioning), a new form of ideology comes into being. As production moves to the factory level, Locke's idea of making a gentleman is expanded into one of reforming the habits of the underclass and teaching them the virtues that industrial society calls for. Under the influence of Locke's psychology reformers seek to "educate" multitudes — a program of popularization that seems at last, in our own time, to have popularized psychology itself.[30]

Every one of the pedagogical tactics of Locke is intended to produce a given psychological effect. And so it is with his successors, even as they took his methods beyond his original intentions. Psychology is a means of influence and control.[31] Even before the seventeenth century, for that matter, it was a concern with "how to handle other human beings" that produced interest in psychology — most sensationally in the instance of Machiavelli.[32] Although the scandal of psychology broke out again in that English Machiavelli, Mandeville (also reviled as a teacher of evil for insisting that we choose between the precepts of Christian virtue and the good of the polity), the main line of the Locke tradition sought to influence and manage others in the name of the moral good of improvement. It was a shared belief of those progressives who created the very discourse of psychology in eighteenth-century Britain that "the mind could be comprehended scientifically, and could be controlled" accordingly.[33] As the rationalization of production breaks processes down into steps, so the management of others demands an understanding of the first principles of human motivation — the springs of action. Said Bacon: Who would master Nature must know how she works.

Few, I imagine, would deny that the theory of woman as nervous, given to "vapors" or hysteria, prey to illusion and fancy — in other words, as psychological case par excellence — served to justify restrictions *on* women. Nor do such measures require sinister intentions; benevolence will suffice. A fictional case in point appears in Charlotte Perkins Gilman's "The Yellow Wallpaper." Written in a remarkable jabbing prose, the story tells of a troubled wife whose physician-husband orders a regimen of mental rest that is worse than her disease, whatever it may be, and finally drives her mad. The husband, like an ideologue whose mind is locked fast, is so bound to the theory of nervous womanhood that he fails to see that his very benevolence has become his wife's affliction. There is also the famous case of Emma Bovary, read by some as a confirmation of their own received ideas about woman in spite of the author's contempt of received ideas as such. As Herbert Marcuse once remarked, in a liberal society Emma Bovary would end up with an understanding therapist. No such society exists within *Madame Bovary* of course, although the production of both things and ideas for popular consumption is already well begun, this being "the first novel to deal with what is now called mass culture."[34] A century later, in the psychological ascendancy that goes along with that of mass culture, Emma would be a neurotic housewife, successor of the victim of that form of hysteria once called in psychiatric textbooks *bovarysme*.[35] The condition of a fictional character — one who confuses fiction with life — was converted to clinical fact.

While psychology springs from the humanitarian tradition, the fascination with probing the innermost being of others, the free attribution to others of motives opaque to themselves, indeed the reduction of others to known quantities to be figured into calculations have conspired to make psychology a slight to human dignity in its own right. To the vast "political, commercial, scientific assaults on privacy that mark our century"[36] we must add the endeavor that targets the most private domain of all more directly than any other. When the knowing explain the mass slaughter of the Jews as the result of a death wish of the Jews themselves, we sense that psychology has introduced a new mode of indecency into human affairs, violating souls, as it were, rather than just graves.[37] Under the regime of psychology, the formerly controversial act of spying into the privacy of others is at once radicalized and endowed with the pretense of science.[38] Closely related to the rise of modern commerce to begin with, psychology has made popular a way of understanding as debased as many another output of the consumer society. Think only of such psychocommercial exploitations as *Sybil*, whose heroine was converted into a multiple personality in order to "make a sellable book"; *Fatal Vision*; or indeed the prurient psychodramas staged daily on television.[39]

Some might counter that the view of psychology as a slur on the self is slanted, that psychology also discloses riches of potential that others could never guess at, much less lay hold of. On this showing the self is a kind of Aladdin's cave where treasure lies waiting to be claimed. But it is the very disenchantment of the world that sends us in search of this charmed place: the romance of self is just the complement of the forces that strip value and meaning. Later I will sketch some of the damage done to the very language of value by the jargon of potential. The practical emphasis of pop psychology — how to realize your goal, overcome anxiety, win — is in any case a vivid reminder of the link between the magic of self and the technological mentality even today.[40] Written in the idiom of psychology, Martin Luther King's "Letter from Birmingham Jail" deplores insensitivity to the race problem; today "sensitivity training" is employed by corporations as a management tool, with employees acquiring the courage to feel as a job skill.[41] Chapter 5 of this study looks at a dreamlike work of fiction that seems to parallel the descent into self with the descent into Africa in the employ of a powerful corporation. A sense of the incommunicable privacy of experience (and it was Locke's belief that no one could really convey ideas to another) allows the narrator of *Heart of Darkness* to feel less implicated in the dirty business of the commercial assault on Africa than he really is. In this work the riches waiting to be claimed are ivory, and plunderers will do anything to get their hands on it. Psychological readers like to look for symbols. The "symbols" on the poles around Kurtz's station in *Heart of Darkness* turn out to be human heads.

Much as the heavily psychological tone of *Heart of Darkness* measures the narrator's complicity in colonialism, America's infatuation with the psychological indexes the manipulativeness of our way of life. Thought like Locke's, permeated with the language of *using*, helped establish the therapeutic program in the first place. A striking example of manipulation, Stanley Milgram's celebrated experiment on obedience to authority, furnishes the subject of my third chapter. Professing to have uncovered a disturbing tendency to submit to the commands of authority no matter how brutal, Milgram is squarely in the Locke tradition of enlightened benevolence. (The classic statement of the right to rebel against unjust authority is after all Locke's.) That people are capable of inhumanity, and all the more so when absolved of responsibility for their acts, no one would deny. Not satisfied with common knowledge, and thinking to remove the dramas of moral decision and default from the pages of history and literature to the more reliable ground of the laboratory, Milgram set out to measure the capacity for inhumanity and, in a stronger sense than he intended, produced results. I believe Milgram's study, while revealing much about the arrogance of science and *its* claim to authority, leaves us about where we were in our understanding of ourselves. His finding that a monster lurks inside the grocer seemed, however, to lend support to a psychological culture's belief that inside everyone is a heart of darkness, or a secret he has never let himself be conscious of.

So great is the mystique of psychology that to many it is the omega of political debate. They do not simply argue with their opponents but diagnose them. Judging them infected with mental corruption — "false consciousness" — they seem unaware of the actual horror of practices designed to cure incorrect thought, practices such as thought reform, a kind of forced penetration of the mind.[42] When they write off arguments on the other side as symptoms of a fear of social change (as though their opponents couldn't equally claim that "revolutionary creeds are rationalisations of neurotic impulses" or some such thing),[43] they do not say what it would really mean to transform society into a clinic. In his proposal to convert universities into treatment centers, Herbert Marcuse gave some idea of what it would mean. Chapter 4 accordingly examines Marcuse's blueprint for political therapy. Also moved to liberate minds en masse was Martin Luther King, who favored the popular yet academically authorized language of self-realization in contrast to the esoteric Freudianism of Marcuse. Of special concern to me is the corrosive effect of the kind of idiom used by King on moral argument. Had he lived, King would have witnessed the strange spectacle of the language of psychological affliction used in the "Letter from Birmingham Jail" — pent-up resentments, latent frustrations, repressed emotions, unconscious bitterness — becoming the lingua franca of affluence itself. Translating moral or political questions into psychological ones doesn't work. However enticing it may be to think there exists a key to everything and that psychology is that key, this is no less a fallacy of reduction than the belief that some conspiracy is sure to be the underlying cause of events.[44] Political psychologists are always looking for underlying causes, as Benjamin Rush once did for the fever behind all diseases and Marcuse did for "the factors behind the facts."

Milgram, Marcuse, King, even Bernays: all adopt the story of a few who help many in the dark about themselves — a psychological version of John Stuart Mill's model of the few in advance of the multitude. Milgram in the interest of an enlightened society acquaints citizens with their own second self: he belongs to the psychological vanguard. Marcuse would have citizens reeducated at the hands of a revolutionary elite that knows their true motives and interests as they themselves do not. For King, civil disobedience is a way to sting many out of their state of numb conformity and denial, while the people's very ignorance (combined with his own diagnostic ability) allows Bernays to manipulate them for their own good. "Through the application of . . . psychology [one] is able to bring about changes in public opinion that will make for the acceptance of new doctrines, beliefs, and habits," writes Bernays, like the John Stuart Mill of a psychological age. In the same spirit, high school teachers as far back as the 1930s were advised to help students discover the "blind spots and emotional fixations" responsible both for their misreadings of literature and their resistance to new beliefs. Once made conscious of the reasons for their resistance to change — a process the author likens to psychoanalysis[45] — students will be in a position to break their servitude to the normal and the customary. Though by no means identical, all of these tales of emancipation draw on the same powerful cultural cliché: the psychologically enlightened ministering therapeutically to the masses. Hence Arthur Miller's understanding of his own work as a playwright: "This is what you see every day, or think or feel; now I will show you what you really know but have not had the time, or the disinterestedness, or the insight, or the information to understand consciously."[46] The kindly condescension of paternalism thus takes a psychological form.[47] Miller leaves no doubt that he shares John Stuart Mill's sense of the dead weight of received ideas. Long ridiculed by conservatism as shallow and naive,[48] progressive thought found in depth psychology an aspect of profundity that made the opposition itself seem just that.

Perhaps the first to claim public recognition for defying public conventions, in the manner of Mill's elite, is Rousseau. The act of baring the self — then so singular that Rousseau could take pride even in the exhibition of his shames — has been normalized in the psychological society, as though here too an original had been reproduced by the thousands. Before Rousseau, those best known for tearing away the public trappings of identity to reveal their naked humanity may have been the tragic heroes — Oedipus, Lear, destroyers of their own glory even as they uncover themselves. The search for self has its roots in literature.

With its passionate and ancient interest in human motivation, literature itself is a sort of alter ego of psychology. When characters are drawn according to nature, said Dr. Johnson, the reader "must dive into the recesses of the human heart."[49] Freud, the most illustrious explorer of those depths, thought the poets the discoverers of the unconscious. The conscious mind was endowed by William James with the rich life of the great novels of the nineteenth century, novels which in their very plotting strongly anticipate his theory of the flow of experienced time. James wrote a prose practically as novelistic as that of his brother, and the "stream of consciousness" discovered by him flowed abundantly into fiction, as indeed fiction fed into it in turn.[50] For that matter, Locke himself is an influence on the novel, a light source refracted even in Smollett and Sterne. It is during the rise of the novel that "narration . . . become[s] entirely a psychological process,"[51] a change sufficiently marked that Swift could ironize it with his descents into the mind, as would Jane Austen in a work like *Northanger Abbey*, with its mordant account of the impression things make on the mind of the heroine.[52]

At one time psychology was the kin of literature and moral philosophy — at one time. In accordance with the specialization of functions, it has since distinguished itself from both — not as sharply as chemistry from alchemy but decisively nonetheless.[53] And the professionalization of psychology, which is also to say its separation from literature, identifies it as part of the order of technical subjects and technical objects. Psychology, that is, owes its existence as a science to the same specialization that shapes all technical work. The establishment of a science is said to require the limitation of the field and techniques for clearing it of foreign matter — the example having been set by the new science of the seventeenth century.[54] The science of psychology removes *itself* from literature, which continues to shadow it nonetheless, as Swift does Locke. The dissociation of scientific psychology from literature is illustrated once again by Stanley Milgram. Long before Milgram laid a trap for his subjects in order that he might educate them, Milton got readers to succumb to the seductions of error in *Paradise Lost* the better to expose to them their own fallenness. Readers are first taken in and then made critics of their own mistakes,[55] much as the Milgram subject first falls for the experimenter's temptations and then, on debriefing, learns to see through his mistake and repudiate it. Nor is this resemblance casual, for as I will argue at the end, the theory that the self gets free of its neuroses by the act of confronting them plays on the Puritan myth of deliverance. Milgram himself has been likened by a defender to the Old Testament prophets in whose tradition Milton wrote, those voices of moral summons that "arouse people to the evil within themselves."[56]

The satirist too provokes us to recognize ourselves — in Swift's case, with the aim of curing delusion and pride; in Mandeville's, to get rid of the delusion that moral reform itself is without heavy costs. Using the greatest possible provocation as he does, Mandeville is in the top rank of the world's debunkers. Indeed, long before Milgram theorized that those who refused to inflict torture in his lab did so to relieve their own strain, Mandeville maintained that we give alms to beggars to relieve our own suffering and not theirs. "Thus thousands give Money to Beggars from the same motive as they pay their Corncutter, to walk Easy."[57] Milgram, a psychologist with a leaning to cybernetics, claims for his conclusions the authority of the laboratory; Mandeville claims to be stating what everyone knows even if no one has the nerve to admit it. Nor does he use a pseudoclinical term like "denial" to denote this willful failure of cognition. Between literature and the science of psychology at any rate is this cardinal difference, that literature speaks a public language — not in the sense that it has no conventions but that they too are common knowledge (and by the same token readily bent); public above all in that every professional or specialist idiom, whether that of social science as in Swift or the law as in Dickens or scholastic philosophy as in Rabelais, is subject to demystification in literature. In addressing his poetry to a reader envisioned "not as a lawyer, a physician, a mariner, an astronomer, or a natural philosopher, but as a Man," Wordsworth acted in the spirit of Enlightenment universalism, and yet he was also in good traditional company.[58] In the General Prologue to the *Canterbury Tales*, featuring among others a lawyer, a physician, and a mariner, Chaucer mocks the terms of art of a number of professionals by the very act of relating them, and by placing their owners on a pilgrimage that equalizes them in spite of their various pretensions to excellence. The psychologist among the pilgrims, in the double sense of being an analyst of other minds and a provider of psychic remedies, is the most forsaken of them all, the Pardoner.

In common with all other jargons, that of therapy ill suits a public realm in which we figure as equals, not bringers of problems to the holders of special knowledge. Literature for its part has so little regard for jargon that it parodies even its own formulas and clichés. Like the language of Shakespeare, that great solvent of jargon (think of the deprofessionalizing of legal terms in the grave-digger scene in *Hamlet*), literature encroaches on every linguistic special inter-est, every closed corporation of words.[59] When teachers of literature cite "men-tal hygienists" as authorities,[60] they have for certain lost touch with the spirit of their own subject, and not just because it is hard to imagine a mental hygien-ist — Flaubert's Homais perhaps? — as anything but a figure of ridicule in any literary work of merit. As citizens of the republic of letters we speak a language different from any used by specialists to perform their work and render it great in the eyes of others: we speak a lingua franca, not a jargon. With the ever sharper division of functions in modern society and the professionalization first of medicine and then of its spin-offs, issues of motivation once in the public domain of literature become as it were the property of psychology, as though all these matters were handed over to the physician whose knowledge Wordsworth thought no more important finally than a mariner's.[61] The dou-ble irony of this privatization of the entire human question is that once psy-chology has established its claim as keeper of the mystery, the language of psy-chology floods even the public realm, as we see today. In what some call the new Puritanism of our era,[62] "every man a psychologist" returns with a differ-ence.

With his investigations of the brain itself as the home of folly and vice, Swift participates in the inward turn of narrative. But if this makes him a psy-chologist, it must also be said that the business of probing "the guts of modern brains" — getting into heads possessed by manias and brewing poisons — is to him a sordid one.[63] Somewhat similarly, psychomedical ills themselves are put into question by the medically trained Smollett in *Humphry Clinker*. Even as he inveighs against the fashions of the age, Matthew Bramble affects illness, and like the worriers of a psychological culture, makes a perpetual study of himself. "For my own part," he writes his doctor, "I have had an hospital these fourteen years within myself, and studied my own case with the most painful attention."[64] Brought back to life at the end of the novel, he begins to see that his obsession with illness *was* his illness. The true precursors of those affluent enough to devote themselves to their ailments — for the affluent society is also the sick society — may be the wealthy in *Humphry Clinker* who flock to the spas of Bath as though flaunting their own debility.[65]

Like Smollett, Sterne ironizes the Locke tradition he belongs to — *Tristram Shandy* being written in a kind of seriocomic deference to the shade of psychology's founder. From the story of his own begetting, which turns on the linkage of his parents' marital observances with the act of winding a clock, *Tristram Shandy* follows the principle of association discovered by Locke.

> From an unhappy association of ideas which have no connection in nature, it so fell out at length, that my poor mother could never hear the said clock wound up, — but the thought of some other things unavoidably popp'd into her head, — & *vice versa:* — which strange combination of ideas, the sagacious *Locke*, who certainly understood the nature of these things better than most men, affirms to have produced more wry actions than all other sources of prejudice whatsoever.[66]

The logic of association becomes in Sterne a method of madness, a formula of whimsical regression that undoes the structure of narrative even as it traces the flow of ideas. If Locke's thought is dedicated to the ideal of "a human agent who is able to remake himself by methodical and disciplined action"[67] (which becomes the patient in therapy who proverbially really wants to change), Tristram Shandy is not only mismade by his parents but tells that story and all the others in a way that carnivalizes the very concept of method. The narrative itself, that is, in drifting ever further from an end instead of advancing toward it, mocks the methodical pursuit of a goal through a series of means. (During the time it takes Mr. Shandy to construct a system of education, his son outgrows it.) So, too, Sterne ridicules the philosophical standard of clarity set by Locke even as he adapts Locke's own critique of abuses of words. Advising us in the interest of clarity that in his book the word "nose" means "nose" and nothing else, while it plainly has an ulterior meaning, he parodies the Locke style much as though it too were a jargon. Even the language of his own philosophical master is treated as a sort of professional affectation by Sterne.[68]

Literarily speaking, the first professional may actually be the "amateur" — the lover. If a profession is supposed to ennoble those who serve it, and has a code of conduct as well as ritualized modes of expression, all this is true in the highest degree of the medieval cult of love. In his mastery of the intricacies of his calling the lover is a technician of sorts, just as his single-mindedness and constant deferral of pleasure remind us of the professional's discipline. And lovers do, of course, profess their passion. The point is, though, that literature's handling of this profession of love is as free and various and contradictory as *Tristram Shandy* itself, ranging from the reverential to the parodic. (Among the parodies we might count the Wife of Bath with all her professionalism.)[69] And it is in the depiction of love, with its sweet delirium and ecstatic melancholy, that literature discovers an interest in the mind's marginal states. The modern novel of course begins with a tale of love-madness whose hero, at once ennobled and befooled by his passion, has drunk too deep of one kind of literature — *Don Quixote.*

Possibly the most concentrated attack on professionalism in all of literature is Tolstoy's *Death of Ivan Ilych*, portraying the very "virtues" of a judge as a sin for which he is arrested by death, almost in the manner of a medieval mystery play. In the course of the work the imposture of medicine, too, is unmasked. Also containing something of the mystery play, *The Brothers Karamazov* explores the mind's marginal states even as medical expertise, intelligentsia jargon, and psychological diagnostics are all debunked.[70] Dostoevsky, reputedly the most psychological of all novelists, denied that he was anything of the kind. In his last and greatest work he satirizes psychology in figures like the lightheaded Madame Hohlakov, in her own estimation "an experienced doctor of the soul," and a prosecutor who, also thinking himself a deep reader of the human soul, not only supposes Dmitri Karamazov guilty of murdering his father but has him figured out. The author's powerful sense of the indeterminacy of human action leads him to question the pretensions of those who think they hold the key to other minds.[71] As M. M. Bakhtin, one of his best and strongest readers, argues, Dostoevsky's opposition to the notion of mastering others in this way ran so deep that it influenced not just the content but the very form of his fiction. There are additional grounds for the author's dislike of psychology, I believe. As a political thinker Dostoevsky battles those who think to transform the masses by changing the conditions that "cause" them to be as they are, a project that plays off, even as it departs from, the bourgeois program of forming minds by rigorous conditioning. That practice in turn is solidly rooted in the psychology of Locke. If, as Bakhtin argues, Dostoevsky denies that another mind can be grasped like a thing, it was bourgeois reformers armed with the new psychology who first espoused the view that other minds are "knowable and manageable,"[72] as they also created the theory and practice of social engineering and introduced therapy on a public scale. Dostoevsky's attitude toward x-ray vision, with special reference to *The Brothers Karamazov*, is considered in chapter 6.

Also a member of the anti-utopian tradition that includes Dostoevsky is Orwell, the subject of chapter 7. In *Nineteen Eighty-Four* Winston Smith seems to be the subject of an experiment that produces the very rebellion he is then cured of — his treatment at the hands of O'Brien presenting a demonic parody of the paternal benevolence called for by Locke's theory of education. In that he himself spoke for common sense and agreed in spirit with Locke's criticisms of obscurity and ornament, Orwell's reply to Locke is especially interesting. And yet if we look into the seeming simplicity of Orwell's writing, we find it gets richer and richer, as though it could never be broken down into elements like "ideas" in Locke. It baffles reduction. I've noted the parody of professional jargons by Dickens, Swift, Chaucer. Orwell knew the work of Dickens from one end to the other and shared his opinion of circumlocution; like Swift, he perfected the art of ironic plainness; and like Chaucer (as well as Swift), he worked in the Menippean tradition. The prose of Orwell is a river fed by many streams, the anti-utopian tradition being but one. In the same way, perceptions don't reduce to simple apprehensions of the object even in Orwell's more factual writings. As Bakhtin might put it, the object is laced with evaluations. Orwell is a moralist, albeit not in the narrow or clerical sense of the word, which is also to say that he disagrees with those who think morality a mere figment of class society, a line preached to the oppressed to keep them oppressed, an illusion fated to wither away in the scientific society of the future. In his distrust of abstractions and recognition of persons and (beginning in his own case) the responsibility that goes with *being* a person; in espousing political causes without absolutizing them; in granting the claims of equality without effacing questions of quality, Orwell beautifully illustrates the possibilities of real pluralism.

A boon to psychology was the cultural prestige accorded it in the university, especially at the hands of other disciplines. One of the seminal literary critics of this century, I. A. Richards, pictured literature as an aid to mental health, toning the psyche of the reader. The work of M. H. Abrams, great in its influence, centers on Wordsworth and his creed that

> the mind of man confronts the old heaven and earth and possesses within itself the power, if it will but recognize and avail itself of the power, to transform them into a new heaven and new earth, by means of a total revolution of consciousness.[73]

which sounds strangely like pop psychology. The work of Northrop Frye, perhaps the most learned as well as urbane of the critics of his generation, centers on an artist who held an even stronger version of the same creed: Blake. Although the writing of Frye is dotted with terms like "reflex" and "therapeutic," neither he nor Abrams, I imagine, thought the malady of modernity a literal

clinical condition to be treated medically. Could these students of the imagination have viewed a culture that reduces the vision of the imagination to the
business of clinical practice any less coldly than Wordsworth himself greeted
the idea of producing genius under controlled conditions?[74] It is the rebels
against the humanism of Abrams and Frye — those inverting their claims for
the liberating power of the imagination, maintaining that "the canon" induces
false consciousness and holds minds captive — who seem to believe literally
in the therapeutic.

What Wordsworth and Blake have most in common, perhaps, is Milton;
each adopts his prophetic role and recasts his epic sublimity. When Stanley
Milgram stages a temptation in his lab, when the teacher draws students into
uncritical responses that can then be "worked through," they too enact Milton,
but in a way that reduces a vision of emancipation to a managed process. And
in thus committing a Miltonic vision to a set of procedures, they follow one of
the pioneers of method and the founder of the psychological paradigm. If tests
in the Miltonic sense temper the will, education in the Lockean sense is a long
course in temperance, and this with the end of producing, as Milton would
wish, someone disciplined enough to be free. The careful procedures devised
by Locke to translate this ideal into practice mark a new mode of ideology
itself, one devoted to the fashioning of human beings. It is with Locke's theory
of education, and its adaptations and sequels, that this study therefore begins.

CHAPTER 1

Locke and His Successors

In accordance with the fancy for psychological explanations, historians have traced a "paranoid" streak in the American character back to the Founding Fathers and their fears. "One by one the Founding Fathers are psychoanalyzed and their unconscious fears and drives brought to the surface." Some investigators use the term "paranoid" loosely, with others leaning to a clinical interpretation of what is said to be a peculiarly American obsession with the threat of conspiracies. The Revolution itself has been accounted "a delusion explicable by the principles of psychology." Weighing heavily against all such diagnoses of an American pathology is that the belief in conspiracies and secret causes was neither uniquely American nor for that matter a sign of mental disturbance. On the contrary, it was common to the enlightened on both sides of the Atlantic, believers in cause and effect who were quick to see behind events the hand of human malevolence. Not a disease of the mind but an enlightened belief in causality — a belief that would underwrite psychology itself — lay behind the eighteenth-century fixation with plots and the search for the hidden springs of action. In turn, the conviction that human events have human causes was nourished by Locke's theory of civil society itself as a product of human decision.[1] Here, though, I am concerned with Locke's thoughts on the fashioning of a person *for* civil society — a corollary both of his political theory and his philosophy of mind.

That we are each the product of our past, that to understand someone is to understand how he or she came about — this doctrine, now part of the creed of the psychological culture, itself arose in part from a philosophical treatise. Concerned to refute the theory of innate ideas, Locke in the *Essay concerning Human Understanding* tracks knowledge back to its origin in sensation, in the process establishing the "genetic" method. The way to understand the mind is to trace the genesis of its ideas. (No doubt the historical turn of Locke's method helps account for the affinity the novel feels for it, the novel being the literary form that makes the most show of historicity.) To be sure, the *Essay* concerns the formation of no mind in particular. That is where Locke's manual on education comes in.[2]

The aim of the handbook on education is to raise up, in fact produce, a gentleman free of the obstinacy, love of dispute, and other incivilities described in the more famous *Essay*. Quite literally concerned with the making of a gentleman, Locke lays down a method for the production of the kind of character called for by civil society, just as in the *Essay* he tries to get the principles of cognition in order so that controversies can be avoided and civility flourish. Education, then, means more than instruction. It means the formation of a person. And this in turn requires that the tutor calculate everything he does to leave the deepest impression on the mind of the learner. Locke's entire educational method, then, is psychologically conceived, for only if you understand the workings of the mind can you hope to mold it. By extending the Puritan practice of self-discipline to the disciplining of another, and at the same time removing the hindrance posed by original sin to the tutor's shaping power, Locke inaugurated an educational project that would expand in time by orders of magnitude.[3]

Beginning with ice-water treatments that break him in and introduce him to the notion of mastering his desires, the child undergoes a long course of conditioning, acquiring proper habits through a carefully designed training regimen. If Locke isn't averse to the use of ice, and even occasionally the rod, in measured doses, his psychological approach nevertheless leads him to prefer subtle measures to harsh ones. For as a rule, the method likeliest to produce the desired effect on the child will work with rather than against him. In any event the test of every educational tactic is psychological: What effect will it have on the child's mind? Because tendencies cement into habits over time, a wise tutor forecasts the long-term result of any given tendency in the child and acts on it accordingly. Because nothing impresses as profoundly or instructs as well as example, illustrations of vice and virtue are kept before the learner. Because the child has a natural love of esteem and fear of disgrace, the tutor keys his system of discipline to those motives. Well-calculated policies like these implant good habits more effectively than blind force ever could. The Lockean method, then, is one of habituation.

This Method of teaching Children by a repeated Practice, and the same Action done over and over again, under the Eye and Direction of the Tutor, till they have got the habit of doing it well, and not by relying on Rules trusted to their Memories, has so many Advantages, which way ever we consider it, that I cannot but wonder (if ill Customs could be wonder'd at in any thing) how it could possibly be so much neglected. (Para. 66)

According to Isaiah Berlin, the "policy of deliberate psychological conditioning" is new to the twentieth century.[4] So it is — in the hands of the state. In private hands it is not new at all, for what more aptly describes Locke's educational program than deliberate psychological conditioning? Admittedly, between education under the eye and direction of a loving father and education at the hands of Big Brother stands a great divide. But as will be seen, Locke's methods were removed from the household by his successors, and with some of these experiments in "reeducation" ideology takes on a more ominous cast.

Since fallacious ways of thinking are not only errors but symptoms of a disordered mind to Locke, it will not surprise us that he construes education as a process of curing. Once good habits take root, Locke finds, they continue as if of their own accord. And so, "having this way cured in your Child any Fault, it is cured for ever" (para. 64). Not until I behave with a decorum that seems entirely natural, as though there had never been any contrary tendencies to overcome or "cure," is civility achieved. The becoming ease of good behavior, the regard for others shown so naturally, certify a healthy mind. No doubt the sheer beauty of Locke's vision of civility contributed to the influence of his educational theory. In any event that influence was profound. Reformers before and during the Industrial Revolution who sought to eradicate bad habits, correct "ill customs," instill discipline, and control influences, all in the name of health, stood squarely in the tradition of Locke even as they worked on a scale he never intended or envisioned. Locke wants to imprint precepts on a child's mind. (" 'Tis as impossible to draw fair and regular Characters on a trembling Mind as on a shaking Paper" [para. 167].) Later pedagogues, also arguing for "gentle" punishments, would seek to print the lessons of morality on the *public* mind.[5]

According to Locke, if education is to sink in, the tutor had better abandon the brute force method and work with, not against, the child's own motives and inclinations. Subtle and well considered rather than crude and arbitrary, this seems just the kind of education called for in the society envisioned by theorists of the civilizing effect of commerce — a society where the more tractable passions are called into play and pressed into the service of political stability. If in civil society we are softened and tempered — "wherever there is commerce, there the ways of men are gentle"[6] — education according to Locke has the same effect, gradually bending the will to the love of virtue, using the subtle power of example in preference to power per se. But the principles of gentle discipline, influential example, and careful supervision guiding Lockean education also lend themselves to the endeavor to civilize on a larger scale. The first such effort to be considered here is that of the periodical essayist Joseph Addison to temper passions and promote civility, as well as vindicate commerce, all in the name of the philosophy of Locke. Taken to a higher level, the pedagogical method of gentle correction and persuasive example yields the Addisonian "Spectator" who surveys the nation, gently correcting its faults and offering an example of civility.

Considering that Locke's theory of instruction hinges on the subtle use of influence, and that the civility he aims for is the harmonizing of wills under mutual influence — considering the captivating quality of this power called influence near the center of his vision — it seems fitting that his work went on to enjoy great influence in its own right.[7] With Addison infusing his ethic into the *Spectator*, Locke entered into the construction of the public realm itself. Originally intended to produce a few good men (as his *Essay* was meant for a private circle of some half dozen), his education in civility was now opened to the public at large in a journal of notable popularity, the prototype of civic journalism as we know it. Locke is in fact Addison's philosophical master, his authority on everything from the Chain of Being to the nature of true wit.

As Locke describes it, the fashioning of a gentleman is a laborious process calling for concentration on one thing, or in this case one person. Not much can be expected from a schoolmaster with fifty or a hundred boys, writes Locke, the "forming of their Minds and Manners requiring a constant Attention, and particular Application to every single Boy, which is impossible in a numerous Flock" (para. 70). And so education must take place within the household. In order for civility to advance, however, ways must be found to economize this kind of training, for in Locke's account it seems prohibitively inefficient, better suited to the world of handcraft than the rapidly modernizing one of commerce. The treatise on education is truly a manual, showing how to do something by hand. Addison scales up the Lockean model. His *Spectator* papers are experimental attempts, or "essays" (and Locke's magnum opus called itself just this) if only in the sense of trying to expand the process of fashioning minds and manners. This means adapting Locke's method — applying the guiding principles of his pedagogy, such as gentle reproach and the sweet power of example — to broader ends. The popularization of Locke begins, then, with the Addisonian project of educating the public in civility.

In Addison's essays the follies of the day are censured in a style at once easily decorous and lightly admonitory, and so pleasant it can hardly fail to carry the reader. In fact the Addisonian style serves to lure the reader into the very habit of reading.

> Stout volumes and lengthy treatises would have rebuffed readers so lacking in self-confidence as those of Addison's day. They would not even have been opened. . . . The paper that consisted of short essays tempted the timorous by its brevity and variety, and held them by never overtiring them. Its unambitious modesty won their confidence. People who would otherwise never have read at all, unconsciously acquired the habit, and the taste for reading became widespread.[8]

The policy of inculcating a good habit gently rather than by force — how well this comports with Locke's strategy for building up the moral habits of the child. Note too the psychological cast of the language just quoted: "unconsciously," "lacking in self-confidence" (today "self-esteem"). Addison was praised by an admirer in these terms:

> Nor harsh thy Precepts, but infus'd by Stealth,
> Please while they cure, and cheat us into Health.[9]

"Cure" and "health" place Addison appropriately in the culture of the therapeutic. Seeing that Locke writes as a physician in his handbook on education, Addison's medicinal approach is itself a sort of testimony to his philosophical mentor.

Addison was but the first, however, to translate Locke's educational project from the domestic to a broader context. Simply as a method of fashioning, of production, that project contains the possibility of expansion. And Locke does mean production. A gentleman is *made*. "To make a good, a wise, and a vertuous Man, 'tis fit he should learn to cross his Appetite" (para. 52). "He that is a good, a vertuous and able Man, must be made so within" (para. 42). Children should "from their first beginning to talk, have some Discreet, Sober, nay Wise person about [them], whose Care it should be to Fashion them aright" (para. 90). Maybe it was this aspect of Locke's thought that recommended his methods to many interested in extending the process of fashioning minds even further than Addison. The adaptation of the Lockean method to wider contexts served to broaden a project of construction forbiddingly costly and time-consuming in its original form, with Bentham, for example, trying to raise what is really hand labor to a factory process. Bentham thought of his now infamous prison, the Panopticon, as a benign device for reforming men whose lack of discipline made them like children; we might think of it as a technology for extending to many the "constant Attention" Locke trains on one, with the similar end of producing a fit member of society. An attempt to reform the habits of "children" by subjecting them to close supervision under controlled conditions (in fine, deliberate psychological conditioning), the Panopticon is clearly a Lockean education on a larger scale. Bentham is one of many who sought to extend Locke's theory of judicious punishment, above all its paternalism, "beyond the master-pupil relationship to the society at large."[10]

In paternalism, we might say, the "worry and care about the self"[11] underlying modern psychology broaden into care for others. Paternalism, of course, refers to the control, manipulation, and occasional deception of others in what is alleged to be their own best interests. Justifying the subordination of others even as the grounds of subordination erode under the force of modernity, paternalism ranges from the subjection of workers to the watchful eye and care of the master, to the protection of women in consideration of their frailty, to the deception of human subjects in the laboratory. Broadly speaking, in modern society the exercise of power over those of inferior status has been justified in paternalistic terms. It bears remembering, though, that at root paternalism refers to a father's rule over a child — and of this Locke supplies a classic example. The Lockean father, with or without a tutor, directs the education of his son, chastening and at times deceiving him for his own benefit. When we speak of paternalism, we mean a relation modeled on one like this, or even, as in the case of the Panopticon, an enlargement of the relation itself. If ideology is understood not just as the projection of ideals but the effort to mold human beings in their image on a general scale, so influential is the Lockean model that in going to work in schemes like Bentham's it helps initiate the age of ideology itself. That it was the activation of psychological ideas that had such an effect speaks to the hold of psychology over our culture. "General psychology," wrote the Scottish philosopher Dugald Stewart, is "the center whence the thinker goes outward to the circumference of human knowledge."[12]

Accordingly, the psychological question — What is the effect on the human mind? — runs through Enlightenment thought. Of every educational tactic Locke asks "what influence it will have upon [the] Mind" of the learner (para. 107). The tactics used by "wary politicians" to manage the mind of the human animal are of interest to Mandeville.[13] Religion is reduced by its most radical critics to mind control. Sterne calls on those "who govern this mighty world . . . who wind and turn the passions" to reflect on the way the heart is really moved.[14] What effect has the novel on the mind of the reader? asks Johnson. Burke's discourse on the sublime and the beautiful examines the action of these powers on the mind of the beholder. The mind-maiming effect of the division of labor concerns Adam Smith. The effect of public punishments on the mind of the spectator concerns Benjamin Rush.[15] Bentham theorizes that the sensation of being watched will exert a wholesome effect on prisoners' minds. So "general" is psychology that it informs all of the human sciences.[16] According to Wordsworth, rural life has a purifying influence on human affections. Even he speaks of the association of ideas, displaying "the same scientific interest in psychology, which is typical of the Enlightenment."[17] However, when asked to serve as a tutor in a scheme to form superior minds by controlling the influences on them, Wordsworth will have nothing of it.[18] That ambitious plan, in turn, seems to belong to the line of adaptations of Locke's tutorial model.

As the word "psychology" came into use in eighteenth-century Britain, theorists under the influence of Locke and his medical concept of the mind explored the possibility of reforming habits of thought by regulating the conditions in which those habits (called associations) were formed in the first place.[19] Education as Locke himself prescribes it, after all, is just such a program of habituation. The most famous of the theorists of association, David Hartley, convinced that "Children may be formed and moulded as we please," looked forward to the application of his doctrine in education.[20] But where Locke had in mind the fashioning of a few, reformers fired by the theory of association had larger ambitions — a leap of scale characteristic of eighteenth-century adaptations of Locke. Psychology is the clue to all things: he who understands the formation of ideas can reform the world. He can do so because once the mechanics of the mind are understood it becomes possible to "form and mould" humanity itself.

Only if a kind of Lockean education, one that builds up good and reforms ill habits, is extended to many can the full benefits of the new psychology be realized. By keying in on the insecurity of his readers and instructing gently, in effect using Lockean tactics, Addison fostered the habit of reading among the public itself. Psychology powers a virtually technological expansion of the educational project. Others, as I have said, thought to expand that project well beyond Addisonian dimensions. Concurrent with the rise of psychological theory in Britain was a surge of thought on education, also in the tradition of Locke and also therapeutic in intent. (It was after he declined to take part in the plan for the education of genius that Wordsworth turned to tracing his *own* education at the hands of Nature in *The Prelude*.) But the most aggressive and politically charged applications of Locke took the form of paternalistic schemes to reform the habits of laborers, the poor, criminals. Armed with the new psychology, energetic men undertook to redesign institutions from the prison to the factory — the Panopticon was to be both at once — in the hope of reforming the character of those inside their walls. As though bent on institutionalizing Locke, they sought to construct the machinery to correct numbers of people as he does a single child. Many of these engineers of humanity were physicians like the philosopher himself: the cult of the therapeutic had begun. As in a hospital — of which one of the reformers, Thomas Percival, designed the modern type — workers and prisoners were to be placed under a regimen intended to cure bad habits and produce moral health. The physician administers medicine to the mind, treating "the prejudices, the caprices, and the passions of the sick and their relatives," in Percival's words. By a sort of heroic magnification of his role, then, the physician heals both body and mind, both the sick and society itself. And driving this expansion of the role of medicine as well as the theory and practice of social engineering, all of it unprecedented, is psychology. It was the new psychology with its doctrine of the malleability of human character that authorized the belief that the many could be reformed by learning the habits of discipline.[21]

If their psychology viewed human beings as clay, one of the reformers took the fashioning of actual clay to a new level: the great potter Josiah Wedgwood. Any number of the devices used by Wedgwood to excite interest in his products — the catalog, the showroom, the trademark, celebrity endorsements, artificial "news" — are still with us, and in fact his techniques anticipate those of Edward Bernays, architect of public relations and psychologist of the public mind. But for now it is Wedgwood's practice as a factory master and disciplinarian that concerns us. Wedgwood's efforts to promote habits of industry among his workers and to root out the contrary, his overall paternalism, and his system of supervision read like transcriptions of the Lockean method of instruction into a new context. In place of the manual production of virtue carried out by the father inside the household, he engaged in something like human engineering, as befitted a factory master. Especially noteworthy for our purposes, perhaps, is Wedgwood's use of a corps of inspectors to watch over workers in detail, an arrangement that enabled him to place many "under the Eye and Direction" of the master as called for by Locke. Meticulously enforced, strict, yet from his point of view benign, the Wedgwood ideal of industrial discipline reflects the method of Locke and is underwritten, like other schemes of correction, by the latter's psychology. At the same time that the psychologically focused literature of sensibility was being popularized "on an unprecedented scale,"[22] a master of the theory and practice of popularization was using psychology to take production itself to a new level. Not only in translating theory into practice, but in attempting to transform workers themselves in accordance with theory so that production might advance, the Wedgwood system dramatizes the coming of modern ideology.

"Having . . . cured in your Child any Fault, it is cured for ever," writes Locke. "And thus, one by one, you may weed them out all, and plant what Habits you please" (para. 64). Weeding and planting might well have been on Wedgwood's mind as he strove to uproot traditional habits and accustom his "hands" to a modern regimen of work; that the process took years suggests he would have agreed that it requires time for good habits to establish themselves. Among Wedgwood's innovations, in addition to systematic supervision, were a number of disciplinary measures designed to improve punctuality and break traditional practices like "St. Monday" to which workers were attached as a matter of customary right. ("You cannot imagine of what Force Custom is," says Locke [para. 14].) In the story of the subjection of labor to the clock Wedgwood holds an important place, for it was he who introduced the punch-in system as well as using bells to divide the working day.[23] Along with the division of time went the division of labor. By segregating workers according to task Wedgwood raised the division of labor from the level of the Smithian pin workshop to that of industrial production. The workers

> were trained to one particular task and they had to stick to it. Wedgwood felt that this was the only way to improve the quality of the ware — "We are preparing some hands to work at red & black [ware] . . . constantly & then we shall make them good, there is no such thing as making now & then a few of any article to have them tolerable."[24]

On the Lockean theory that only "constant use" (para. 64) cements actions into habit, Wedgwood wants workers to keep at the same task.

The manager, writes Alasdair MacIntyre, is the therapist in another skin: the former concerned with "transforming raw materials into final products, unskilled labour into skilled labour, investment into profits," the latter with transforming the maladjusted into what are called productive members of society.[25] The justice of this analogy is confirmed by Wedgwood, in that "curing" workers and getting the most out of them were for him the same act. And no less than his marketing tricks, his therapeutic attitude has caught on. It has caught on to the point that people now seek to get the most out of themselves. As innovative as Wedgwood was, however, his originality in this case lay in adapting to adults — people with a history — the habit training that Locke proposed for well-born children. Thus was Locke's psychology of instruction transposed to a field well beyond what he had in mind. But the adaptation remains true to the spirit of the original.

For Wedgwood aspired to make his "hands" as well as his ware good. He too, that is, engaged in human fashioning — and, like Locke, said so. Again and again Wedgwood speaks of making men something, as if charmed by the audacity of the usage. He strives "to make Artists [of] mere men," to "make such Machines of the men as cannot err." Few can be found who paint in the requisite style; therefore "we must make them." Needing craftsmen and finding "none ready made," he undertakes to train them himself.[26] Much as he took the division of labor to a new level by refining the categories of work and separating his workshops themselves, Wedgwood also raised the techniques of human fashioning from the manual or household stage of Locke.[27] He too wanted the training process to begin early. "To achieve perfection he demanded he had to train his workmen from youth."[28] So it is that a straight line runs from Locke's paternal theory of education to the potter's paternalistic attempt to reeducate his workers, both schemes dependent on minute supervision and methodical training, both aimed at instilling habits of "Application, Industry, Thought, Contrivance, and Good Husbandry" (para. 130). To build up habits of application Wedgwood had a supervisor "encourage those who come regularly to their time, letting them know that their regularity is properly noticed, & distinguishing them by repeated marks of approbation," with marks of disapprobation going to the tardy.[29] As we might suppose, this scheme too agrees with the Lockean model, built as the latter is on the stated assumption that "Esteem and Disgrace are, of all others, the most powerful incentives to the Mind, when once it is brought to relish them" (para. 56). Industrial discipline is psychology in action.

If psychology enables Locke to fashion a gentleman by adjusting the means of instruction to the end in view, it assists Wedgwood in producing not only goods for the fashion market but reliable workers. And this sort of enlargement of the category of fabrication to include working on "human material" has left its print on modern political history, as Hannah Arendt has observed.[30] Not only, it seems, does psychology expand its dominion under the technological paradigm, but the very concept of technique expands as well, bringing expressions like "making" institutions — or revolutions — and "making" a better humanity into political parlance. (The very term "the masses" implies unformed stuff awaiting the shaping power of the hand to be made into something. Clay comes to mind.) Jeremy Bentham had something of this fabrication mentality, and in his plans for a Panopticon we seem to see the complete industrialization of the Lockean method. That is to say, Bentham envisions the mass production of virtue using techniques of conditioning analogous to those Locke intends for children — Bentham viewing the undisciplined *as* children. Not just the Panopticon but the edifice of Bentham's thought itself is psychologically based, grounded as it is on the author's theory of elementary human motives, desire for pleasure and aversion to pain. These are the forces a wise legislator knows how to work with, and it is significant, in view of our interest in the therapeutic tradition, that even this figure is imagined by Bentham a healer. The

> art of legislation is but the art of healing practised upon a large scale. It is the common endeavor of both to relieve men from the miseries of life. But the physician relieves them one by one: the legislator by millions at a time[31] —

another example of the expansion of the Lockean project that brought into being a new mode of ideology. What with Hartley's construction of a vast system out of a sort of aside in Locke, and Priestley's popularization of Hartley in turn, and Bentham's dream of simply infinitizing the educational project, it is hard to avoid feeling that psychology had a hand in creating the world of popularizations we now inhabit. It was Addison, a most adept popularizer of Locke himself, who in expanding the reading public created a model of modern civic journalism. Two of the undoubted masters of popularization, Benjamin Franklin and Wedgwood (the one became an icon, the other produced them), were also squarely in the Locke tradition — members of the Royal Society and figures of both industry and civility. That psychology should now find itself so thoroughly popularized is from this point of view poetically fitting.

Almost simultaneously with the publication of *Conscious Autosuggestion* by Emile Coué came *The Little Engine That Could* (1926), whose refrain "I think I can, I think I can" is autosuggestion in action. The prodigious success of this little parable is itself a sort of parable of psychology's popular appeal.[32] The linkage between psychology and the very mechanism of popularization comes clear when it is recognized that *The Little Engine That Could* descends from the children's literature of the Industrial Revolution — the first of its kind, and fully in the spirit of Locke's educational precepts. As Isaac Kramnick argues in tracing *The Little Engine That Could* back to the Locke tradition, the emergence of a children's literature in late eighteenth-century England coincided with the enlargement of the market for consumer goods of all sorts, from buttons to buckles to the cameos and tea services of Wedgwood. The new literature in fact sought to imprint values like Wedgwood's on the minds of the young: psychology even then was engaged in the packaging of ideas. Probably it is because of its historical connection with the theory and practice of popularization — and the Enlightenment itself refers to an intellectual movement grounded in psychology and concerned with the propagation of ideas — that psychology alone among the social sciences born in the Enlightenment finds itself mass marketed today. There is no pop economics, no pop sociology to compare with pop psychology.

Bentham, like Wedgwood, adapted the psychology of Locke to the industrial era. In the tradition of Wedgwood's pottery works run by mechanical men who "cannot err," Bentham envisioned the Panopticon as a kind of mill that grinds the deviancy out of its inmates, transforming paupers and felons into honest workers. Predicated, like Wedgwood's system, on a scheme of inspection both detailed and comprehensive, the Panopticon would expose inmates to constant surveillance by their warden, himself concealed by the ingenious use of screens.[33] If Locke believed that "the ideas and images in men's minds are the invisible powers that constantly govern them,"[34] Bentham thought to put minds right by himself becoming their invisible governor. And in theory Bentham's charges would be transformed like patients in therapy. In a secular version of contrition, they would be compelled by their very solitude to reflect on their misdeeds and hence "would . . . undergo psychological regeneration."[35] The Panopticon strikes us as a slow-torture device. To be subjected at all times to the eye of power, to be watched into submission — this seems unbearable. Yet Bentham considered himself a man of benevolence, and the Panopticon was intended to do away with the barbarity of the existing prison; indeed the eeriness of the design derives in no small part from its complete rejection of all the familiar features of a Newgate. Fetters and gangs would have no place in the

Panopticon. The hatred of barbarism that led others to favor the nonviolence of solitary punishment over chains led Bentham to propose a mechanism of correction that outmoded brutality altogether.[36] And in this he follows Locke, who repeatedly criticizes childbeating and propounds a theory of education as a steady process of gentle correction under the paternal eye — the theory underlying Bentham's own correctional designs.

In Locke's time, as labor moved out of the household into factories, laborers "were hidden away and segregated from the community like criminals behind high walls and under constant supervision."[37] Wedgwood, we know, kept workers under watch. Bentham turned his attention to criminals, whom he regarded in the manner of a Lockean father. As I've suggested, one way to construe the Panopticon is as a technology for subjecting many to the "constant Attention" Locke concentrates on one, with the similar end of molding character by rigorous conditioning. The ambition of stepping up the work of Locke seems implicit in Bentham's statement that legislation is "the art of healing practised upon a large scale." Locke, a physician, conceives of education as a process of curing the mind. It was Bentham's hope to extend this kind of therapy to multitudes, and to those even farther from Locke's thoughts than wage laborers: the criminal and the indigent. In fact the Panopticon is a machine for the reconstruction of human character and the solution of the humanitarian problems of the age. No matter whether your purpose is "punishing the incorrigible, guarding the insane, reforming the vicious, confining the suspected, employing the idle, maintaining the helpless, curing the sick, instructing the willing in any branch of industry, or training the rising race in the path of education," the Panopticon is your answer.[38] Like one who thinks he possesses the key to everything, Bentham sees in the Panopticon the cure of the world's ills. Dreaming of a machine that would automate an education on Lockean lines, he symbolizes the mechanization of thought itself under the influence of ideology — its repetition of formulas, self-rapture, drive for universal conclusions.[39] So too, in his plans for "a vast extension" of the Panopticon beyond its original scope,[40] he brings to mind the sheer expansionism of the therapeutic culture of today and the excess of its output. It is as though Bentham's device for human reformation, a device that would build in the kind of transparency he called publicity, had been transformed into a publicity machine.

Though the Panopticon never quite came to life, it did leave its stamp on the construction of many schools, barracks, and similar facilities. The influence of Bentham took other shapes as well. His godson John Stuart Mill grew up in a virtual Panopticon, strictly segregated from other children, subjected to the all-seeing eye of his father, and so resolutely engineered that in the midst of his depression he came to suspect he was a machine and not a living being. In a way his suspicions were well grounded, too, for in order to reconstruct others as Bentham wants to, you would have to see clear through them like a piece of machinery shown in a diagram disassembled down to the bolts. Your vision would have to be panoptic in the sense of rendering them completely known. But it is a kind of presupposition of narrative that we can never be known in this way, because in the trials and chances of life our qualities come out in ways that defeat prediction. In crisis, conflict, or competition the element of uncertainty is at its highest. It is noteworthy that Bentham's famous disciple began his divergence from Benthamism in what he terms his mental crisis, and that his essay on liberty centers on the trial of idea against idea, a test charged with conflict and competition.

Mill's argument with the majority in *On Liberty*, his most enduring work, records his departure from the Benthamite standard of "the greatest number." In Mill's conception liberty serves above all to safeguard the few, benefactors of an often ungrateful multitude. Bentham for his part distrusted talk of liberty as emotive and dangerous — firewater. Resolving liberty into security, he did not shrink from asserting that "If security against anything that savours of tyranny be liberty, liberty, in the instance of . . . [paupers] can scarcely ever have existed in anything near so perfect a shape" as in the Panopticon.[41] From this kind of argument Mill must have learned something about the defects of single-mindedness, for it seems the product of someone in the grip of a fixed idea, a sort of ruling passion of the brain. In any event, where Bentham reduces liberty to security Mill insists on the difference between them, arraigning in *On Liberty* a middle-class society that has simply sold the first for the second. It is as though Mill's contemporaries had submitted to living in a Panopticon, there to be taught by a grinding routine that their own advantage lies in conformity to house rules. The morality Mill objects to — a compound of outward propriety, mechanical habit, and narrow self-interest — is that of the Panopticon. He himself knew what Panopticon life was like, having grown up a virtual prison, secluded, inspected, drilled, all with the aim of making him a model soldier in the cause of Utility.

The reform of prisons and the very law with the aim of making a gothic system of justice both humane and rational — this, the grand design of Bentham, exemplifies the penal project of bourgeois society as described by Michel Foucault. Under the new regime penalties are more regular and less barbarous than before, and the entire system of discipline more vigilant and comprehensive. It is in just these terms that Mill characterizes the Victorian system of surveillance in *On Liberty*. Subjection is no longer imposed on society but by society, manners are softer, censorship itself no longer uses indelicate methods like the chopping off of hands or the burning of books by the common hangman, and behind this waning of severity is a system of moral surveillance that bears down universally like the weight of the atmosphere itself, just as a reformed penal code was intended to. The old creaking apparatus of authority is put away in the closet of history like some relic of an ungentle past, or some process of manual labor replaced by one of more efficient design. The barbarism of the pillory gives way to the enlightened reformism of an improving society. Doing away with the unpleasantness of actual coercion, the machinery of conformity exhibits something of the same modernizing impulse that led Bentham to claim his Panopticon was incomparably more humane and efficient than any known method of correction, antiquating whips and fetters as it did. Before Foucault mocked the "automatic docility" of the modern citizen,[42] before he wrote of the "gaze" of moral overseers and the dread power of the Norm, Mill decried the reduction of citizens to automata, the paralysis of will by surveillance, and the despotism of the Norm. Did Mill share Foucault's understanding of psychology as a technique of control, a way of disciplining the mind and not only the body (just as in Locke's theory of punishment)? Perhaps in part. In *On Liberty* he protests the practice of judicial inquiry into the sanity of anyone sufficiently odd, adding that

> all the minute details of [the] daily life [of the suspect] are pried into, and whatever is found which, seen through the medium of the perceiving and describing faculties of the lowest of the low, bears an appearance unlike absolute commonplace, is laid before the jury as evidence of insanity.[43]

Testimony in favor of Foucault's account of psychology as an instrument of discipline.

If Wedgwood took pottery production into the industrial era and Bentham designed a sort of factory for the mass production of virtue (it would produce goods too, with Bentham holding a state-secured monopoly on the prisoners' labor), Mill's argument belongs to the age of steam. Only because of the railway and the newspaper, only because of steam power do the Victorians "read the same things, listen to the same things, see the same things, go to the same places."[44] And with this reign of uniformity Mill associates a terrible malaise — what the republican tradition understands as a loss of the power to sustain freedom, but which modern consumers are more likely to experience as an impairment of health calling for some kind of psychological remedy. It is at this point in the story, then, when industrial power is such that it dwarfs one and all into insignificance, that psychology seems to become a countermeasure, a reclamation of one's own being, as well as the management tool it was designed to be by modernizers like Bentham. But is the quest for psychic well-being therefore linked to the very powers that threaten individuality so formidably? I believe so. If Alasdair MacIntyre is right and in social life "we are trying simultaneously to render the rest of society predictable and ourselves unpredictable,"[45] then as the forces rendering us predictable grow more powerful ("they now read the same things, go to the same places"), the more urgent is the need for private depths known to oneself alone. In a world where you try to see through others without being seen through in turn — and this, as it happens, is the privilege of the inspector in the Panopticon — psychology both enables you to read others and supplies a sense of inner depths. Surely it is no coincidence that detective fiction, with its psychological eye, gets going in Mill's society and takes as its setting the very conditions of protective anonymity and aggressive inquisition that he describes.

Historically speaking, *On Liberty* stands on the threshold of that society in which the complaint of malaise is general and psychological tonics become consumer goods. Through its membership in the republican tradition, however, *On Liberty* holds a quite different conception of health.

> From Plato and Aristotle, through Burke and De Tocqueville [Mill's immediate precursor], the therapeutic implication of social theory is remarkably consistent: an individual can exercise his gifts and powers fully only by participating in the common life. This is the classical ideal. The healthy man is in fact the good citizen. The therapeutic and the moral were thus connected in the Western tradition of social theory.[46]

What is it but this ideal that underwrites Mill's vision of citizens flourishing in the exercise of their gifts and powers, equal to the preservation of freedom, untouched by the debility that worries the republicans? If pluralism doubts the unity of truth, and especially the value of monological formulas, *On Liberty* is richer, more pluralistic in qualifying its "one very simple principle" of laissez-faire[47] with a classical ideal that is never definitively stated but whose presence is felt everywhere in Mill's argument. So complete has been "the triumph of the therapeutic," however, that the republican dimension of Mill's argument has slipped from our sight.[48] Psychology conceives of us as potential patients. But "patient" is related to "passive," and Mill, writing in the twilight of the republican tradition, worries about a new mode of oppression that saps the power to *act* or, in the words of Tocqueville, "enervates the soul and noiselessly unbends its springs of action."[49]

Within half a century of the publication of *On Liberty* the themes of Mill's lament were being heard in the press and the advice literature of the United States: the rise of the mass society; the enervation of middle-class life; the decline of vitality; the lost intensity of being. While these complaints, like Mill's, spoke to the mechanization of life in an industrial society, the effect in America was to drive middle-class readers into the arms of psychological helpers who themselves, clearly, shared industry's concern with proper adjustment and sound functioning. (Industry in fact now had a "psychology of management" showing how to get the most out of the worker.) The malaise cited by Mill, now a quasi-medical condition, had a quasi-medical cure. The loss of "vital power" deplored in the last sentence of *On Liberty*, now the common theme of a society worried about health of mind and body as never before, was answered by spiritual tonics, pep literature, and consumer goods from toothpaste to malt extract. With the outpouring of therapies and public excitement over hypnotism and depth psychology; with the publication of books with titles like *Jesus, the Christ, in the Light of Psychology* (1917) and *The Psychology of Advertising* (1903); with the popularization of "the subconscious," the psychological society had arrived.[50] Consumers of all these things no doubt provided the audience for psychologically knowing critics, reformers, and publicists (among them the subject of my next chapter) who over the decades established their cultural authority by casting themselves in the role of Mill's minority even as they declared their revolt against the Victorians.

With the ascendancy of psychology, then, Mill's story of the few leading the many turns into one of the psychologically enlightened leading those unacquainted with their true selves. Mill asserts our freedom, within limits, to do as we like. Psychology identifies the mental constraints that seem to keep us from doing as we might wish even in the absence of other checks. It claims, in effect, to complete what Mill began. Considering William James's kinship with Mill — "My fancy likes to picture [Mill] as our leader were he alive today," James said[51] — it appears in retrospect as though Mill were on the threshold of psychologism already. He never took the last step, and indeed James himself brought literary qualities to his psychology that would not survive the passing of the Victorian era.

While Mill in the tradition of republicanism etches a sharp line between the public and private realms, that line blurs in a consumer society where publicity itself, much of it psychosexual, becomes a favorite item of consumption. Pop psychology in particular subverts Mill's categories by probing into private life at once more radically and less menacingly than the intrusions he was concerned to check. Mill made his protest against a stealthy form of oppression "penetrating much more deeply into the details of life" than the old frank modes of political tyranny, so that to most it doesn't feel like oppression at all.[52] In Mill's own name, as it were, the institution of psychology reaches still more deeply into the details of life, breaching the last limits of privacy in a way that doesn't even feel invasive.

The dwindling of differences observed by Mill, and before him Tocqueville, became for some an axiom of the technological age. The social psychologist Gabriel Tarde, for example, foretold an empire of uniformity spreading over civilization. The sort of expansion of influence by orders of magnitude that we have seen in the case of the Locke model — this Tarde identified as the very law of social existence, analogous to a law of nature, the "key to almost every lock." As this last phrase suggests, Tarde's exposition of the law of radiation, in spite of its scientific dress, has as much in common with myth or indeed propaganda as with science. His divination of the future ("And this will undoubtedly continue until the political uniformity and unity of the whole human genus are achieved"); his categorical tone; his vision of a single charismatic with thousands bound hypnotically to his example; his racial postulations, heavy use of the metaphor of contagion, glorification of military service — all would find equivalents in the propaganda of conquest.[53] If propaganda derives Z from A by a "law" of necessity,[54] Tarde proclaims the law that impels the propagation of ideas themselves in the direction of the ultimate. Ideology claims a scientific basis: Tarde helps provide it. Now it is a fact of some political consequence that the most adept propagator of ideas in twentieth-century America did not go in for heroic visions of conquest. A liberal self-identified with the tradition of Mill, Edward Bernays undertook neither to dominate nor dazzle the many but simply to beguile a nation into health.

It was in a society marked by the concentration of industrial power, and, on the consumer side, the search for health of mind and body that Bernays rose to prominence and flourished. Analyst of the public mind and consultant to the corporations that supplied cars and radios, bread and cigarettes to the new consumer society, Bernays illustrates the link between the fascination with psychology and the modernization of production. The coming of the consumer society was accompanied by a broad shift from the Victorian ethic of self-denial to a therapeutic ideal of well-being. Bernays for his part made use of physicians, health commissioners, and sanitarians, and in fact got started by breaking Victorian conventions for the discussion of venereal disease. He broke them in the name of health. How well his tactics caught on can be judged by the mass marketing of the belief that the taboos of tradition have at last fallen — a topic to be discussed later.[55]

Reflecting in 1950 on the ascendancy of social sciences whose program it was "to manipulate and adjust" human beings in the name of their own well-being (and the policy of Bernays was just that), Lionel Trilling traced the liberal style of management to the model of a parent's oversight of a child; specifically,

> the paradigm of . . . the child who is *understood* by its parents, hemmed in, anticipated and lovingly circumscribed, thoroughly taped, finding it easier and easier to conform internally . . . [and] yielding to understanding as never to coercion. . . . The act of understanding becomes an act of control.[56]

Although the target of this description is a novel style of solicitude, overbearing even in its benevolence, in essence the paradigm is as old as Locke. Understanding the child the better to mold him; making the mind and not just the body yield; using a sort of calculated kindness along with a policy of constant oversight — these are the very principles of Lockean education. Blown up to political dimensions, the parental model becomes (Trilling suggests) the Grand Inquisitor watching over his children with a show of love. It is in fact fraught with ambiguous potential. Precisely as a technique or "act of control" (one that seems to promise mastery not just of nature but our own nature), the Lockean method lent itself to applications far from the warmth of the household. A scheme like the Panopticon is ambiguous in the highest degree, embodying a kind of ruthless benevolence. As the product of a technological mentality it seems to dramatize the ambiguity inherent in technique itself as a thing that can be applied to different ends. And this quality belongs as well to psychology itself.

To many psychology, the study of the mind, is the key to every lock.[57] In fact it has been put to such various uses that some simply clash. Having helped construct the image of woman as hysteric, psychology is now the woman's friend, filling the columns of magazines with intimate counsel.[58] In turn, the therapeutic bent of American culture dates back to the time when psychological nostrums promised relief from the ills of the industrial system that "the psychology of management" helped support.[59] Standing as a sort of figure of the entire therapeutic complex is Edward Bernays; but if Bernays believed in the manipulation of public opinion, so did Joseph Goebbels, whose stagecraft went well beyond the construction of media-events and the perpetration of innocent shams. If the nonviolent protester wants to shake the public out of its stupor, so does the terrorist.[60] If Martin Luther King reminds us what it is to be afflicted with inferiority feelings, defeatism, frustration, and hostility, so does the "Unabomber."[61] Indeed if psychology is the password to the inner self, it was also the code of the superpowers — nuclear deterrence "above all depend[ing] on psychological criteria."[62] Like physics claiming cognizance over the infinitely small and the infinitely large, the psychological domain seems to encompass both the self and the systems that dwarf and deride it. Along with the expansion of private therapeutic services, too, has gone the conversion of politics into a full-time publicity operation — a play for "the public mind." Psychology, it seems, lends itself in the manner of a technique to conflicting purposes. It possesses a kind of open-ended utility enabling those committed to a given position to offer a show of hard scientific support. In other words, as well as authorizing the transformation of human beings in line with the prescriptions of theory, it falls into the category of ideology as an argument produced to defend given interests. To the degree that the modern age is an age of ideology, then, it is also an age of psychology.

CHAPTER 2

Puppet Government:
The Art of Edward Bernays

The founder of public relations as we know it, Edward Bernays was Freud's nephew twice over, his mother being Freud's sister, and his father's sister Freud's wife. Born in 1891 into an upper-middle-class family, Bernays grew up in privilege in New York. His father, conventionally authoritarian but independent in matters of religion, prospered as a grain broker. Bernays sat through an education in agricultural science at Cornell but soon enough found his true calling elsewhere: in shaping public opinion, or as he put it, engineering consent. Over the years Bernays promoted everything from sexual candor to tobacco. Already rich by the Depression — for it was in the period between the World Wars that big business discovered the efficacy of public relations — he kept his fortune through that desperate decade. Later, in the manner of an industrialist turned public benefactor, he devoted himself to causes. Perhaps his dearest cause was public relations itself: he began promoting it, and not incidentally himself, in his twenties, and by old age saw it as one of the highest and most morally demanding of vocations. Into his nineties, in fact, he was still campaigning to have it licensed like Freud's original profession, medicine. Bernays died in 1995.

The imagery that today fills our public space as ether was once thought to fill space itself is an homage to Edward Bernays. His traces are everywhere, from the professional tailoring of the presidential image (Bernays spruced up Coolidge) to the therapeutic content of television to the subculture of the "facilitator," a role he practically invented. Bernays had a hand, it appears, in the introduction of sky-writing,[1] and it is indeed as if his own name were on the public realm, albeit in vanishing characters. In *The Presentation of Self in Everyday Life* (a work influential in its own right), Erving Goffman portrays simply everyone as a Bernays, stage-managing their own performance of themselves, creating "the kind of impression that will lead [others] to act voluntarily in accordance with [their] own plans."[2] The art of inducing others to go along with a design was reduced by Bernays to a formula.

Bernays made his start after World War I, when the collapse of conventional fictions in Europe cleared the way for the fictions of Mussolini and Goebbels. In contrast to those impresarios of the public stage, however, Bernays sets out to induce conformity all over again, albeit in a more liberal key. His credo in fact isn't so different from that of the famous prewar publicity agent Leopold Bloom: "Commerce, Operatic Music, Amor, Publicity, Manufacture, Liberty of Speech, Plural Voting, Gastronomy, Private Hygiene, Seaside Concert Entertainments, Painless Obstetrics and Astronomy for the People."[3] Bernays conducts a media-event in a campaign against venereal disease and sexual hypocrisy — Liberty of Speech and Private Hygiene in one. He creates a fashion for Spanish combs. As an advance man for Caruso and the Ballet Russe he fosters the cult of celebrity that still reigns. He promotes Lithuanian independence and salad dressing, Cartier jewels and racial equality. He organizes a moderation craze. He is the one, it appears, behind the carving of Ivory soap in schools — the Oz behind the curtain. He orchestrates a celebration of Edison that has been called "one of the most astonishing pieces of propaganda ever engineered in this country during peace time."[4] In his work for the American Tobacco Company his unseen hand coaxes physicians to issue pro-tobacco findings, stage manages a Fifth Avenue demonstration under the banner of women's rights, and in the midst of the Depression gets fashionable New York to go crazy over green, the color of a pack of Lucky Strikes. In the tradition of Josiah Wedgwood's use of "impartial" others to puff his goods and the leaders of taste to adopt them, he pulls strings again and again, achieving his end by a crafty obliquity in preference to more direct methods. Such a taste for the covert characterizes the public relations expert, who "hides his business intentions in the role of someone interested in the public welfare," as distinguished from the mere ad man.[5] In 1941 the maverick literary theorist Kenneth Burke published a satire on American electioneering in which the inhabitants of an imaginary island pretend to cure their ills by throwing out one ruler after another even as the same businessmen retain their power. The name of the island is Psychoanalysia.[6]

A kind of social engineer with a fancy for trickery, Bernays advocated the reconciliation of interests and emancipation from archaic attitudes. Certainly he imagined himself to be doing something nobler than selling. With an ancestrally dubious reputation, the figure of the huckster is altogether too traditional for a modern like Bernays. As medicine stands to quackery, so in theory stands public relations to the marketing of goods. Asserting the medical virtues of public relations therefore enabled Bernays to raise his work above the disrepute — the smell of fakery and "the public square" — that traditionally surrounds advertising and that once induced Josiah Wedgwood to explore more indirect means of marketing.[7] In its main points the Bernays method in fact recreates that of Wedgwood (himself closely associated with physicians who spoke of curing a sick society). Nor is this coincidental, for Bernays too follows a modernist program of reforming habits and engineering well-being by "manipulating [people] and their motions."[8] He has exactly this sense of puppetry. The very role of the popularizer he inherited from those in the Locke tradition who thought to bring the fruits of education to "multitudes," to "millions."

Indirectly his way of thinking did reach millions as it penetrated the American classroom. Louise Rosenblatt's *Literature as Exploration* (1938), the English teacher's equivalent of Dr. Spock's *Baby and Child Care,* is just what Bernays would have written had he been an educational theorist.

> We of the older generation know that many of the habitual attitudes and ideas that we took for granted have with changed conditions become inappropriate and even anti-social. We possessed much prized habits of thrift, only to have the economists tell us that the socially valuable rule is to spend, not save. Women dutifully restricted the scope of their interests to the home, only to find that the functions of the home itself had changed. . . . We assimilated the doctrine that punitive measures would prevent crime, only to find social scientists asserting that the criminal is to be cured, not punished.[9]

So Bernays could have said verbatim. Both the authority on public relations and the authority on human relations seek to liberate minds from the power of received ideas even as they reduce liberation to a cliché. And completing the analogy is that Rosenblatt as well as Bernays speaks in the name of psychology. Under the Rosenblatt method the teacher performs a generalized psychotherapy, with students first being encouraged to react "spontaneously" to the novel or poem in a classroom version of free association and then to work through more critically their own "projections" onto it; all with the aim of liberating them from unconsciously acquired beliefs and equipping them to choose more rational values. Both Bernays and Rosenblatt, then, envision themselves moderns freeing society from ideas that no longer work, like the locked-up gears of some rusted machine.[10] Yet the proposition that criminals need to be cured (to take but one example) was not born in the twentieth century but in the eighteenth-century movement for penal reform that included Bentham. And so it is with the modernism of Bernays: in spite of a show of novelty, it both carries forward and dilutes an Enlightenment tradition that created the very theory and practice of impressing ideas on the minds of many in the name of progress. That Bernays pursues this program of benevolence even in a world of uprooted moral postulates, even as the Enlightenment faith goes dark — this probably contributes to the feeling of being suspended in space that he leaves with us. But only by looking more closely at his method can we place Bernays in relation to the modernist tradition of "scientific psychology." One of his writings of the 1920s, filled with a sense of infinite possibility, outlines his theory and practice with unusual boldness. Its very title is a flourish: "Manipulating Public Opinion: The Why and the How."

Equipped with a knowledge of "introspective psychology," the manager of public opinion (he says) educates citizens out of old ideas that stand in the way of progress. As one example Bernays cites his work on behalf of the National Association for the Advancement of Colored People (NAACP) in 1920. For publicity reasons it is decided to hold the association's convention in Atlanta — to contest traditional Southern opinion from within the South itself. The conference being designed to jolt the press, blacks and whites are put on the same dais. A certain dramatic strategy governs the construction of the entire event:

> Here, then, were the main factors of a created circumstance; a conference to be held in a southern city, with the participation of national leaders and especially with the participation of southern gentlemen.
>
> The scene had been set. The acts of the play followed logically.
>
> And the event ran off as scheduled. The program itself followed the general scheme. Negroes and white men from the South on the same platform, expressing the same point of view.

Though in retrospect it is plain that NAACP goals like the abolition of lynching and Jim Crow were not achieved, Bernays, writing in 1928, felt warranted in claiming that the conference had its effect and produced "a change, or at least a modification for the better, in the public attitude toward the Negro."

Characteristically, however, after recounting this attack on racial prejudice, the author changes key and turns to his work to save the millinery industry from the incursions of the felt hat. "What to do to prevent débâcle?" Analyzing the problem, Bernays determines that "the habit-using habits of women" are subject to four sources of influence ranging from "the woman at the fountain-head of style who made the fashion by her approval" to "beautiful girls." Mobilizing these powers in favor of the makers of ornate hats is simply a matter of engineering. First "a committee of prominent artists was organized to choose the six most beautiful girls in New York" to show off the productions of the millinery industry at a ball at the Astor. Just as the endorsements of respected figures were enlisted for the Atlanta conference, the support of style authorities is rounded up to make sure the millinery ball has the desired effect. Bernays's account of these events is mock-heroic and tinged with absurdity. Unlike the Atlanta convention, though, the mock event is an unqualified success. The felt hat is beaten back. "In ten days the [millinery] industry was humming." The women of America had "quite rightly accepted the leadership" of the fashion authorities, almost like the multitude that follows the wise minority in the political theory of John Stuart Mill. Emboldened by success, Bernays next undertakes to promote velvet by getting Paris, the capital of fashion, to adopt it. With the help of a go-between he arranges for "the distinguished Countess this or Duchess that" to wear velvet. Success is swift, thousands of jobs preserved. "The fields in which public opinion can be manipulated to conform to a desired result are as varied as life itself."[11]

Bernays writes with the pride of discovery, as though reporting some insight, at once simple and world-transforming, never achieved before. Perhaps he caught the mood of an era when America was declaring cultural independence from Europe.[12] Yet the theory and practice of changing minds by changing the impressions that act on them originated not with Bernays or the pedagogical theorists of his day but the reformers of the Enlightenment, inventors of "the profession of opinion-molding" that he dreamed of licensing *as* a profession.[13] The very role of engineer of the motions of others Bernays inherits, even if his interpretation is novel. So too, it was from the Enlightenment tradition and not from the Christian remedies then on the land (*Jesus, the Christ, in the Light of Psychology*) that Bernays, a secular Jew, constructed his therapeutic program. As a sort of professed doctor of the body politic, he succeeds all those of the Enlightenment — from pedagogues and factory owners and physicians to the fictional Homais, the apothecary-publicist of *Madame Bovary* — who sought to cure backward ways and correct the maladjusted in the name of health. In point of fact there isn't much new about the Bernays method. Though he didn't know it, in outline it reproduces that of a man who died in 1795. In perhaps the first instance of its kind, Josiah Wedgwood carefully orchestrated public opinion as part of a campaign to win parliamentary support for a new canal.14 Evidently the industrialist saw the fashioning of a public consensus as a technical problem in its own right, just as Bernays would in turn. The indirection shown in his approach to Parliament — for he had to proceed "by degrees and by stealth"15 — would also become a Bernays mark. When Wedgwood said that opponents of the modernization of production were suffering from delusion,16 a path was opened to the argument that one who seeks to modernize attitudes, like Bernays, performs a kind of cure.

And for Wedgwood the production process spills over into the effort to produce a market for his goods by techniques that have since become givens of consumer culture — the trademark, the catalog, the showroom, the guarantee. His principal tactic, though, was the celebrity endorsement, and it is here, in his use of powerful figures, that Wedgwood anticipates Bernays most strikingly. Long before Bernays enlisted leaders in the expectation that others would follow, long before he succeeded in using duchesses and countesses to advertise velvet, Wedgwood placed his china with the aristocracy in the well-founded hope that middle-class consumers would then adopt it. "It is plain from a thousand instances," he wrote, "that if you have a favorite child you wish the public to fondle & take notice of, you have only to make a choice of the proper sponcers."17 With something of the same wry delight in his own tactical skill as Bernays, Wedgwood shaped the public reception of his wares by the use of noble "sponcers" — the word later to dominate television. So it is that he filled orders for the royalty of Europe even though in all likelihood he believed in monarchy as little as Bernays. Even the cause of civil rights has a Wedgwood link (beyond his manufacture of antislavery hairpins), for it was Dissenters like him, outsiders in an officially Anglican nation, men excluded from public office, who led the campaign of their day for political reform. Indeed Bernays's father joined a sect founded by one of them — Priestley, the popularizer of the psychology of Hartley.

With the scheme of Wedgwood's son Tom to engineer the reception of ideas as his father did vases, and to create men of genius to convey those ideas to the public as his father "made" workers, we come even closer, perhaps, to the ideal of public relations. Still in the tradition of Hartleyan psychology, Tom Wedgwood dreamed of methodizing the way children receive impressions with the aim of producing genius much like John Stuart Mill's. (The word "impression" would later pass into the lexicon of stage managers like Bernays.) Reasoning that the progress of society depends on "the influence of superior characters," the younger Wedgwood proposed to create those characters with the help of superior tutors like Wordsworth and Coleridge — they declined — and in time send them out into the world to "win esteem and affection" for enlightened ideas.[18] In this scheme of human production we seem to see the outline of public relations — the art of winning good will as opposed to just selling — and the precursor of later efforts to enlighten the many by some mixture of cajolery and indoctrination.

Yet it is hard to take the fashion leaders who carried the public over to the cause of fancy hats as the elite of knowledge. Indeed, as paradoxical as it may sound, Bernays in every way undermines the tradition in which he stands. With his sudden plunges into the absurd as with the descent from race to hats, he seems to be laughing at both himself and others. In the same way he sports with the Enlightenment tradition responsible for his own imagined identity as one who reforms habits, cures prejudices, manages impressions for educational ends, "engineer[s] . . . a good and happy life."[19] From different political positions, both Hannah Arendt and T. W. Adorno maintained that psychology collapsed in the face of events of the Second World War, Arendt arguing that both the victims and executioners of the SS "can no longer be psychologically understood,"[20] Adorno that the enthusiasts of Fascism no longer follow the laws of psychological motivation but identify, in a kind of gross emotional pantomime, with a leader they believe in as little as he does them. If "psychology abdicates" at the Fascist crowd or the death camp,[21] the liberal Bernays marks the point where the psychological tradition of the Enlightenment empties out into the sea of mass culture. The paternalism that runs through the tradition, from Locke's educational prescriptions to Wedgwood's benevolent despotism over his workers to his son's plan for the total control of a child's impressions — in Bernays this declines to a seriocomic pretense of manipulating the public for its own good.[22] The belief in enlightenment itself is ironically qualified by the pessimistic estimate of the powers of human reason that Bernays absorbed from theorists of the irrational, above all his uncle. The faith in progress that powered the tradition is proclaimed by Bernays even in the aftermath of a World War that demolished its basis. With Bernays it is as though we reached the reductio ad absurdum of the therapeutic tradition, which is not to say it came to an end. Its origins are, however, forgotten. If the displacement of originals by copies is a feature of mass culture, Bernays takes the place of his own originals, who drop from public memory in the culture he helped create.

*

When Ben Franklin undertook to improve the night patrol in Philadelphia's streets, he first "prepar[ed] the Minds of People for the Change" by suggesting a measure to one club after another, but always artfully so that the idea seemed to spread of its own accord. "This Idea being approv'd by the Junto, was communicated to the other Clubs, but as arising in each of them."[23] Here, then, in Franklin's use of a sociable style so different from the old way of prescription, is a sort of first approximation of the Bernays method. On the other side of the Atlantic, Josiah Wedgwood — also a dissenter, entrepreneur, scientist, inventor, member of the culture of sociability, master of salesmanship — experimented with tactics of influence as well as dyes and glazes, producing the very prototype of the Bernays method. Wedgwood organized fads, used notables, manipulated the press. But what seems like a stroke of art in Franklin or Wedgwood's hands seems less original two centuries later. Wedgwood took pottery into the industrial era. Bernays in an already mechanized society designed mechanisms of compliance, chief among them the use of powerful others to execute his schemes.

Following Wedgwood, Bernays's favorite way to reach consumers was to enlist their "group leaders," the figures who influence them. The formula he came up with was to rally the prominent to whatever his cause happened to be, in the expectation that others would follow: an indirection that raises him above common salesmen and lends his endeavors an aspect of civic merit.[24] Bernays makes optimum use of insiders. Editors, municipal worthies, physicians, health commissioners — all are quite willing to be used by him. Newspapers are his special toy: he places material in their pages at will. In what may be the first cosmetic enhancement of a president's image, Bernays undertakes to endear Calvin Coolidge to the public by having him breakfast with Hollywood stars. The press obliges by reporting the sessions as news. This sort of thing is repeated time and again as the press plays into the schemes of the engineer of consent:

> To get publicity for a new soap when Procter & Gamble was expanding
> its line of soaps, I wrote to newspaper editors asking why they shouldn't
> critically appraise a new soap, just as they criticized music, drama and
> literature. A flood of publicity resulted.[25]

As poor a light as such incidents throw on the "objectivity" of journalism, they were nothing unusual. It is estimated that by 1930 press agents, as they were

called, "had come to outnumber journalists in New York City" and "were responsible for at least half of all news items in the papers."[26] ("Pray get another
article in the next paper," Wedgwood once wrote his partner.)[27] Few could have
been more successful than Bernays at planting news and gaining the civic
authority of print for their private designs. With its influence over opinion, the
newspaper provides the mechanical advantage that enables Bernays to work
the motives of the public.

To Bernays publicity is a technique, a means to an end. The ends he
believes in include equal rights, emancipation from archaic attitudes, sexual
enlightenment, getting along, and indeed getting ahead. In liberalism he sees
a happy end to the conflict between private gain and public good. He misses
no chance to affirm the "coincidence . . . between the public and the private
interest" as if it were the solution to the riddle of history.[28] Now engineering
a "coincidence" of interests — designing institutions in such a way that people
need only consult their own advantage to promote the general good — was
the passion of Jeremy Bentham. The reconciliation of public and private interests was for Bentham the great task of legislation, and the Panopticon a perfect tool for the purpose. As we might imagine, Bernays too takes a kind of
panoptic position. Working out of sight and claiming to see into the public
mind, even down to motives obscure to itself, he is the hidden one at the center of things, the eye from which there are no secrets. Who possesses more
penetrating insight than the man like Bernays in touch with people's springs of
action? When Bernays speaks of the "invisible governors" of society, those able
to "control the public mind" because they understand it, he uses the very language of the Panopticon.[29] His role, then, derives from the tradition of
Bentham as much as from Freud; between Bernays and the architect of transparency come those American sexual progressives who thought to render
human life itself transparent by throwing on it the light of science.[30]

Strange to say, Bernays persuaded himself that by shaping opinion he was
actually teaching the public "how to express itself," and by "pull[ing] the wires"
of the public he was preserving liberty.[31] His puppetry metaphor was far from
original. "To guide the motions of the human puppet," wrote Helvétius, mentor of Jeremy Bentham, "it is necessary to know the wires by which he is
moved."[32] So Bernays believes as well, although his manipulations resemble the
tricks and appeals of the mass media as much as the benign ruses of the edu-
cator. Bernays pulls our wires, television pushes our buttons. Either way, the
result is a plain mockery of the ideal of citizens who speak and act for themselves. Implied in the manipulations of Bernays, indeed, is a certain contempt

for those he works on. As he describes his aim — "teach[ing] the public how to ask for what it wants"[33] — it sounds like teaching a dog to beg. Did Bernays imagine that by his maneuvers he was somehow arming the public against the demagogues of his era who in *their* cynicism undertook the staging of events?

As shown by his comparison of soap to drama — a foreshadowing of the soap opera, that showcase of the psychological culture — Bernays has a flair for the banal, and in the era of the self-dramatizing Mussolini his methods are almost mercifully trifling. If hired to boost the sales of ping-pong sets, Bernays would round up a committee of experts to extol the physical and civic bene-fits of ping-pong, elevating himself over those who use more commercial meth-ods while yet leaving the leading roles to others. He contents himself with get-ting people to cooperate — with "facilitating." In the Bernays vision of social harmony it seems people are the willing agents of others. Physicians act at the behest of a tobacco company, editors open their columns to the hokum of hired pens, consumers heed the prompting of both editors and physicians. And mov-ing it all along is Bernays. If Charles Lindbergh, conqueror of the air, symbol-ized the man of power in his day, Bernays was an antihero, invisible to the pub-lic that deluged the other with fame; acting through others while the Lone Eagle proclaimed the purity of solitary achievement and promoting liberalism in the face of the other's fascist leanings and affection for Germany.[34]

Acting on the public indirectly, by means of people better placed than himself, gives Bernays leverage. His chosen role is that of the go-between, the stage-setter, the prompter. In one case he introduces John D. Rockefeller Jr. to President Hoover. He seems to be everywhere, this Zelig of history, and to have his hand in everything, but contrary to those at the time who spoke of the Jew as the secret power of the world, Bernays does not wield power but something more like influence.[35] Influence was the ineffable something women were conceded instead of power — the consolation of marginality. For a cen-tury women had been said to possess unbounded power to act through others but not in their own persons: Bernays habitually acts through second parties, exerting far greater power by that means than he possesses in his own right, being neither a man of politics nor of business, science, or even the press. In his use of the mechanism of influence as well as the indirection and craft so commonly if unfairly imputed to women, he adopts a "feminine" model greatly at odds with the stern masculine values of his uncle, Freud. Woman, says Rousseau in *Emile*, is the influence expert. She is because she has to be. "Her sci-ence of mechanics is more powerful than ours; all her levers unsettle the human heart. She must have the art to make us want to do everything which her sex cannot do by itself and which is necessary or agreeable to it."[36] If Allan Bloom is right that for Rousseau the purpose of education is to preserve Emile as far as possible from becoming "a skilled psychologist, able to manipulate others,"[37] the scheme seems to require that women take on that very function — the old tactic of displacement onto the Other. Whatever one may think of Bernays's ruses, at least he doesn't employ that one. The same liberalism that distinguishes him from other stage managers of public events also places him in a kind of identification with women, how sincere it is hard to tell.[38]

Like what is called a functioning person, a functioning society calls for the adjustment of conflicts and the adaptation of one interest to another. As a liberal, Bernays likes finesse and fluidity more than brute power, and when he deplores old ideas he has in mind the authoritarian style. His way of dealing with chieftains of business, of meeting force with wit, is illustrated by a case already referred to. In 1928 Bernays was retained without knowing it by the president and patriarch of the American Tobacco Company, maker of Lucky Strikes, with the intention of keeping him out of the hands of the competition. Usually, however, George Washington Hill preferred a "simple, direct approach" (the very antithesis of the other's artifice), and indeed is portrayed by Bernays as a hard-charging dominator whose emblem is the Bull Durham poster of that animal with sexual organ conspicuously concealed. Possibly as a way of showing this ogre what finesse can do, Bernays promotes Lucky Strikes with all the indirection he can summon. Informed by a prominent psychoanalyst that to some women cigarettes symbolize freedom, he organizes a Torch of Freedom parade on Fifth Avenue on Easter Sunday of 1929. Like many other events he staged, this "protest of man's inhumanity to women"[39] seems half parodic, tinged with fakery. Soon, though, all across America women are sighted smoking on the street. "Age-old customs, I learned, could be broken down."[40] In the midst of the Depression, still dissatisfied with the numbers of women smoking, Hill again consults Bernays, who decides the way to promote Luckies this time is to make the color of the pack, green, the rage. In the spirit of Wedgwood he sets out to manipulate the mechanism of fashion. Green events are organized. Artists and psychologists, happy to place their talents at his service, lecture on green. Magazines, department stores, all the forces of fashion pick up the chant of green. France joins in. A Green Ball takes place in New York, a faint imitation of the parodic dinners of a single color staged in ancient Rome. It is all a master stroke of obliquity. Throughout the craze no one but the impresario knows the purpose of it all is simply to glamorize a pack of Lucky Strikes.

It was the opinion of Margaret Mead that scientists in the habit of trickery and deceit fall into a contempt for those they manipulate — or else weave
theories of their own heroic benevolence to excuse their acts. In the second
case, writes Mead,

> the need to justify demeaning other human beings . . . is compensated
> for by [a] kind of delusion of grandeur: that of becoming someone who
> benefits mankind on a large scale, the omnipotent theorist, the all-know-
> ing teacher, the scientist working for the intelligence agency of a par-
> ticular government or conspiring with some secret plot to save the
> world.[41]

In the social scientific writings of Bernays both the note of cynicism and that
of benevolence are distinctly audible. Especially interesting, though, is Mead's
reference to scale, since it calls to mind the effort to scale up the educational
model of Locke — a model featuring trickery. Do not scold a child into reading, says Locke; "Cheat him into it if you can."[42] Here at the very origin of the
modern therapeutic tradition we seem to discern the outlines of Bernays's own
dislike of bullying as well as his love of finesse and happy ruses. For its part,
the Panopticon is built on deception in that the inmates are made to feel they
are being watched even when they aren't. As the dimensions of the deceit are
scaled up, so too are the claims of benevolence: the Panopticon may not be
capable of saving the world, but it is, according to the promotional literature
of the designer, the cure of the social problem. With Bernays both the scope
and the benefits of manipulation rise toward infinity. "The fields in which public opinion can be manipulated to conform to a desired result are as varied as
life itself."[43] And yet in his impersonation of the all-seeing, "panoptic" scientist, Bernays makes a mockery of the role itself.

One experiences a feeling of levitation in reading of Bernays's enactment of the
Enlightenment role of the engineer of the good even after the faith in progress
ran into the twentieth century and the faith in reason into the force of the irrational. And the most mythopoetic and powerful theory of human irrationality
came from his own uncle. Freud's theory, especially its nucleus the unconscious,
possesses great fascination, but is not, I think, to be taken as science or for that
matter religion. The risks of a too literal belief in repression are illustrated in
the present craze of "repressed memories," which would be laughable were it
not for the accusations it fuels, and which probably couldn't have caught on

in the first place if some loosely Freudian notions weren't already public property. Edward Bernays not only belongs to the era when Freud first became an "offstage influence" on American culture,[44] but he himself, Freud's nephew, was as close to being the stage manager of that culture as any single person could be. Seemingly impossibly, in building on the Enlightenment tradition of the malleability of human character and adapting it to a society with an anxious belief in infinite possibility, he identified himself with one who portrayed the intractability of our nature, and the slender prospects for reform, with a power rarely seen before. Bernays went so far as to brag of his "ability to understand and analyze obscure tendencies of the public mind" in a book he presented to Freud.[45]

Like Freud's challenge to theism, Bernays's aim of engineering social harmony derives from the Enlightenment, and so it was, perhaps, that he came to see himself as a co-worker of his uncle, opening up a new science of the mind and battling prejudice and convention — an American Freud whose "new psychology" liberates the public mind from slavery to habit.[46] If Wedgwood moved the movers of taste, Bernays thought to get hold of the ultimate movers, those springs of action hidden in the group mind, in order to promote health and correct the malfunctions of industrial society. In the George Washington Hill story one of Bernays's most characteristic touches was to consult a psychoanalyst, as if to demonstrate to the brutish Hill that a seemingly impractical "Jewish science" can yield the most impressive and tangible results. Yet Bernays considered himself an analyst as well — analyst of the public mind. Drawing a parallel between his services and Freud's researches, he writes that "My uncle, Sigmund Freud, encountered almost insurmountable obstacles in gaining acceptance for psychoanalysis. I decided to establish public acceptance for the work I was doing and have made this an avocation ever since."[47] As already noted, Bernays never gave up on the fantasy of getting public relations licensed like Freud's original profession, medicine. Did he not claim in effect that he manipulated the public for its own good with the same care as a physician?

If Freud denied that psychoanalysis belonged to medicine and never wanted it to become a medical specialty, his nephew by contrast craved the repute of medicine and late in life pled over and over for public relations to be recognized as a profession with medical status. In affecting medical stature, Bernays recalls not only the social workers and other meliorists who cast themselves as "doctors to a sick society" and claimed the authority of medicine[48] as well as Homais, the "chemist" — and publicist — of *Madame Bovary* who got in trouble for practicing medicine without a license, but, again, the early believers in social engineering in the Wedgwood circle, many of whom *were* medical doctors. (Among the thirteen members of the so-called Lunar Society, five were doctors.) Descendants of Locke — another physician and reformer of the mind — believers in both physical and moral hygiene, and, significantly in this context, effective publicists of their cause,[49] these men saw themselves as restoring the body politic to health. With medical status Bernays could claim to be their successor. Medicine, with its tradition of paternalism, might also excuse his little acts of guile as benign deceptions in the interest of the patient.[50]

In his paper "Manipulating Public Opinion," Bernays adverts to the psychological findings that are the secret of his art, to the "diagnostic ability" required to read the public mind. Implicitly he casts himself as a Freud, except that where his uncle emphasized the stubborn survival of the archaic, Bernays stresses the ease with which his new science can overcome the habits of the past — a single stage-managed event sufficing to overcome women's reluctance to smoke.[51] Probably by design, Bernays even got himself publicized as a Freud. In a 1932 piece written somewhere between jest and wonderment, he is described as "a nephew of that other great philosopher, Dr. Sigmund Freud. Unlike his distinguished uncle he is not known as a practicing psychoanalyst, but he is a psychoanalyst just the same. . . . His business is to treat unconscious mental acts with conscious ones."[52] Bernays therefore ranks as a founder of the therapeutic culture now flourishing in America. With his puppetry he mocked the ideal of autonomy: today Americans in large numbers claim to be victims of addiction and abuse with no autonomy at all, and seek psychological help. As a mimic and popularizer of Freud, Bernays also had something to do with introducing the "approved loquacities of psychoanalysis" and the conventions of intimate revelation into public culture, as well as with blasting traditions of reserve.[53] Bernays talks of instinct and superego, of greeting cards that "appeal to the unconscious."[54] In view of the psychosexual content of the mass media, we can say that Bernays's doubling of Freud helped constitute the very culture we inhabit.

The early Bernays joined those campaigners against Victorian morality who crammed everything they hated into the epithet "Puritanism." Curiously, though renowned for his own defiance of prudery, Freud admired the Puritans, to him figures of self-command.[55] Deep differences of vision and temperament evidently divide uncle and nephew, the latter employing a sort of guile traditionally identified with women, and incompatible with the austere masculine values of the former; while the older man's powerful sense of the past, and indeed fascination with the archaic, rule out the younger's easy modernism. The one leans to a Great Man view of history, the other is an antihero in the shadow of the great, unnoticed next to Edison and Ford, Rockefeller and Hoover. Where the uncle shunned the radio and despised the American mad rush for happiness, the nephew did publicity for CBS, contributed to the creation of mass culture, and helped convert the pursuit of happiness into the purchase of hats, refrigerators, cars. And of course where the uncle spoke of the fearless pursuit of truth, the nephew was a man of tricks. Those who brand psychoanalysis a hoax and its founder a showman certainly hit a tender point. In effect they reduce Freud to the nephew who subverted his own stated principles.

As the epigraph to his memoirs Bernays chooses a passage from a work by Freud's favorite poet, Milton, seemingly unaware that the words he reproduces are those of a notorious deceiver:

> . . . that grounded maxim
> So rife and celebrated in the mouths
> Of wisest men; that to the public good
> Private respects must yield.

Thus Dalila in *Samson Agonistes*. Yet Bernays was hired to paint the interest of his clients *as* the public good, a task facilitated by his belief that private and public interests coincide — the same ethos that today depicts the timber lobby as stewards of nature and the education lobby as a force for "excellence." While others before him believed in the ultimate harmony of public and private interests, perhaps no one worked like Bernays to rig that outcome, and few can have held a more facile version of the harmony thesis. Certainly his thinking bears but slight resemblance to Mill's. Never could Mill really get himself to believe that the public good would come about if only people dedicated themselves to their own concerns and forgot about wider spheres of action and more expansive ideals of virtue. When Bernays presents himself in the character of a man of vision enlightening the people in spite of their servitude to habit (a Miltonic role in its own right) — when he entitles his memoirs *Biography of an Idea* as though after Mill's intellectual autobiography — he pantomimes Mill just as he also does Mill's German translator, Freud.[56] The uncle ranks Milton first among poets and considers Mill, in all his ethereality, "perhaps the man of the century who best managed to free himself from the domination of customary prejudices,"[57] the nephew seems to identify himself as the inheritor of the Milton-Mill tradition.

Retained by the American Tobacco Company, Bernays looks for "some way to link public interest in a new sanitary method of cigar manufacture with the private interest of American Cigar in selling more" of its machine-made products.[58] When he sends Freud a box of cigars, however, they are Havanas. Were the cigars a royalty for the use of the title of psychoanalyst? In gratitude his uncle sends him a copy of the *General Introductory Lectures*, which becomes America's introduction to the new psychology. I doubt Freud cared for his popularity. Though he established the notion of the Freudian slip in the public mind — Frederick Crews calls this a "public relations success"[59] — he was too much of an elitist to regard the market, much less court it. At the prompting of Bernays the editors of *Cosmopolitan* once proposed that Freud furnish articles on popular topics (the kind of pieces Bruno Bettelheim would write in later years). He rejected the offer with indignation. Apparently he despised celebrity as much as he loved fame.[60]

> This absolute submission of your editors [Freud wrote Bernays] to the rotten taste of an uncultivated public is the cause of the low level of American literature and to be sure the anxiousness to make money is at the root of this submission. A German publisher would not have dared to propose to me on what subjects I had to write. In fact, the subjects brought forward in your letter are so commonplace, so far out of my field, that I could not give them the attention of my pen.[61]

Particularly offensive to Freud is the editors' assumption that he is as yielding, as interested in getting along, as they. Getting along is Bernays's watchword. "It is now generally recognized that people, groups, and organizations need to adjust to one another if we are ever to have a smooth-running society."[62] If the mechanization of life at the hands of industry and the consequent dulling of the sensation of being once sent Americans in large numbers in quest of therapy, Bernays uses a mechanical term — "adjustment" — to denote a state of health.

To many of the generation of immigrants' children that included Bernays, adjustment to society meant learning such things as sanitary practices, regular work habits, and the English language. In adult life Bernays carried out this ethic of assimilation, fitting different interests together like Pandarus orchestrating the union of others and associating himself with progressive causes from medicine and soap to industrial bread and machine-made cigars.

The second phase of his memoirs Bernays entitles "Adjustment." When he drops a friendly hint to someone important and things begin to happen — when at his suggestion art galleries put together an exhibit to promote salad oil, much as Wedgwood promoted his pots by getting them into the paintings of famous artists — the wheels go around because everyone is in adjustment. Ideally, all the meshings are frictionless.[63] For the purposes of Bernays, adjustment is a mechanism of infinite utility. With its indirect methods and teasing suggestions and wondrous efficacy, the ethic of getting along must have seemed to him an advance over the authoritarianism of men like George Washington Hill — a sleek, streamlined, modern design as against the massive, monumental shapes of the past.

According to Bruno Bettelheim, Freud in contrast to Bernays "cared little about 'adjustment' and did not consider it valuable," although, significantly, his American interpreters set great store by it.[64] How could Freud promote adjustment to society when his own thinking went well beyond what society considered decent and when he took upon himself "the fate of being in the Opposition and of being put under the ban of the 'compact majority' "?[65] If Freud challenged public opinion in the tradition of John Stuart Mill, Bernays offers himself as Mill's successor, no longer just bemoaning public opinion but doing something about it. Mill laments the power of the newspaper over public opinion, Bernays plants news. But when Bernays sends Freud a copy of his first book, *Crystallizing Public Opinion*, Freud responds with disdain. "I have received your book through Boni and Liveright. As a truly American production it interested me greatly."[66] That is all. Can Bernays have missed the icy contempt in Freud's voice? (Can he not have thought twice about his own methods when he learned that Goebbels, the mover behind the campaign to "crystallize" Jewish windows, used the book as a guide?) Freud's sharp reply hints at his differences with the nephew who styled himself after him and who, in his own fashion, took part in the Enlightenment tradition.

Freud spoke in the name of the Reality Principle. What meaning could the Reality Principle have to one who conjured a fortune into being with sleight of hand, who dealt in the production of imagery with a reality content approaching zero, the owner of a method with a potential, as he believed, as open as the sky? In the hands of Bernays, Freud's severe skepticism becomes a belief in the manipulability of events and the prospects of human reform; Freud's disdain of adjustment, promotion of adjustment itself. Such are the ironies attending the Americanization of Freud. Adam Smith, a man of stoic ideals, justified a consumer way of life that turns out to be as alien to stoicism as any could imaginably be; just as ironically, in American society Freud's sternly neutral treatment of sex — his analytical stoicism — yields to constant excitation. In this translation, it seems, all but the name of the author was lost. And among the translators was his own nephew. Lionel Trilling once observed that Freud enables us to oppose the seductions of our culture — to resist and not adjust to its appeals and demands.[67] The remark brings out the conflict between Freud and his nephew, the prince of seduction; between Freud's rather ironized esteem, and the nephew's impersonation, of John Stuart Mill; between Freud's modernism, qualified by an admiration of Moses and those neo-Israelites the Puritans, and the unqualified modernism of Bernays. As this may suggest, whatever the merits of Freud's thought,[68] its adaptation to America and conversion into the common coin of American cultural life amount to a sort of contradiction in themselves. Freud's subtle and highly personal blend of modernism and stoicism did not survive translation at the hands of his nephew. If the logic of enlightenment calls for ideas to be conveyed to "multitudes," to "millions," Bernays subverted Freud in the very act of popularizing his thought and putting it to work in an industrial society.

The Green Ball, exhibitions of salad: it all seems a conjuror's trick, a folly lighter than air, too much like make-believe to be of any account. The oddity is that Bernays's methods had real and even grave effects.

The mobilization of public opinion in World War I — a fateful step in the totalizing of war — opened possibilities that political hoodlums and charlatans as well as comedians like Bernays were sure to seize on. Hitler, an orator, asserted the supremacy of the Aryan race even while proclaiming in print his contempt for the German masses. Also full of contempt for the public he sought to dominate, Mussolini got his start as a journalist concocting news. As we know, Bernays too staged fake events, planted news, pretended insight into the public mind, attempted to impress his purposes on a passive citizenry. Unlike Mussolini and Hitler, however, he had liberal views and used his craft not to glorify himself but to camouflage his role and, as he thought, outwit brutality and ignorance. In the tradition of the liberal he apparently considered public relations a neutral instrument usable for good or ill, his own uses of it of course being good — a persuasion not shaken by his discovery that Goebbels studied and employed his methods. Evidently he simply concluded that his own white magic had been perverted. It turns out, though, that Bernays's practices were not as innocent as he imagined.

Bernays takes delight in exposing his methods in print, as though marveling that such impressive results could have sprung from such simple formulas. No success is too large or too small for his ledger. "From Lithuania to silks is a long distance," he writes. "And yet the same technique of creating circumstances [that is, staging events] which freed the Lithuanians helped to create a market for more beautiful silks"[69] — a dizzying descent characteristic of the man's mock-heroic mode. Today the American publicity machine beams the message that there is no limit to what we can produce, consume, achieve, or indeed become. (The infinite *self*-malleability of human nature?) Encountering Bernays one begins to suspect that the line "You can be anything you want" is simply a presentable version of the manipulator's belief that there is nothing *he* can't achieve. Didn't Bentham dream of a manipulator's utopia where an unseen hand would be capable of everything from "reforming the vicious" to "instructing the willing"? Now, however, rather than acclaiming their own powers aloud like a quack or a Faust, the American heirs of Bentham promote the notion that there is no limit to what anyone at all can do. America, says Bernays, is "the land of unlimited possibilities," especially so, perhaps, for engineers like himself.[70] It is true that Bernays plays down his abilities as much as he vaunts them. He concedes his powers are limited by the nature of the material he deals with. But he doesn't feel very constrained. "Human nature is readily subject to modification," wrote the nephew of Freud.[71] Bernays came close indeed to claiming omnipotence when he asserted that "The fields in which public opinion can be manipulated to conform to a desired result are as varied as life itself." With his seductive demonstrations of the uses of his methods, Bernays contributed richly to the culture of manipulation that now defines our public life.

That our politicians style their images, that politics itself is largely given over to the production of imagery for public consumption, everyone knows. And here the innocence of public relations ceases. No great gap separates Bernays's vision of the wondrous possibilities of "Manipulating Public Opinion" from Nixon's belief that presidents "must try to master the art of manipulating the media not only to win in politics but in order to further the programs and causes they believe in."[72] (It irked Bernays that Nixon gave public relations a bad name.) But Nixon was no more obsessed with publicity than his predecessor. The other side of the public myth of infinite possibility is the infinite profit of duping the public, and it was in the Vietnam War, construed by Johnson as a public relations drama and plotted by men taken with "the unlimited possibilities in manipulating people,"[73] that the worst fallacies and the heaviest costs of the engineering of consent really came out. At the very time the

United States was pouring violence beyond all measure on a small country, the authors of this policy spoke of the struggle to impress audiences and win over their hearts, using a language that looked back to the origins of publicity in show business. As the Tet offensive began, Johnson's first move was a psychological one: "to orchestrate a public relations drive designed to promote optimism."[74]

During World War I, writes Bernays, "evacuation hospitals . . . came in for a certain amount of criticism because of the summary way in which they handled their wounded. The name was changed to 'evacuation post,' thus changing the *cliché*. No one expected more than adequate emergency treatment of an institution so named."[75] As a sly proof of the power of a name, the anecdote brings to mind Wedgwood's idea of naming a cheap line of vases after the Duchess of Devonshire. As a specifically military coinage, though, "evacuation post" calls up the code-words later to envelop the Vietnam War like some vile if odorless gas: "protective reaction" for B-52 bombing, "pacification" for the burning of huts, "refugee camp" for concentration camp, "weed-killer" for defoliant, "Incinderjell" — which has both "Cinderella" and "Jell-O" in it — for napalm.[76] Rigging language, Bernays observes, is a quick and easy way of "changing people's ideas."[77] It is psychology in action. The same manipulative mentality lay behind the campaign for hearts and minds, as they were called, during the Vietnam War.

When Bernays wrote that the public relations man has to know "how to speak in the language of his audience,"[78] he little imagined the fruit his advice would bear forty years later in Vietnam. In a manual on the art of shamming produced there in 1967, American "psyoperators" were given the same counsel. It seems that the Joint U.S. Public Affairs Office (JUSPAO), the center of psychological operations in Vietnam, found that its own "communicators" were such blunderers that their propaganda gave itself away.[79] As a corrective it issued a manual on the dos-and-don'ts of shamming, including instructions on how to make propaganda undetectable. The idea was that if the Americans spoke the peasants' language convincingly enough, they wouldn't identify the messages as propaganda and their hearts and minds would be ours. In Vietnam we tried "to understand and change a people strange to us,"[80] which is to say the project Bernays inherited from men like Bentham — that of figuring people out in order to reshape them — became a kind of national imperative. The pseudo-science of manipulation, what the manual calls PsyOp, wasn't invented on the spot in Vietnam. It was shipped there from the nation that first made an industry of public relations. But the art of selling imagery found little success in Vietnam, for it found little market. Unable to win the hearts and minds of the people, we avenged our failure in fire.

The technicians of deception who drafted the JUSPAO paper were filled with the idea that if only they did their work skillfully enough their audience might be won over. The document is made up of warnings and cautionary examples that impress the technical nature of the assignment on the busy communicator:

> *DO* use photographs instead of sketches whenever possible. Appropriate photographs increase the credibility of a message. Numerous Vietnamese seem to regard photographs as positive proof of the events being depicted, and they seem to be unaware that photographs can be altered.

> *DO* try to be subtle; attempt to develop PsyOp items which do not appear to be "obvious propaganda." . . . The Psyoperator should always be alert to the need for developing and discovering innovations in the dissemination of persuasive messages so that they are difficult to identify as attempts to persuade. PsyOp items which are not readily identifiable as propaganda are more credible than any other type of message.

> *DO NOT* produce messages which contain obvious lies *OR INCREDIBLE TRUTHS.*

> *DO* attempt to be objective. A message which "rants and raves" at the enemy is not likely to induce them to perform the desired act.[81]

How reminiscent of Goebbels it all is — the pretense of scientific detachment and psychological insight, the stress on the persuasive power of images, the preference for a straight style that doesn't appear propagandistic, the doctrine that credibility is all, the anxiety that something said might backfire.[82] And yet the Joint U.S. Public Affairs Office did not model its work on Goebbels but on American public relations. Its project of manufacturing attitudes is the project of Bernays (the unwitting mentor of Goebbels), as its strategy mirrors the man's own maxim that the best way to get people to perform the desired act is exactly *not* to bid them to do it in the manner of an advertiser. As Habermas remarks, public relations "must absolutely not be recognizable as the self-presentation of a private interest"[83] — a caveat Bernays took to heart when he organized a vast celebration of the light bulb without mentioning General Electric, and that the "psyoperators" observe in their own way by trying to fashion propaganda not recognizable as what it is. Bernays remains offstage, works through "impartial" others, avoids the vulgarity of selling; the psychological warriors of JUSPAO dream of making propaganda that does not advertise its own nature.

Nor are these resemblances an accident, for it is out of the American culture of manipulation that the thinking of the "psyoperators" arose. Moreover, as advisor to the United Fruit Company, Bernays himself was deeply involved in what now looks like a prelude to the Vietnam War — the campaign against the communist insurgency in Guatemala. In his introduction to *The Engineering of Consent*, published in 1955 and containing an essay likening public relations to military tactics, Bernays issues some cautions on the art of winning hearts and minds which, banal as they are, virtually predict the Vietnam manual.

> Bernays: The use of pictures to illustrate text is sound tactics. But if you were preparing a promotion piece on new fashions about town, you would want to make sure no out-of-date gowns or accessories were worn by anyone in the picture.

> JUSPAO: *DO NOT* use illustrations which contradict specific statements in the text. For example, if refugees are supposed to be "happily receiving gifts" from GVN officials, the illustrating photographs should include, at the very minimum, someone who is smiling. The refugees should not look like apathetic automata.[84]

> Bernays: A careless misprint may convert an otherwise effective mailing piece into a subject of ridicule and make it boomerang upon you.

> JUSPAO: Literally dozens of PsyOp items have been reviewed which contained ambiguous sentences, and many of these were capable of an interpretation which could be counterproductive to the Allied PsyOp effort.

> Bernays: In public relations necessity for care extends to every aspect of tactical effort.

> JUSPAO: Every item produced should be viewed as putting the entire PsyOp program on trial.[85]

In the world of publicity, not only are high abstractions like progress reduced to teapots and cameos, silks and hats, but tips on the way to promote fashions grow into counsels of war.

The language of scene staging used by planners and prosecutors of the Vietnam War suggested, in fact, that events themselves can be constructed and managed as a Green Ball. The same fabrication metaphor responsible for "making" a person or "making" an institution also inspires the crafting of events. In her report on publicity operations in Vietnam, Mary McCarthy produces a number of examples of this fabrication mentality, including a "showcase" concentration camp and a colonel's "painted scale model . . . of an ideal Vietnamese hamlet, which will probably really be built."[86] All of these constructs seem to reflect a belief in the power of sheer ingenuity, like that of Bernays as he managed events and molded outcomes. Apparently, though, the Bernays method presupposes the existence of a consumer society that was absent in Vietnam.

At one time a show business publicist, Bernays thought he saw the transformation of his art into a social science. The mind-readers of the Joint U.S. Public Affairs Office in Vietnam seem to have believed that if only their output were more scientific they would win or at least be able to compete in the battle for the hearts and minds of the peasants; it was only a question of employing well-chosen means to their end. This belief was a delusion. It presumed that the peasants were simply material for them to engineer, like those once subjected to factory discipline and other correctional schemes in the name of their own improvement; it also presumed a market for what they had to sell. The American "psyoperators" in Vietnam exhibited an intellectual version of the contempt that led others to call the peasants gooks and ravage their land. In Vietnam Bernays's facile philosophy of liberating people in spite of themselves — an ironic postscript to the humanitarianism of the Locke tradition — grew into an attempt to liberate people if we had to kill them to do it. It is as though all the ambiguities of Bernays's liberalism were heightened in Vietnam, dramatized in the paradox of aiding a people one despised and rescuing a land one would willingly burn.

The manual I have quoted from is entitled *Lessons Learned from Evaluation of Allied PsyOp Media in Viet Nam*. What the nation learned in Vietnam it is hard to say. To General William Westmoreland, commander of American forces in Vietnam, however, the lesson is clear to this day: "They defeated us psychologically."[87]

CHAPTER 3

Entrapment as Science: The Milgram Experiment

"This is a proof to which you have no right to put a man"
— Samuel Johnson

The pedagogy of Locke, melding paternal benevolence with the technique of an engineer; enlargements of this design also uniting the spirit of benevolence and the "science" of control — both bear out Charles Taylor's analysis of a modern paradigm both humane and technical. We turn now to a psychological experiment that seems to dramatize these traits, conceived as it is in a spirit of humanity and accompanied by a concern for the well-being of subjects even as those subjects are lured into a carefully engineered trap in the name of science and driven, some of them, to fits of hysteria. I refer to Stanley Milgram's famous experiment on obedience to authority. Deep in the background behind this study stands Locke, author of the classical statement of the limits of obedience. I am so far from denying the importance of questioning authority in the spirit of the modern that I question Milgram's own.

As is well known, Milgram camouflaged his experiment as something else. Recruited for "a study of memory," subjects presenting themselves at his lab at Yale were briefed in studiously vague terms, in order not to give the game away. "We want to find out just what effect different people have on each other as teachers and learners, and also what effect *punishment* will have on learning in this situation."[1] A rigged drawing assigns all subjects the role of teacher, after which they are informed that electric shocks (painful but, they are assured, not dangerous) are to be administered to learners for wrong answers. Specifically, they are to read a list of word pairs for a learner to repeat and give shocks of increasing severity for each wrong reply — the learner being a confederate of Milgram's and the shocks fictitious. At this stage in the experiment the situation begins to close in on the subject. The learner deliberately gives one wrong answer after another, so that the subject is caught in the position of having to defy the experimenter and give in to the screams and pleas of the "victim" or disregard them and carry on with his grim duty. A high percentage of the subjects go all the way up the dial, administering what appear to be dangerous levels of shock in spite of the "victim's" entreaties. Subjects who hesitate are told by the experimenter that they must proceed; some break off nonetheless. Variations of the experiment are performed in which elements of the situation, like the distance between subject and "victim," are juggled.[2] This, then, is the experiment that Milgram and many others thought exposed an appalling tendency toward blind submission, even though it took a contrived situation and intense pressure to bring this tendency out and even though there is no evidence that any participant in the experiment ever inflicted suffering on a helpless victim, at the behest of authority or not, either before or after.

The experiment, as I have said, was designed to close in on the subject like a vise. Without really knowing what they are getting into (for the experimenter wants to keep them off guard), the subjects are drawn little by little into an excruciating dilemma: keep shocking the person in the next room or defy a Yale University scientist to his face, in his own lab, in spite of your agreement to perform the experiment and his pressure to continue. Trapped in this bind, many "tremble and sweat"[3] and fifteen go into "full-blown, uncontrollable seizures" of hysteria — a detail mentioned by Milgram in a 1965 write-up of the experiment[4] but not in his book *Obedience to Authority*. (Do the fifteen then have a "tendency" to go into hysterics?) I fail to see that Milgram had any more right than I to inflict such anguish. Perhaps if he had subjected his own actions to the kind of searching analysis he performs on others he might have confronted this question. Does science possess its own authority, so that in its name one can do things that would never be condoned otherwise? But if Milgram robes himself in the authority of science, claiming rights and privileges as an experimenter that I don't possess, then he is in no position to lecture about those who pushed the shock button in the belief that *their* action was covered by authority. They, at least, had to be pressured and fought with themselves. Nor I think was it honest of Milgram to lecture about indifference to suffering we cause, seeing that he himself was perfectly indifferent to the torment of the subjects.

Milgram does not fail to point out that all reasonable psychological care was offered to the subjects upon exit and that no lasting scars resulted from their ordeal. In the attempt to prove his own beneficence — to portray himself as one who cared for the welfare of his subjects more than they knew — he places himself in the tradition of the Lockean father, who possesses authority to the full and is not above the use of deceptions but in the end exhibits "the good will of a compassionate friend."[5] After the experiment

> each subject had a friendly reconciliation with the unharmed victim and an extended discussion with the experimenter. . . . Obedient subjects were assured that their behavior was entirely normal and that their feelings of conflict or tension were shared by other participants. . . . When the experimental series was complete, subjects received a written report which presented details of the experimental procedure and results. Again, their own part in the experiments was treated in a dignified way and their behavior in the experiment respected.[6]

Had Milgram respected his subjects he never would have deceived and racked them to begin with. The unmistakably patronizing tone of his remark signals its falsity. "There is something repulsive," Lionel Trilling once wrote, "in the idea of men being studied for their own good" — to which I would add, doubly repulsive when they are so mastered by their investigator that they return thanks for being deluded with dignity. "The paradigm of what repels us is to be found in the common situation of the child who is *understood* by its parents."[7] As we know, at the origin of the psychological paradigm in which Milgram himself worked is just such a parental model — a model scaled up in a number of Enlightenment projects.

The Enlightenment science of the mind sometimes seems to mean the investigation of *other* minds, and the removal of the investigator himself into a higher category. While for Bentham it is an axiom that human beings in general are driven by self-interest, he claims for himself the purest benevolence; even his scheme to profit from prisoner labor he deemed benevolent. Like those who believe that human beings are the product of conditions but that to some few it is given to construct those conditions, Bentham seems the beneficiary of a double standard.[8] Similarly Milgram. Under the rules of his experiment Milgram excepts his own conduct from critical scrutiny as Bentham excepts himself from the generality of human beings. Milgram seems unaware, however, of the implications of his membership in a tradition of fashioning human behavior.

"Very often," wrote Edward Bernays, "the propagandist is called upon to create a circumstance that will eventuate in the desired reaction on the part of the

public he is endeavoring to reach."⁹ Milgram rigged a situation that "eventu-
ated" in a given reaction.

Everyone knows of cases in which people are lured, pressured, or impor-
tuned into doing things they wouldn't do otherwise. When the police themselves lay the trap, perhaps in a Milgram-like belief that they are merely drawing out a criminal tendency "already there," we speak of entrapment. An
informant for the state takes up residence in a college dormitory and begins
badgering his neighbors to buy drugs. He keeps it up for months, finally sup-
plying the stuff himself, at which point the buyers are arrested. This then is
entrapment. The students were free to resist the agent's importunings of course,
just as Milgram's subjects were free to get up and walk out (and some did), but
surely the case reveals as much about the arrogance of those who feel entitled
to play God as it does any kind of criminality in those they tricked. And so
with Milgram. That in order to get his results he had to construct the experiment and stage-manage its performance with the utmost art, as well as apply
constant pressure on the subjects, suggests that he in fact induced those results
in the same way the state induced drug use. In both cases people are set up.
Arguably Milgram's findings are even more far-fetched than the claims of the
police, for while students are surrounded with drugs and will run into them
sooner or later, the odds are that few of those who underwent the Milgram
experiment ever met or would meet a situation remotely resembling the one in
the lab. To claim that the behavioral sciences "aim to reduce man as a whole,
in all his activities, to the level of a conditioned and behaving animal"¹⁰ is exorbitant, but that the Milgram experiment both degraded its subjects and cued
their responses seems to me beyond dispute. The twist of the knife is that the
experimenter looked down on others for performing acts he did everything
possible, by fair means and foul, to bring about.

But if Milgram's results are so dubious, why have many felt that they tell
us something important?

Not, I think, because he discloses something new but practically the
opposite: because the notion that a torturer lurks inside the average man seems
to agree with the cliché of "the dark side of ourselves" that circulates widely in
the psychological society and has somehow become dear to it. Subjects were
"duped into revealing sides of themselves they would never voluntarily have
exhibited,"¹¹ a critic of Milgram has written. That a person can be said to have
a torturing side as a result of what he did in Milgram's lab and, for all we know,
nowhere else, seems to me an overstatement, but as the cult interest in "multiple personalities" shows, the notion that we have sides has surely caught on.

(The triggering event of the multiple personality craze, the publication of *Sybil*, took place in 1973, one year before the Milgram book.) In every one of us, some believe, lies another self as yet unknown. A student once countered my critique of Milgram in these terms: "You can't face the ugly truth about yourself," she declared. Not that she actually claimed to know my dark self. To her it was just axiomatic, first that I have one and second that it would propel me up the dial; not to recognize these things is not to let myself be conscious of the truth. One might just as well say that Smith abused his children on no other grounds than that theory of abuse demands that he did; or that the holder of incorrect thoughts is statutorily sick, as in a totalitarian state.

But how could such a way of thinking take root in America, which is not a totalitarian state but a largely permissive consumer society? One answer is suggested by Hannah Arendt in a discussion of the difference between worldly things possessing duration or cultural worth and consumer goods that are used up even as they fulfill a need — the fulfillment of needs being, as we know, the very theme and flag of psychological language. So generally persuaded is the consumer society that the things we do are driven by some private need that "the innermost recesses of the human heart"[12] become a topic of public chatter. The heart of darkness receives the illumination of Broadway. Did not Edward Bernays, that American Freud whose business it was "to treat unconscious mental acts with conscious ones," help usher in the consumer society?[13] With its incessant talk of needs and desires, consumer culture is the richest sort of medium for psychology to grow in. Psychology is the determinant of all else — and "the dark side of ourselves" an undeniably romantic enrichment of psychology itself. It is true that Milgram doesn't impute a craving for submission or similarly lurid motives to the compliers, and in this sense goes only so far with the theory of the dark side. In a psychological society, though, his findings resonated. If Milgram concludes that normal people in effect became someone else in his lab, early studies of hypnotism and alternate personalities feature mysterious cases of a second self that lodges within like a perfect stranger[14] — exotica that has since passed into popular psychological lore.

If entrapment is well understood, so too all know of cases outside the lab where people show the most callous indifference to the suffering in front of them, even suffering they themselves caused. The mention of Hannah Arendt brings up the notorious example of Eichmann, the deporter of millions of Jews to the death camps, whose trial Arendt covered in Jerusalem around the same time as the early runs of the Milgram experiment. Numbed by bureaucratic routine, insulated from the killing itself, and perhaps most important possessed of a belief that destroying the Jews was not an excusable act but a moral imperative, Eichmann has come to stand for the human cog whose sheer mechanical functioning enables the mass production of death. In Jerusalem the psychiatrists found nothing wrong with Eichmann, and Arendt concludes it was not a warped mind but dull normality and lack of any heroic capacity even for evil, along with plain lack of thought, that fitted him for his work. Milgram himself was impressed with *Eichmann in Jerusalem*, and seems to be making a similar case about the normalization of evil even while ignoring Hannah Arendt's stated antipathy to the jargon and methods of social science. Yet it took more than an authority standing over Eichmann to get him to do what he did — it took an ideology that sanctioned murder, that portrayed the ridding of the Jews as a disinfection of the body politic, in effect a medical necessity. And psychological dead end though it is, I think the case of Eichmann more instructive, more pertinent to historical experience, in every way more significant than the findings of Stanley Milgram.

"You can call yourself Eichmann," the wife of one of Milgram's subjects told him.[15] How comforting it would have been to the actual Eichmann to know that what he did was no worse than punish a learner for getting his words wrong! He might well have been gratified, too, with the finding that ordinary people are potential Eichmanns, for it was his contention that in his place anyone else would have done the same thing. He just happened to be the one the lot fell to; between those who "would have" acted like him and himself, the actual deporter of the Jews, no moral distinction exists. But who can believe that Eichmann, instrumental in the murder of millions, is morally in the position of someone who performed no act at all? Were bloody hands ever wiped clean more nimbly? Between "might have" and "did," between what one has the potential to do and what one actually does stands an abyss. In many cases it doesn't even make sense to speak of potential. What is potential, that is unproven, courage? Literature, our best guide in these matters, concerns itself precisely with the proving of human beings — the encounters and tests that bring human qualities to the light of actuality. Probably it makes no more sense to speak of a potential Eichmann than of a potential hero.

No one stood over Eichmann ordering his every move, nor did he suffer the pangs of misgiving like so many in Milgram's lab. As a loyal subordinate he certainly carried out the directives and policies of superiors, but in keeping with Nazi doctrine carrying them out meant more than mere compliance with the terms of an instruction as in the Milgram experiment — it meant going beyond the call of duty. This is one reason why his claim in Jerusalem that he had merely followed orders rang hollow. (In one significant case recounted by Arendt he went so far beyond mere literal compliance as to defy an order completely. It told him to let up on the execution of the Jews.) Again one is struck with the artificiality of Milgram's model. It may be that Milgram thought Eichmann too easy a target and wanted to shatter the complacent belief that crimes against humanity could not be committed by average Americans, as Orwell attacked the complacency of the English by setting *Nineteen Eighty-Four* not in Moscow but London. To make the point one need only cite the My Lai massacre in which American platoons systematically murdered almost five hundred villagers on March 16, 1968. This was no case of a superior standing over reluctant executioners telling them they "must go on." Men sick with grief and rage were given a command (for many it might as well have been a license) to kill and debauched themselves utterly. On the eve of the slaughter, one of the men later recollected, "your adrenalin started to flow just thinking about the next day. . . . Finally, at last, it was gonna happen." A number of Americans became "double veterans" at My Lai, slang for one who rapes a woman and then murders her. Others mutilated the dead.[16] This was frenzy, not a recital of word pairs. In order to learn about the suspension of moral inhibition or blind indifference to suffering or the moral stupor of bureaucracy, we need to look to history or literature, not the laboratory. Milgram's findings, so plainly the product of his own methods, and revealing as much about himself as about his subjects, add nothing to our knowledge of real crimes against humanity.

With the sense of the other possibility that literature conveys (and that informs any true pluralism), an experimenter in Milgram's position might have asked whether his judgments of the subjects applied also to himself. Milgram never does. In "The Yellow Wallpaper" by Charlotte Perkins Gilman, a physician out of sheer benevolence drives his wife mad by subjecting her to a regimen of absolute rest. Never does he doubt his right to imprison her, never does he envision her tortures or grasp his own responsibility for her madness. Claiming as he does the authority of science, he simply cannot imagine himself wrong, in spite of the evidence before his eyes.[17] There is something of the same blindness in Milgram. If we judge Milgram like anyone else, according him no special rights by virtue of his lab coat and no points for the humanity of his political views, we can only conclude that he himself displays the indifference, the dissociation, and the desertion of ordinary moral standards that he points out in his subjects. If subjects who go right up the dial show an indifference to the effects of their decisions, what of Milgram's indifference to the writhings of the conscience-stricken? Consider the responses of one subject:

> "I can't stand it! I'm not going to kill that man in there! You hear him hollering? . . . He's hollering. He can't stand it. What's going to happen to him? . . . I'm not going to get that man sick in there . . . know what I mean? . . . I refuse to take the responsibility. He's in there hollering! . . . There's too many left here; I mean, Geez, if he gets them wrong, there's too many of them left. I mean who is going to take responsibility if anything happens to that gentleman? . . . What if he's dead in there? I mean, he told me he can't stand the shock, sir. I don't mean to be rude, but I think you should look in on him. All you have to do is look in on him. All you have to do is look in the door. I don't get no answer, no noise. Something might have happened to the gentleman in there, sir."[18]

Again and again the experimenter orders him on. The indecency of the incident lies not just in the way Milgram reduces a man to begging and stammering, but in his cool observation of the subject's suffering, and interpretation of it as evidence of the subject's moral block, not his own.[19]

Self and other indeed seem totally out of relation in this study, with the experimenter training a cold eye on others and, as I have said, exempting his own conduct from critical scrutiny on the grounds of psychological privilege. Where "the dialogic imagination" takes the other possibility into account,[20] Milgram points to the subjects' tendency to get caught up in the technicalities of their task, never considering, apparently, that in telling the story of the experiment he himself does much the same: he gets stuck in the technical details of the experiment's construction, the twists of its variables. And if some of the subjects seem dissociated not only from the "victim" but from themselves — delivering shocks even as they protest, as in the case above — what of the dissociation of an experimenter who takes notes on subjects as they go into fits and continues to believe in his own benevolence no matter what? Indeed it was Milgram who dissociated subject from "victim" to begin with by placing them in different rooms, just as he himself went up the dial in a manner of speaking by configuring the experiment to yield the most sensational result. Milgram marvels at the ability of average people to lay aside their ordinary scruples. Again and again, he finds, "good people were seen to knuckle under to the demands of authority" — that is, his demands.

> Men who are in everyday life responsible and decent were seduced by
> the trappings of authority, by the control of their perceptions, and by
> the uncritical acceptance of the experimenter's definition of the situa-
> tion into performing harsh acts.[21]

But did not Milgram himself put aside his scruples against lying when he mis-
led subjects about the sort of trap they were walking into, and his inhibition
against causing pain when he sent fifteen into "full-blown, uncontrollable
seizures" of hysteria? No doubt Milgram believed his actions justified by the
interests of science. So did the complying subjects. Only those convinced that
the cause of psychology excuses everything Milgram did can fail to perceive
that he acted no better than most of his subjects, but with less excuse.

   If Milgram hadn't disarmed criticism of himself by refraining from moral
censure of those he deceived, surely his experiment would have appeared the
trap it is. Suppose he had recruited people into his study only to send them
home judged, shamed: who reading of this wouldn't perceive that the subjects
had been set up? Instead he debriefed his subjects "in a dignified way" and with
friendly assurances of their own essential decency, as though demonstrating
his own at the same time.

The Milgram experiment leaves an image of a "teacher" in some sort of chamber with his hand on a dial, shocking a "learner" in calibrated doses. Some of
Milgram's readers may have had the feeling they had encountered this before.
In *Nineteen Eighty-Four* we find a similar scenario. In a torture chamber in the
Ministry of Love, O'Brien, the curer of souls (he combines the intimacy of a
confessor and the authority of science, as if in parody of the psychologist),
demands answers to questions and with each wrong response goes up the dial.

   The root of the resemblance lies deeper, however. Milgram produces the
evidence he cites — entraps people in a way that incriminates them, as it were.
Although Winston Smith in *Nineteen Eighty-Four* rebels, it emerges that his rebellion is supervised by the state itself, which places in his hands the forbidden
diary and later the forbidden Book and probably even introduces the germ of
rebellion into his receptive brain in the first place. As nearly as a reader can
determine, the state is conducting a kind of psychomedical experiment on
Smith with the double aim of creating the Enemy it needs and perfecting its
knowledge of the telltale signs of rebellious thought. It makes Smith a criminal before curing him, just as "We make the brain perfect before we blow it
out."[22] If Milgram entraps his subjects, entrapment seems too light a word for

what happens to Winston Smith. As O'Brien with his lab coat and his caring manner reads like a psychologist gone demonic, so the state's plan to set Smith up in order to torture and finish him reads like an ordinary case of entrapment gone mad.

With the modern age and the rise of scientific experiment, writes Hannah Arendt, the idea that "one can know only what he has made himself" took hold. Decisive here was "the element of making and fabrication in the experiment itself, which produces its own phenomena of observation and therefore depends from the very outset upon man's productive capacities."[23] Normally not troubling, this aspect of fabrication leaps into significance in the Milgram experiment, which places subjects in a situation as artfully contrived as a play[24] and elicits behavior probably shown nowhere else, leaving us to suspect that it produced its own phenomena of observation. Presumably some form of the maker theory of knowledge was held by Milgram himself, or else he could have contented himself with the moral trials of literature rather than trying to fabricate such trials in the laboratory. The irony is that all the fabrication compromises the very thing the experimenter seeks in the first place, data.

The Locke tradition sketched earlier adopts the maker theory of knowledge — to understand something is to construct it, or to reconstruct how it came to be. Locke reconstructs knowledge. Wedgwood makes clays, dyes, glazes, earning a membership in the Royal Society. With Bentham the matter becomes more ominous, the Panopticon in theory both making the prisoners into new men (and Bentham means "making") and laying them bare as objects of knowledge.[25] "One can know only what he has made himself." Subjecting inmates to the total control of an all-seeing power, the Panopticon prefigures the totalitarian state, although not until the means of human production were taken over by the state did totalitarianism become possible. Milgram echoes *Nineteen Eighty-Four* in that both his practice and that of the psychological O'Brien (he knows Smith's dreams) take off from the Lockean model — Milgram placing himself in the high tradition of enlightened benevolence by seeking to cure the illusion of our moral immunity, O'Brien enacting a diabolical parody of the Lockean father who educates his son using a policy of careful watching and judicious punishment. Irving Howe was right that the Party's ideology in *Nineteen Eighty-Four* is a perversion of the ideology of progress,[26] for what else but that introduced the theory of making and remaking a person that totalitarianism seizes for its own uses?

Both Orwell and Milgram sought to warn of totalitarianism and to shake up the complacency of those who thought "it couldn't happen here." While

Orwell contented himself with fiction, Milgram undertook to *prove* our vulnerability just as he also sought — most ironically — to confirm in the laboratory Arendt's conclusions about Eichmann, and for that matter to remove the drama of moral decision from the shadow world of literature to the light of positive science. Likening himself to a dramatist,[27] he seems to say that science verifies what the stage only imagines. His verifications, however, fail. Milgram produced submission as artificially as the state in Oceania produces rebellion. If we take to heart the injunction to question authority, not excepting that of social science, we find the Milgram experiment illuminating less for what it reveals about any presumed human tendency to dumb obedience than for what it says about the beliefs of a culture where such manipulations could be prized as a contribution to knowledge.

CHAPTER 4

Herbert Marcuse: Political Therapy

Shortly after World War II, in an attempt to get to the root of fascism and prevent its recurrence, a group of researchers including T. W. Adorno conducted a clinical investigation of "the authoritarian personality." Justly appalled by Fascism and its brew of power worship, irrationalism, and race hatred, they studied it as one might a disease, trying to determine its warning signs if not its cure.[1] In the tradition of the philosophes' campaign in medical metaphors against the disease of fanaticism,[2] these researchers, free in their use of terms like "syndrome" and "diagnose," believed they were not only in the right but scientific, their opponents not only wrong but sick.[3] In a modern age where the standard of proof is set by physics — an homage to Newton as the medicalization of the mind is to his contemporary Locke — having science behind you is the secular equivalent of having God on your side. Even with other forms of authority in question, that of science has survived, indeed thrived. "Physics envy" is not new.[4] All those in the eighteenth century esteemed as the "Newton" of this or that — among them the Newton of psychology, David Hartley — shared in the glory of physics. The investigators of the antidemocratic personality also borrowed the authority of science. Perhaps it was the arrogance that comes of believing the laws of science on your side that led an associate of Adorno's in the Frankfurt school of social thought to advocate turning the universities of America into clinics for the treatment of ideas he opposed.

One of many intellectuals who fled Hitler, Herbert Marcuse first made his mark in America with the utopian speculation of *Eros and Civilization*, that his utopia claims a foundation in Freud, a political skeptic, would seem to make it doubly improbable. Yet it was a kind of dystopia that became Marcuse's signature work. Published in 1964, *One-Dimensional Man* is a passionate tract whose main allegation — the snuffing-out of opposition in American society — would shortly be mooted by protests against the Vietnam War. The author himself was to become an intellectual patron of the student revolt. Though Marcuse well knew that America was no Nazi Germany, he perceived here a new, soft form of totalitarianism all the more deadly and effective, perhaps, in that the machine gun and barbed wire were no longer needed. (In this Marcuse may remind us of John Stuart Mill's protest of the velvet tyranny of his society, "more formidable than many kinds of political oppression.")[5] The old technology of oppression loses its point in a system where ideas — false ideas — do the dominating. In the affluent society, Marcuse maintains, an Emma Bovary's revolt against the narrowness of her existence would be cured rather than lived out and defeated. With psychology "institutionalized,"[6] Emma becomes just one more neurotic, and her rebellion an illness understood to death in the therapist's office; thus does the one-dimensional society deal with protest. Marcuse with some reason prefers the hazard of a failed revolt to the sedations of liberal society. How could such a society be awakened? Perhaps in the spirit of the dialectical turn, Marcuse once proposed to cure the very quieting of the will to revolt.

Potentially, radicalism and the project of curing evils and errors come to the same thing. As the agrarian populist William Cobbett stated a century and a half ago,

> If a man has a fever, he must be cured *radically*, not *partially* or *moderately*. On the same principle the honest political physician will prescribe a course of medicine which will go to the *radix*, or root, of the national disease. He will physic, purge, bleed, — he will ERADICATE, — he will be a RADICAL.[7]

It's unlikely, though, that Cobbett had in mind the inspection of people's thoughts to the end of rooting out political errors. His language points to traditional "physic," not psychiatry. Marcuse descends from the philosophes rather than the agrarians, and his radicalism points to psychiatry in its political guise: thought reform.

A body of lies dominates American life: of this Marcuse was so convinced that he concluded the only hope of liberating minds from their influence and clearing the way for more scientific conceptions was to ban them entirely and convert schools into centers for the correction of thought. In 1965 he called for the withdrawal of toleration of speech and assembly from groups and movements which promote aggressive policies, armament, chauvinism, discrimination on the grounds of race and religion, or which oppose the extension of public services, social security, medical care, etc. Moreover, the restoration of freedom of thought may necessitate new and rigid restrictions on teachings and practices in the educational institutions which, by their very methods and concepts, serve to enclose the mind within the established universe of discourse and behavior.[8]

The notion that students "need to be liberated from . . . narrow ideas" and made conscious of the forces responsible for their resistance to change — for such is the reach of the psychoanalytic model — had already entered the discourse of educational philosophy a generation before *One-Dimensional Man*.[9] Marcuse ran with it. He too judged it essential to cure the student of antisocial attitudes and "create a new way of life,"[10] but abandoned the liberal idiom in which these goals were once framed as well as the fiction that the outcome of therapy is not given in advance. Persuaded that a law of history comparable to one of science decrees the policies he favors (and who can tell all that is comprehended in the three letters of "etc."?), Marcuse knew exactly what the outcome of therapy had to be, and by the same token considered the dominant discourse on a par with pseudo-science — flat-earthism — but more dangerous because more seductive. In his call for the prohibition of everything injurious and reactionary he helped set in motion what is now known as political correctness, although no one so far, perhaps, has been sentenced to counseling for opposing the extension of a bus line.

Marcuse's case comes down to this: The false ideas circulated in a "totalitarian democracy" dominate the public mind so completely that the only way to break their power is to outlaw them and reeducate society as a whole. Only a public already cured of propaganda is in a position to be self-governing — that is, to exercise the power of choice presupposed by the theory of democracy. At present, "tolerance is administered to manipulated and indoctrinated individuals who parrot, as their own, the opinions of their masters, for whom heteronomy has become autonomy." If they are ever to be free, those opinions have to be rooted out. And this in turn can only mean subjecting people to the probes of political examiners. As Marcuse states, "false consciousness" is so advanced that the wide allowance customarily given thought and speech as opposed to acts can no longer be afforded, and in fact has become a mechanism of tyranny in its own right. Only "intolerance even toward thought" can promote the cause of liberty. The perversion of values peculiar to the one-dimensional society — doesn't it start, after all, "in the mind of the individual, in his consciousness"? Although he never quite states the corrective measures he has in mind, Marcuse's argument points straight at the compulsory inspection and reform of consciousness itself — in fine, political psychiatry. Demonizing the opponent to justify fighting fire with fire is a common tactic. Marcuse turns schools into indoctrination centers as oppressive, and mental hospitals as violating, as all that he hates in the one-dimensional society. Perhaps most violating of all, his psychiatry requires me to recognize the compulsory "truth" as my own, as though in some parody of Plato I were but reknowing a truth once known to my soul (or recovering a repressed memory). The preknowledge of the Platonic soul becomes the ready-made truth of Marcuse's Republic.

Considering that the Marxist state deems psychoanalysis bourgeois decadence (weighting sexual rather than political motives as it does), Marcuse's coupling of Marx and Freud is a strange one. The actual affinities between Marxism and Freudianism, it seems to me, are unflattering to both. The Marxist state makes decoders of us all in that we read works authored under dictatorship with an eye for "possible motives, hidden meanings, and Byzantine strategies,"[11] as well as a sense of the all-presence of censorship, much like a Freudian wielding the tools of suspicion. On the other side, in Freudianism, with its own brand of leader-worship and its own strained claims to the deepest truth, is a creedal quality analogous to that of the Marxist faith. It is a trait of Freudian readings of literature, for example, that anyone not already of the faith will find them simply bizarre. From Freudian doctrines come Freudian conclusions, a process that to an outsider seems hopelessly circular. Ironically, it is just this kind of tendentiousness — this drive toward conclusions already given — that Marcuse objects to in the discourse of the one-dimensional society. He fights fire with fire: fights one closed language with another. There are psychoanalysts who take any criticism of their doctrines as signs of pathological resistance to be interpreted according to the very doctrines in dispute. (The critic of psychoanalysis fears the power of the unconscious.)[12] Marcuse, psychoanalyst of the people, takes disagreement with his ideas as a malady to be cured by indoctrination.

With his belief in an all-powerful enemy that has stolen into the very minds of the masses, Marcuse, like many ideologues, tends toward conspiracy theory. In this respect his thought grows out of the Enlightenment and its search for the causes of events and the springs of action. "The enlightened men of [the eighteenth century] were ready to see plots and conspiracies everywhere," a spectacular case being the conspiracy of the enlightened themselves alleged by Rousseau.[13] With his heart as its hero, the *Confessions* marks the psychologization of autobiography, and the baring of Rousseau's heart sets up his persecutors' concealments much as helplessness before his own emotions sets up his helplessness before *them*. Less sensational but also instructive is the case of Bentham, convinced that his Panopticon was blocked by a sinister cabal. Intended as it was to bare the inmates to the eyes of the inspector as though behind walls of glass, the Panopticon was to build in something like the "transparency" Rousseau demanded. Now it is hard to imagine the scrutiny of minds by a political elite not yielding readings as weirdly forced as Freudian readings of literature on the one hand or conspiracy theories on the other (and the sort of crypto-logic at work in Freudian interpretations themselves, where the lock is made to fit the key, offers a kind of unwitting recognition of the Founder's link with the Enlightenment). It is also hard to imagine universities run on Marcuse's rules not turning into so many panopticons, with thought policed by guardians and unwholesome influences barred as in Bentham's utopian scheme for the rehabilitation of the untaught. The theory is much the same in both cases, too: control every influence with the aim of reforming the mind. Bourgeois thought after all introduced any number of doctrines, from the malleability of human nature to the progress of society through historical stages, later deployed against it by the Left. Most pertinent in this discussion of a plan for reeducation, it was the successors of Locke, thinking to extend the benefits of education to already formed adults, who first saw the possibilities of reeducation itself. Hence Hartley's conclusion that "not only can children be educated to think and feel alike, but also men can be *re-educated* to the same effect."[14] The Panopticon is a reeducation device. It is in the tradition of Marxism's use of the doctrine of progress against its own authors that Marcuse takes over the fabrication imagery used by Bentham when he described the Panopticon as a factory for producing honest men, but also by Wedgwood when he undertook to make the workers he needed and by Locke when he spoke of making a gentleman. Says Marcuse: "If the people are no longer (or rather not yet) sovereign but 'made' by the real sovereign powers — is there any alternative other than the dictatorship of an 'elite' over the people?"[15] The elite will undo what has been made of the people — and make them anew.

Although Bentham is never mentioned, Marcuse's polemic on the subject of tolerance is a running dialogue with Bentham's godson John Stuart Mill and, implicitly, with the entire liberty tradition. In the manner of the Marxist announcing himself as the destined inheritor of history — the political

Christ — Marcuse presents himself as the successor of the libertarians of old, one who fulfills even as he negates the original terms of the toleration argument. It is in this spirit of reversal that he plays up the limits on freedom of speech written into the toleration argument as far back as Milton and Locke, but by them played *down*. When he cites the people's natural "right of resistance," it is as though he turned Locke's words back on him, as he also does those of Mill. For what else is it but a reversal of terms to cite the "tyranny of the majority" against Mill, who gave Marcuse the phrase itself? Or to propose educating people for freedom in a way that contradicts the spirit of Mill's own recommendations? And much as Marcuse turns Mill's argument against itself, so with his talk of "making" history and "making" facts he appropriates the bourgeois tradition that uses the language of fabrication, even going so far as to speak of the making of a human being.

If Marcuse dreams of curing the false ideas that infect minds and obstruct progress, as though raising medicine to a political art, Locke as philosopher "resembles the physician (that he was) who seeks to cure diseases."[16] Long before Marcuse imagined a benevolent elite curing the people of errors of thought and preparing them to be free, Locke told the benevolent father how to root out the faults of his son and prepare him for accession to the freedom of civil society. Only practice can drive lessons home, Locke maintains. Until committed to practice, skills are not really learned; once practiced they become habitual. "Having this way cured in your Child any Fault, it is cured for ever: And thus one by one you may weed them out all, and plant what Habits you please."[17] With the eighteenth-century expansion of civil society, and the program of fitting minds for it, Locke's ideas on instruction were picked up by "educationalists." The theories of these reformers, aimed at making people virtuous by bringing wholesome influences to bear and shutting out the sources of corruption, also had the "sanatory" intention of curing wrong ideas and bad habits.[18] Marcuse's dream of turning the university into a kind of political sanatorium takes its place in the history of aggressive expansions of the Lockean model, even as it repudiates the bourgeois good of liberty itself. As we know, one stage in the expansion of the educational project was Bentham's fantasy of shaping a multitude of minds at once and his scheme for a prison where paupers and felons would be turned into honest citizens by a kind of mass production. With his philanthropic intentions Bentham stands as an exception to the selfishness that, according to him, rules the generality of human beings; Marcuse's elite, similarly, is immune to the baneful influences that claim common minds. (This elite, a kind of saving remnant, is thus the answer to the riddle of how a monopoly that seems in control of everything can neverthe-less be broken.) In the hands of Marcuse's few, schools acting as ideological reformatories would turn out large numbers of right-thinking citizens. They would become panopticons in the additional sense that those in charge discern what ordinary minds are blind to in themselves (their "true" interests and "true" motives) just as the warden sees more than the inmates. And this analogy between Bentham's prison and Marcuse's schools — with guardians in both cases keeping watch over the minds of their charges — is a grounded one.

Curiously, the unpoetic Bentham traced his awakening to the reading of a romance where family groups live under a benevolent Father-King, safe from the sources of strife and corruption. "[Bentham] was a man with a vision; a vision that had its origin in the English utopian tradition and in the Arcadian romance of the pastoral idyll."[19] What allies the visionary Marcuse with Bentham is not just his fantasy of treating large numbers under conditions strictly controlled "for their own good," but his membership in the utopian tra-dition. Like other utopias of Bentham's time and before, utopias constructed to preserve humanity from the contagion of envy and excessive desire, Marcuse's would cure the effects of consumer society. Like those who sought to restore a golden age, Marcuse thought to return "the people" to their true identity and equip them to exercise the sovereignty that was theirs by a decree of history. As though in a Platonic belief that the soul can re-cognize knowledge it has lost, he imagines people returning to their senses — coming back to con-sciousness — in universities as tightly governed as Plato's Republic. For now, though, the people are unconscious of their true position, seemingly hypno-tized, in that state of dazed submission to the established reality that the author deplores in *One-Dimensional Man*. In order for Snow White to be restored to her-self she must first be lying as if dead.

Linking the two utopians is another, less evident similarity. Both, as has been noted, are conspiracy theorists, Bentham in his belief that an alliance of insiders thwarted the Panopticon itself (in his sense of injury Bentham wasn't far behind Rousseau); Marcuse in his belief that the one-dimensional society controls even people's thoughts. Margaret Mead once observed that faith in the power of science and social science is but the other side of the dread of fluoridation and of psychiatrists who "can see right through you."[20] It isn't only the populace, though, that combines conspiracy thinking with faith in science. Bentham did so; he had such faith in the Panopticon just because it would enable him, the "inspector," to see right through the inmates as he could also see through the screens and ruses of the powerful. Marcuse, analogously, believes in his ability to transform others precisely because he knows their inner workings with the powerful certainty of one who sees through a plot.

Nothing could be farther from the respect for human differences than Marcuse's conviction that the minds of others can be known by formula — known, indeed, in spite of themselves. For by the terms of his argument Marcuse must consider others as being in an ideological coma, incompetent to speak and act. To anything you might say in disagreement he has the ready reply that, suffering from false consciousness, you don't really know what you're talking about. "More than ever," he writes in "Repressive Tolerance," "the proposition holds true that progress in freedom demands progress in the *consciousness* of freedom" (emphasis in the original). Even if the laws of history and science were behind Marcuse, receiving enlightenment at the cost of autonomy would still be a bad bargain. As Alasdair MacIntyre has written of Marcuse, "To make men objects of liberation by others is to assist in making them passive instruments; it is to cast them for the role of inert matter to be molded into forms chosen by others."[21] Add to this that the future is not determined and that in history as we know it "liberation" by a dictatorial elite turns out a mockery, and it seems that Marcuse himself is offering a poisoned apple.

Just as he appropriates the bourgeois tradition, arguing that fulfillment of its promise demands the suspension of tolerance, so too Marcuse turns to his own uses that favored practice of the consumer society, psychology. The utopia of B. F. Skinner, in which humanity itself is subjected to techniques of production (Benthamism carried to infinity), turns out on analysis to be a dictatorship of psychologists.[22] And so I believe would Marcuse's. The psychology that reduces everything to happiness and unhappiness — this, it is true, Marcuse has no use for. Nor would Marcuse ignore the political ironies of the adoption by the affluent of the language of psychological affliction. Rather than simply abandoning so dubious a practice, however, Marcuse seizes on psychology as an instrument of political conversion. In the spirit of using the adversary's own weapons against him, he turns psychology into a means of getting into the minds of the masses and revealing their enslavement (a revelation that in psychoanalytic fashion frees them). Marcuse gives you psychology, and indeed altered states of consciousness, with a vengeance. First searching your mind to make sure no prohibited thoughts are harboring there — for the guiding policy is "intolerance even toward thought" — political inspectors correct your entire mentality, your consciousness. Though again no details are given, in practice this can only mean "struggling" the patient in the manner of thought reform, a technique so violating it reduces a police search of the body to a common courtesy. As I will argue, standing just behind Locke like an eclipsed sun is Milton, and the poet of of *Paradise Lost* "forces to the surface the deceitful and self-serving thoughts employed by the [reader's] subconscious to avoid uncomfortable truths, and insists that they be submitted to the correction and judgment of the revealed word."[23] Excepting only that Milton's reader is a free agent and his own revelation secular, this is just what Marcuse's therapy would come to. Forcing thought out into the open where it can be rectified is, after all, the very mechanism of thought reform as actually practiced.[24] Fortunately Marcuse's correctional scheme was never realized. But much as the Panopticon caught on without ever actually being built, so his design lives on in university classrooms where students must testify to their injuries so that they can be made whole, or, only somewhat more innocuously, submit personal journals for inspection.

In the tale told by Marcuse a hero (the elite) rescues the people from a spell that enchants its powers. Marcuse is a romantic. But romanticism and the Enlightenment have their own affinities, even if the first is also a revolt against the excessive abstraction of the latter. Bentham, bane of the romantics, was inspired by an arcadian romance, while on the other hand Wordsworth himself is tied in with the Locke tradition.[25] So too Herbert Marcuse carries forward an Enlightenment dream of the reformation of humanity through education, and the creation of a new earth.

In the history of the stepping-up of the Lockean program, a major role belongs, as we know, to Hartley. Building on Locke's psychology, Hartley constructed a theory of "association" that seemed to promise the improvement of human character through the control of the circumstances in which it is formed. Coleridge named his first son after Hartley. John Stuart Mill was brought up in the thought of Hartley, minus his piety. And in America Benjamin Rush was an enthusiast of Hartley and "the revolutionary uses of psychology."[26] In the belief that human character could be perfected with all the certainty of science (since the mechanism of its formation had been revealed), Rush dreamed of a new republic that would reform its citizens like one great university with rigid restrictions. Not only slavery but public punishments, dueling, hunting, affected language, militarism, smoking, and apparently all other reactionary practices were to be banned. In order to cure the young nation of its prerepublican habits — and Rush, like Hartley a physician, meant to cure — nothing less was required. ("And thus one by one you may weed them out all, and plant what Habits you please.") Through science, utopia. "The new physiology and metaphysics (i.e., the science of the mind) afforded nothing less than the scientific mechanisms by which the Christian utopia could be realized in this world."[27] But more than the passage of laws is required to bring this transformation about: the population as a whole has to be educated in Christian and republican principles. Schools must become the nurseries of virtue, and all of society a school. Omit the Christian element and Rush's plan for national reformation offers a sort of good first approximation to Marcuse's dream of reeducating the populace and delivering it from bondage to the existing reality.

Not that Marcuse consulted Rush. He didn't have to, for he belonged to the Enlightenment tradition even in breaking away from it. The curing of error; the pupil/teacher model; the shaping of minds through the control of their surroundings — all of these elements of his revolutionary paradigm derive from the tradition of Locke. Before Marxism consigned people to the role of inert matter to be molded according to the will of their liberators, Locke viewed the child as "Wax, to be moulded and fashioned as one pleases,"[28] and it was by removing this program from the household and projecting it to a higher level, whether in factories, reformatories, or nurseries of virtue, that the successors of Locke set in motion the practice of human engineering.

CHAPTER 5

We Dream Alone:
Heart of Darkness

The journey, that staple of narrative, can be transformed into a passage through time, rendered fantastic in the romance quest, vaporized in the psychedelic trip. In Conrad's dreamlike *Heart of Darkness* the symbolic possibilities of the journey not only prevail over the journey itself but seem to get in the way of narrative. Things are told as if in ellipses, with any number of events critical to the story simply passed over.[1] By the eighteenth century, writes Erich Kahler, "the narrator's observation and command post is set up inside, in man's innermost self, and consequently events themselves are more and more shifted to the interior of the narrating ego."[2] Read by many as an allegorical descent into the interior of the self, *Heart of Darkness* dissolves events themselves in a blur. So brokenly and obscurely is the tale delivered, and with such strange insistence on the impossibility of narration, that it seems to be disputing the notion of telling a tale. Our foremost impression is of the narrator himself, Charlie Marlow, who so predominates that other voices appear in passing when they appear at all. His own rendition of events, as strange as it is, thus stands undisputed.

Heart of Darkness concerns Marlow's journey into the Belgian Congo as a steamboat pilot in the employ of an unnamed corporation headquartered in Brussels. Before undertaking his voyage, though, he has to visit the company psychiatrist.

First the doctor measures his skull. " 'I always ask leave, in the interests of science, to measure the crania of those going out there,' he said." And when they come back? " 'Oh, I never see them,' he remarked; 'and, moreover, the changes take place inside, you know.' He smiled, as if at some quiet joke."[3] Although Marlow bristles at the questions of this "alienist," characteristically he tells his tale in accordance with the man's predictions. Ponderously subjective, Marlow's narrative tells us far more about the impression events make on him — the changes they induce inside — than about the events themselves. (And a silent inflection of mockery plays around most of what Marlow says, as if he too were having a weird joke.) Marlow bears out the man of science he despises, as he serves loyally the corporation he loathes. Convinced that meanings lie well within the cranium, Marlow seems to say that he's telling things too deep to be told.

Chain gangs of natives; a trek through the jungle; the exploits of Kurtz, the most glorious and murderous of the company's agents; the human heads atop poles at his compound — things like this one would think deserve to be told, and Marlow does tell of them, but with a kind of ostentatious obscurity that reminds the reader constantly of how incommunicable it all really is ("You can't understand. How could you?" [p. 50]). The key word of the tale seems to be "inconceivable." Narrating the tale is as futile as narrating a dream. "Do you see the story? Do you see anything? It seems to me I am trying to tell you a dream — making a vain attempt, because no relation of a dream can convey the dream-sensation." The truth of his journey, Marlow asserts, is too mysterious to be told. "We live, as we dream — alone" (pp. 27, 28). Only a narration with the quality of a dream — the most purely psychological experience — can capture the truth, yet a dream can never really be told. By wrapping his tale in such strange silence, Marlow effectively ironizes the Victorian ethos of reticence, just as his broken and incomplete way of telling reads like a rejection of the fullness and consecutive manner of Victorian narration. In withholding the truth of Kurtz's depravity from his betrothed, it is as though Marlow subjected the Victorian practice of preserving the decencies to the direst parody. Even as he keeps the truth to himself in an act of discretion, he seems to be saying that truth cannot really be conveyed from one mind to another at all.

And with his insistence that the picture of things inside his head can't be communicated, Marlow affiliates himself with the Locke tradition. Words being signs for private ideas, it was the belief of Locke and indeed an entire modern line that meaning cannot be conducted from one mind to another, strictly speaking. Ideas are

> absolutely incommunicable except through the radically imperfect medium of language — "the sad incompetence of human speech." Each individual has his own language, a principle stated expressly by Locke, Condillac, Turgot, Herder, Destutt de Tracy, and Wilhelm von Humboldt.[4]

Nor does the tradition stop there. In the landmark *Principles of Psychology* — a work that appeared but a decade before *Heart of Darkness*, and that has been described as a revision of Locke's *Essay concerning Human Understanding* — William James asserts that

> Each [mind] keeps its own thoughts to itself. There is no giving or bar-
> tering between them. No thought even comes into direct *sight* of a
> thought in another personal consciousness than its own. Absolute insu-
> lation, irreducible pluralism is the rule.[5]

Hence Marlow's rhetorical demand, "Do you see the story? Do you see anything?" According to the Locke tradition, as sociable beings we are nevertheless spared the worst of this sentence of a life incommunicado. Marlow, however, insists on the final impossibility of understanding, and even invests his
tale in it somehow. Why tell a tale on the condition that no one can understand it? Why this hyperbolization of solitude? Let me offer a speculative
answer that is consistent, I believe, with the evidence of the text.

That our inmost being is finally unknowable seems to me a fact; yet there
is much that Marlow knows but will not tell. This narrator's strange insistence
on the futility of narration points not so much, I think, to the mysterious nature
of one's own being as to the unspeakable nature of the work he is part of.
Marlow, a man of moral intelligence, contracts his services to a company in the
business of rapine; he implicates himself in the same imperialist venture that
revolts him. Consider this typical incident:

> Once a white man in an unbuttoned uniform, camping on the path with
> an armed escort of lank Zanzibaris, very hospitable and festive — not
> to say drunk. Was looking after the upkeep of the road, he declared.
> Can't say I saw any road or any upkeep, unless the body of a middle-
> aged negro, with a bullet-hole in the forehead, upon which I absolutely
> stumbled three miles farther on, may be considered as a permanent
> improvement. (P. 20)

Marlow recoils in revulsion, and yet he himself is complicit, if not in the murder of this man, in the work of imperialism generally. And he knows it. As he
says after describing in unusual detail the passage of six black men chained
together, with iron collars around their necks, "I also was part of the great cause
of these high and just proceedings." Even around this admission, however, is
something of the flicker of mockery, the play of negation, that seems to be

Marlow's characteristic note. By delivering his tale in a tone so ironically detached, Marlow manages to dissociate himself from men he despises, crimes he deplores, and a cause he more or less disbelieves in. And I believe that the psychologization of the narrative of *Heart of Darkness* — its transformation into a dream too private to be told — accomplishes the same end. If Marlow's tale cannot be understood, he cannot be judged. If his experiences are so singular as to be incommunicable, he can't possibly be mistaken for an ordinary imperialistic adventurer. Psychology defuses morality. Just as it was only with the rise of consumer industries that depth psychology caught on in the United States; just as it is only amid the anonymity of mass society that the task of finding the well of creative power inside every self becomes an urgent one; so the fact that he is working for the Company along with so many others makes it important for Marlow to separate himself absolutely from those around him.

As Marlow hears reports of a remarkable agent named Kurtz in the Inner Station, he becomes practically magnetized by this figure who stands out so strongly against the vile similarity of the Company's men. Kurtz went down to Africa filled with exalted ambitions but once there, as it turns out, depraved himself and gave in to desires as unholy as his original intentions were pious, even going so far as to deify himself. (Having written that whites "must necessarily appear" to Africans "in the nature of supernatural beings," he apparently started believing his own words [p. 51]). Those heads on the poles were put there by Kurtz; why and how Marlow does not say, even though he knows. Neither does he tell of the ceremonies used to worship the self-deified Kurtz, or indeed any of his debaucheries, as though he the narrator were observing the last propriety and at the same time guarding the memory of Kurtz as he does at the end with Kurtz's Intended. Marlow thinks of the journey upriver as a journey toward Kurtz, affirms Kurtz in spite of all that he knows of him, and finally lies for the man despite his own professed hatred of deceit.

Why this strange alliance? Why does Marlow elect Kurtz as his doppelgänger, why cast his narrative as a tale of psychological discovery even though he never reveals "the horror" of Kurtz's deeds and could never imaginably have followed Kurtz's path? Why does Marlow bond with one whose missionary zeal turned to savagery when he himself neither believes in the missionary cause nor condones savagery? Because, as Marlow himself says of Kurtz, "Whatever he was, he was not common" (p. 51). Evidently it is so important to Marlow to distinguish himself from the grubby businessmen (as well as inane tourists) of imperialism that he is willing to identify himself with Kurtz to do so. By making himself the double of one who is not common, while at the same time veiling the deeds of this one and showing his own moral sanity, Marlow is able to dissociate himself honorably from all those company men engaged in their own petty scramble for Africa. Whatever he is, he is not like them. As the teller of so highly meditative a tale has too much depth to be taken for one of the hollow men with "no entrails" (p. 22), so by telling a story that seems to culminate in his recognition of himself in the extraordinary Kurtz, Marlow puts moral distance between himself and the ugly daily business of imperialism.

As he tells the story, Marlow went up to the edge of a precipice that Kurtz plunged over. What drew Kurtz over the edge was "the awakening of forgotten and brutal instincts" (p. 67). But an instinct acts in us identically, practically at the level of a biological force. If Kurtz had really deified himself by instinct, we would surely be seeing a lot of other human beings getting themselves adored or at least acting under that impetus, just as the instinct of self-preservation operates in one and all. Yet in fact we see few other self-deifiers, and those more plausibly under a delusion of glory than the blind direction of instinct. Only by begging the question and assuming the existence of the very "deification instinct" in question can it be said that Kurtz acted out a force that impels all humanity when he set himself up as a god (and the text suggests he did no less). The use of "instinct" in the cited phrase doesn't stand up to analysis; the term does, however, convey an obscure impression of depth that suits both the narrator's style and his penchant for the psychological.

If the portrayal of Kurtz as Hyde to Marlow's Jekyll plays up the theme of the double, the presentation of practically everything else in *Heart of Darkness* as a kind of dream-enigma plays on the fascination with dream material that made Freud's *Interpretation of Dreams* (published almost simultaneously) so much more than a technical work of interest to a few. Not only is *Heart of Darkness* dreamlike, it actually concerns the effort to make sense of material that tempts and resists interpretation with a power comparable to a dream's. As Tzvetan Todorov well observes of *Heart of Darkness*, "we are dealing with a narrative in which the interpretation of symbols predominates."[6] Posted in front of Kurtz's compound are certain round knobs that at first appear ornamental but are later discovered to be "not ornamental but symbolic" (p. 58). Symbolic? Those knobs are human heads. They are not Blake's sick rose, they are not a dream rebus, they are not shadows of the sacred, they are not symbols of any kind, as Marlow himself well knows. In calling them symbolic Marlow uses the same irony he so often employs to dissociate himself from his own words. The heads are "food for thought and also for vultures" (p. 58). When Marlow reports of Kurtz's young aide that "he had not dared to take these — say, symbols —

down" (p. 59), how much more ironic and negating a tone could the word bear? But is it not possible that other symbol-enigmas in *Heart of Darkness* are as much a mockery as this of symbolic heads?

Like the casting of the story as a dream too mysterious to be understood, least of all by others, the seeding of *Heart of Darkness* with symbols has the effect of obscuring the moral issues raised by Marlow's service to the company. Can he be innocent amid the atrocities that seem to take place all around him and that he reports with such an oddly aloof tone as if from the distance of another world? When, during his two-hundred-mile trek through the jungle, porters die under their loads, are we to imagine that *his* gear is not being carried? (On a more psychological journey, a journey to the inner truth rather than the Inner Station, gear wouldn't be an issue.) A number of critical questions are as little considered by Marlow as this one of exhausted porters. "Marlow admires tenacity in driving rivets, but he is notably untenacious in thinking through his own situation."[7] Does Marlow really believe that just doing your duty as it lies to hand — fixing pipes — is a prescription for moral decency? What of the imperialist venture that has Marlow on his boat busy with mechanical chores in the first place? Does he believe in it? From a passage near the beginning of *Heart of Darkness* no one could tell: the entire thing is a conundrum. The Romans, he muses,

> were conquerors, and for that you want only brute force — nothing to boast of, when you have it, since your strength is just an accident arising from the weakness of others. They grabbed what they could get for the sake of what was to be got. It was just robbery with violence, aggravated murder on a great scale, and men going at it blind — as is very proper for those who tackle a darkness. The conquest of the earth, which mostly means the taking it away from those who have a different complexion or slightly flatter noses than ourselves, is not a pretty thing when you look into it too much. What redeems it is the idea only. An idea at the back of it; not a sentimental pretence but an idea; and an unselfish belief in the idea — something you can set up, and bow down before, and offer a sacrifice to . . . (Pp. 6–7)

Quips aside, how can blind murder be proper? How can anything redeem it? To me the enigma of *Heart of Darkness* is how someone of Marlow's intelligence could let questions like these go by. What can be meant by an unselfish act of robbery? Offering sacrifices to an idea — is this any better than worshiping Kurtz, the man of ideas who may actually have received sacrificial offerings?

What is Marlow saying? Perhaps he doesn't mean for us to know. His mystifi-
cations, his practice of darkening the tale with words like "incomprehensible,"
his insistence that it is too singular to be understood, his way of spinning the
reader around with irony and at the same time invalidating voices not his
own — all serve to keep the moral question from *becoming* a question and deter
the reader from looking into it too much. If *Heart of Darkness* tells through Kurtz
of the end of the Enlightenment in depravity and rapine, it tells through
Marlow of the end of the Enlightenment project of the clarification of knowledge in a kind of willed obscurity. "It is the great saving grace of companion-
ship for solitary men," writes Hannah Arendt, "that it makes them 'whole' again,
saves them from the dialogue of thought in which one remains always equivocal."[8] The solitary Marlow uses the occasion of relating his story to his com-
panions aboard the *Nellie* to render himself entirely equivocal.

Heart of Darkness makes such a show of the impossibility of telling that it
reminds one noted critic of a parable, a story that confounds its own listeners
and veils a sacred truth in the very act of disclosing it.[9] As a quasi-parable or
likeness of a likeness, *Heart of Darkness* offers riches to the professional searcher
of texts even as it removes itself from the possibility of comprehension. But
what sacred or remotely sacred truth is conveyed under the figures of *Heart of
Darkness* — the corpse at Marlow's feet, the heads on poles? Arguably, in telling
us that events pass all telling, *Heart of Darkness* resembles less a parable than a
tale of war. "It cannot be told, it cannot even be imagined except by those who
experienced it": this, surely, is the note of the war narrative in the twentieth
century.[10] For that matter, nothing turns Jekylls into Hydes like war, where
ordinary men can become as barbaric as their own image of the enemy. In a
great tale of the fog of war by Conrad himself, an English sea captain possessed
with mistrust descends to the same treachery he hates above all else in others.
Like some Freudian virtuoso of suspicion, he meets (imagined) guile with double guile.[11] So too it is amidst the political warfare of *The Secret Agent* that an
advocate of law and order plots an act of terrorism.[12] In *Heart of Darkness* the
"civilized" descend to murder and rapine. For all of its dreams, *Heart of Darkness*
concerns events as gross and savage as that; reading it as an intimation of the
mystery of self, or of some similar ultimate, dissipates those hard realities.

A powerful current of irony flows through Marlow's speech, leaving us with the
sense that anything he says may be unsaid. The discourse on the Romans,
for example, seems to end in annihilation, with Marlow mocking his own

conclusion. Marlow's turn for negation, his way of denying what he says, seems to go along with his capacity to disengage himself from his own actions.

As Charles Taylor argues in *Sources of the Self*, the modern concept of self stems from the theory of the disengaged subject asserted perhaps most influentially by Locke. The disengaged subject stands not only to things but to his own self in a posture of detachment, especially detaching from his desires to determine if they are really worthy of being satisfied. The mind, writes Locke, has "a power to suspend the execution of any of its desires; and so all, one after another; is at liberty to consider the objects of them, examine them on all sides, and weigh them with others."[13] Standing aloof from and reflecting on our own desires enables us, Taylor says, to remake ourselves (as though we had taken over the process of fabrication once in the hands of our fashioners). Taylor further finds that the ideal of discipline codified by Locke — that of suspending desire and treating it as one more thing subject to rational control — was put into practice in the military and bureaucracy, among other settings. Now it is notable that Marlow, a captain in the employ of a large corporation, tells his tale as one who refrained from the gratification of desires Kurtz indulged. Kurtz "had made that last stride, he had stepped over the edge, while I had been permitted to draw back my hesitating foot" (p. 72) (although it is hard to envision Marlow driven to the verge of the pit with the desire to be a god, like Kurtz). Again, "Mr. Kurtz lacked restraint in the gratification of his various lusts" (p. 58). If Locke would have us weigh our projects and examine them on all sides — in a word, ponder — Marlow delivers a narrative ponderous in every respect, one that time and again simply breaks off, too, as discipline enables us to check desire.

In illustrating the practice of disengagement, Taylor offers two cases: someone who decides the guilt he feels is simply a product of his childhood and tries to disregard it; and someone irritated at a relative's sense of humor, but who on second thought decides he's overreacting and asks what it is in himself that makes him behave so irrationally. In both instances a feeling is checked on reflection. Although these illustrations appear in a discussion of Locke, they point unmistakably to psychology as we know it today. Am I overreacting? Is X a result of my childhood? Am I responding to something in another or *in myself?* So common by now is the psychological idiom of questions like these that it has become, like television, the very currency of our culture.

With Marlow all the practices of disengagement are raised to the level of the extraordinary. Not only does he have second thoughts, he fills a long tale with them. Not only does he find something of himself in Kurtz, he is drawn to the man as to his own dark side. Rather than probing the meaning of his own behavior in the manner of someone troubled with his reaction to an aunt's bad jokes, he presents his African experience as a kind of dream full of obscure portent, and asks rhetorically, What does it mean? Readers have taken up the question. In a review in 1902 *Heart of Darkness* was declared a "psychological masterpiece" that relates "the sub-conscious life within us . . . to our conscious actions, feelings, and outlook."[14] Thus was a tale insistent on the privacy of meaning and the solitude of experience converted into a cliché. That Conrad himself had a notion of the banality of psychology can be inferred from the scene in *The Secret Agent* where Verloc tries to convince his wife that he's morally innocent of getting her brother blown up. As Conrad reports with the heavy irony that distinguishes the work, Verloc wants to tell her things "of a profound psychological order." He wants to tell her "that there are conspiracies of fatal destiny, that a notion grows in a mind sometimes till it acquires an outward existence, an independent power of its own, and even a suggestive voice." A victim of his psychological stars, Verloc was "haunted" by his controller, under the spell of suggestion.[15] Verloc's deepest thoughts, apparently, have the quality of an astrology column.

Nothing is more solitary than dreams, but as it happens, even dreams can be commodified. When Marlow returns to Europe following his African adventure, we are reminded of Gulliver returning to the human race he detests. The humans of Europe are to Marlow practically another species. In point of fact, however, they too had taken dream journeys both surreal and exotic. In the Paris exposition of 1900, attended by millions of visitors, Moorish mock-ups and "savage huts" mingled nonsensically with scenes of Asia, the entire spectacle reflecting both the reach of European power and the fantasia of the department store. Not only Kurtz but the citizens of Europe — and after all, Kurtz is said to be the child of Europe — are Marlow's kin. *Heart of Darkness* tells of Marlow's journey: at the Paris show most of the big attractions "involved a dynamic illusion of voyage."[16]

Like those entertained by the fantastic displays of the Paris exhibition, the consumer society enthralls itself with the fantasia of psychological knowledge. And like the "imaginary wants" coaxed into being by the economy, the psychological problems of that society turn out to be as boundless as the imagination. Yet if the hyperbolization of selfhood is but the other side of the facelessness of modern life, then the mysterious potential of self is never far from the blankness of clichés and the flatness of mechanical reductions. Marlow mystifies us. The next work before us — revered as a psychological masterpiece — has a lot to say about clichés and reductions.

CHAPTER 6

Dostoevsky and X-Ray Vision

"Don't rummage in my soul"

— Dmitri Karamazov

"Listen, I don't like spies and psychologists, at least those who poke into my soul"

— Stavrogin

When Fyodor Pavlovitch Karamazov is discovered murdered, the district doctor, investigating lawyer, and prosecutor happen to be assembled at the home of the local police captain for an evening of cards. All are introduced to us, the prosecutor as

> vain and irritable, though he had a good intellect, and even a kind heart. It seemed that all that was wrong with him was that he had a better opinion of himself than his ability warranted. And that made him seem constantly uneasy. He had, moreover, certain higher, even artistic leanings, toward psychology, for instance, a special study of the human heart, a special knowledge of the criminal and his crime.[1]

At one point in the interrogation of Dmitri when the suspect relates a guilty dream, the prosecutor inquires in the classic psychological manner, "Is that the sort of thing you dream about?" (p. 572). The tone of the question, a falsely knowing one, declares that the prosecutor now understands his man to the very core. Drawing on his special knowledge of the criminal (always assuming that he *is* the criminal), Ippolit Kirillovitch has Dmitri figured out. Indeed, with its show of procedure, inquisition into the suspect's mind, and moral rather than physical tortures, the interrogation of Dmitri dramatizes the coming of those modern "disciplines" like psychology that claimed to render human beings at last calculable.[2] The rest of the prosecution team as well classifies Dmitri as a specimen of guilt. Just as the team is already fortuitously assembled before the news of the crime, all subscribe to a theory of the crime before the "criminal" is even interrogated, the prosecutor's theory being the most refined. The philosophy of M. M. Bakhtin, a great admirer of Dostoevsky, centers on the critique of ready-made ideas. The ideas of the prosecutor are exactly that.

And being ready-made, they do not change. At the trial some two months later, all "the psychological Ippolit Kirillovitch" (p. 608) does is spin out the theory of the crime constructed during a social evening, now in a manner that dramatizes his own imagined powers and converts Dmitri's soul into a sort of public object. Nothing he learned in the interim, none of Dmitri's own testimony, has dented his faith in his own conclusions. Dmitri, he earnestly believes, is a reckless man of passion who nevertheless premeditated the murder of his father and carried it out. So positive is the prosecutor that he understands Dmitri right to the core that he tells the jury in detail what Dmitri *would have* done had he really worn a bag with fifteen hundred rubles around his neck as claimed — little realizing that he is inventing another Dmitri altogether, almost in the manner of a rival if second-rate author.[3] Dissolute yet thirsting for reform, reckless yet not invariably so, Dmitri as we actually see him in the course of *The Brothers Karamazov* is reduced to caricature in the courtroom, caricature all the more effective for claiming the accuracy of x-ray vision. That Dmitri was capable of murdering his father no reader can doubt. He came close enough to killing him with his own hands once, and had every reason to hate the old man as a swindler, trampler of things sacred, and sexual rival. Dmitri could have killed his father but did not, and it is in the space between "could have" and "did not" that the moral drama of the novel takes place. With a brass pestle in his hand he peered into his father's bedroom half-expecting to find Grushenka in there too, hatred for his father surging — yet he did not kill the old profligate but fled. He retained the power to falsify the confident analysis of someone like the prosecutor, to whom it's clear that in such circumstances Dmitri Karamazov could have done only one thing. It is in subjecting Dmitri's moral condition to an interpretation that claims the power, depth, and certainty of a medical analysis that the prosecutor errs.[4]

The pretensions of the prosecutor expose him to ridicule at the hands of the defense, a Clarence Darrow–like figure whose brilliance does Dmitri no good. "Before I started on my way here," he states in his address to the jury,

"I was warned in Petersburg, and was myself aware, that I should find a talented opponent whose psychological insight and subtlety had gained him peculiar renown in legal circles of recent years. But profound as psychology is, it's a knife that cuts both ways." (Laughter among the public.) (P. 882)

He proceeds to show that details cited by the prosecution in support of its theory are capable of the opposite construction. Yet I think from Dostoevksy's point of view what is wrong with psychology isn't so much that it cuts two ways as that it violates a human soul by cutting at all. To pluck out the heart of someone's mystery, as Hamlet says (3.2.365–66), is an act of violence. That Dostoevsky himself has been glorified as a violator, one who "steals from [his characters] their most jealously guarded and intimate secrets,"[5] reveals more about our culture than about him. Invading your characters in this way seems inconsistent, after all, with granting them being and independence in the first place. True, there are those in *The Brothers Karamazov* who want to get their hands on another's secret, who publish gossip, thrill to the revelations of the trial, claim to know others to the very depths — in all these respects like members of a psychological culture taking ordinary voyeurism to a higher level — but they are not the author. The classic novelists, it is said, "seem to leave around men and women a zone of unexplored freedom, a kind of inviolate spring of independent action,"[6] an observation surely true of the author of *The Brothers Karamazov*. Not only do its principals surprise the reader continually, but for all that we know about them there is just as much that we don't and probably never will know, unless and until they themselves disclose it in the act of dialogue. The reader of *Crime and Punishment* has no real inkling of Raskolnikov's motive for murder until he himself, halfway into the novel, launches into his theory of audacity. Not until his confession to Sonya near the end do we actually grasp the meaning of the crime.

Those who imagine Dostoevsky laying bare the soul with all the force of an act of violence seem indeed to confuse him with Raskolnikov. In the early pages of *Crime and Punishment*, as he muses over a letter from his mother, Raskolnikov sees through every word with a power of vision that simply burns away the veil of appearances.

"No, Dunechka, I see it all. . . . Isn't it that [his mother's] conscience is secretly giving her trouble for having agreed to sacrifice her daughter for the sake of her son? . . . But Mr. Luzhin doesn't take much figuring out . . . Showed himself in his true colours . . . Dear, Dunechka, I mean,

I know you! . . . Why, the last time we saw each other you were just about to be twenty; but I already understood your temperament. . . . But what of Dunya, what of her? I mean, the man must be an open book to her, yet she's going to live with him."[7]

In these judgments is something of the same violent bravado that inspires Raskolnikov's crime. As it turns out, Luzhin *is* a pig, but that Dunya agrees to marry him for his sake as Raskolnikov so hastily supposes is never confirmed. She herself in fact denies it:

"The whole trouble with you is that you seem to believe I'm sacrificing myself to someone for someone else's sake. That really is not the case. I'm simply getting married for my own sake, because things are not going well for me; later on, of course, I shall be pleased if I can succeed in being of assistance to my family, but that is not the principal element in my determination. . . . "[8]

Thus is Raskolnikov's x-ray vision called into question. In his obsession with mind reading Raskolnikov writes about the psychology of crime; the detective Porfiry, his match, chatters psychology in an effort to break down his defenses.[9] And what enables Porfiry to get into Raskolnikov's mind is that the latter has *stated* his mind in his article on crime. The detective has the wit to pay attention to a "clue" that is not hidden. In the gamesmanship of Porfiry (who like the defense lawyer of *The Brothers Karamazov* well knows that two can play at psychology), Raskolnikov's own theorizing comes back to haunt him. At his trial the circle of irony closes as the Napoleonic murderer gets off with a light sentence for acting up the part of an ordinary mental case — someone stricken with temporary insanity, the same pat diagnosis applied to Dmitri in *The Brothers Karamazov*.

In histrionic moments members of the cast of *The Brothers Karamazov* will claim to see right through someone, or, more strangely yet, to have been pierced by another's insight. "I know her through and through," says old Karamazov of Grushenka, whom he misreads completely (p. 206), just as he makes a kind of buffoonish boast of Father Zossima's having "read me to the core" (p. 47). The theatrical Madame Hohlakov declares to Father Zossima, "You have seen through me and explained me to myself!" (p. 64), a claim the elder questions immediately. When Dmitri in his self-dramatizing style exclaims, "I see right through [Katerina], as I've never done before! It's a regular discovery of the four continents of the world, that is, of the five!" (p. 185),

Alyosha has to pull him back to reality by reminding him of how grossly he has dishonored Katerina by revealing her secret to her rival. (For someone with an acute sense of honor, Dmitri can be mighty free with the honor of others.) The prosecutor identifies the "special motive at the bottom" of Dmitri's own conduct — jealousy (p. 853). So too Rakitin boasts to Alyosha that in a moment of insight he

> "suddenly understood your brother Dmitri, [saw] right into the very heart of him all at once. I caught the whole man from one trait. These very honest but passionate people have a line which mustn't be crossed. If it were, he'd run at your father with a knife."

Dmitri, this diviner declares, is a sensualist. "That's the very definition and inner essence of him" (p. 90). Now whenever Bakhtin speaks of the "unfinalizability" of human beings, he means their capacity to disconfirm statements like this — to disappoint all who presume to define them. At the outset of *The Brothers Karamazov* each of the brothers is placed in just that kind of acute crisis — Alyosha being between two dwellings, Ivan two intellectual positions, Dmitri two women — that least favors the flat predictive certainty of Rakitin or anyone else who may think he owns the key to other minds. Far more than diagnostic acuity of the kind satirized within the work itself (and it is nowhere more satirical than in its portrayal of medical experts), *The Brothers Karamazov* asks in its readers a traditional feeling for the drama of moral choice — to eat or not to eat the apple, to be or not to be, to protect old Karamazov or leave him to his fate. About each of the brothers, anyway, is a radical indeterminacy that belies pat predictions and diagnoses — an indeterminacy brought out as they wrestle with the sort of moral questions that in the more monological *Heart of Darkness* seem willfully obscured.[10]

From the fact that the brothers cannot be "finalized" or reduced to objects of knowledge, it follows that, like Dunya, they reveal themselves in speech and action and are not revealed by others. As Bakhtin puts it, it is Dostoevsky's conviction that "In a human being there is always something that only he himself can reveal . . . something that does not submit to an externalizing secondhand definition."[11] By contrast, a type — say the cuckold whose horns are visible to all but himself, the snob who stands "ludicrously exposed" for what he is,[12] the Jew marked by every word he says — not only coincides with his definition but stands revealed whether he chooses to or not. Everything he does gives him away. Only if we ourselves were stock types would our very core be revealed for others but not ourselves to see. In point of fact we are not generic but individual, not objects of knowledge but agents in our own right, from which it follows that no one can reveal us to ourselves, no one can administer self-knowledge, and the ideologist's ambition of "unveiling the hidden motives behind the individual's decisions, thus putting him in a position really to choose" is a fraud.[13]

In illustration of Bakhtin's point, hundreds of pages into *The Brothers Karamazov*, in the throes of his interrogation, Dmitri reveals a fact known to him alone that makes us rethink everything we thought we knew about him: up to that evening he has had a bag with fifteen hundred rubles belonging to his betrothed around his neck like an amulet of shame, and it is the torture of hovering between stealing this money and returning it (another crisis of decision) that drove him to act like the distracted creature we saw. No one reveals this *about* Dmitri: he reveals it himself, as he sewed the money in the bag himself. In a sense, Dmitri even weaves the lies that entrap him. The misreadings he attracts in *The Brothers Karamazov* are the counterpart of his theatrical portrayal of himself as a victim of fate and his own passions. In either case it seems to be his very ambiguities that call forth a simple picture. As if his own theatrics came back to haunt him, in the drama of the trial he becomes the victim he declared himself to be.

Convinced as he is that he holds the key to Dmitri, the prosecutor cannot accept information like the story of the rag that doesn't fit with what he "knows." In effect all of the trial's drama — for it is indeed a show — takes place because the prosecutor can't believe that he does not possess the last word about Dmitri. Also a show trial in a sense is the Grand Inquisitor episode in which the old cardinal indicts, convicts, and sentences Christ. The diatribe of the Grand Inquisitor makes a great show of baring the moral core of humanity itself — unveiling its hidden motives. Dazzled by its brilliance and blinded by its rhetoric of totality, we forget that the depiction of humanity in flight from its own freedom contains but part of the truth. That the brothers Karamazov default on their freedom is true, yet neither can they live without it: such is the knot all of them, including Ivan, author of the Grand Inquisitor episode itself, are caught in. Despite its mighty pretense of being the last word, the Inquisitor's prosecution of the human race is no more authoritative and no less partial than the kinds of things that get said in the courtroom per se. Bakhtin maintains that the last word is never spoken by human beings, and that Dostoevsky, under the inspiration of this truth, created a new form of the novel that freed the heroes from an an *author's* attempt to define and determine them in the way other characters do when they tell stories about the brothers, or for that matter the way the Inquisitor does all of humankind.[14]

And the same considerations that led Dostoevsky to experiment with the polyphonic novel led him to repudiate psychology. In his notebooks he writes, "They call me a psychologist; this is not true. I am merely a realist in the higher sense, that is, I portray all the depths of the human soul."[15] In the words of Bakhtin, Dostoevsky considered psychology in all its forms — but especially psychology as practiced in court (still one of its venues) — as a kind of sin against the soul,

> a degrading reification of a person's soul, a discounting of its freedom and its unfinalizability, and of that peculiar indeterminacy and indefiniteness which in Dostoevsky constitute the main object of representation: for in fact Dostoevsky always represents a person on the threshold of a final decision, at a moment of crisis.[16]

By placing the brothers in a state of ultimate crisis at every moment, like someone with a knife poised but not yet thrust, Dostoevsky calls forth capacities in them that no amount of psychology — whatever its pretensions to science — and least of all the diagnostic certainties of the prosecutor, could do justice to.[17]

If another can tear away my mask or persona and still not reveal me, if in me is what only I can reveal, this does not mean that my self is fully formed and ready as it were for display. For it is the nature of tests, and to a degree of events generally, that they bring out qualities in us that cannot be foreknown with certainty. Could Dmitri have known that he would find the resolve not to touch Katerina's three thousand roubles for a month after he stole it? All have heard stories of people who display in war traits of which they give no sign in civilian life; nor is it apparent how a quality like courage can manifest itself, or even be said to exist, before being tested. From the trials and combats of epic and romance to the more familiar encounters of the novel, events that try the self are the very matter of fiction. When Father Zossima bows down to Dmitri, it is because of the trials, the sufferings, that await him. (Significantly, and contrary to the ways of depth psychology, Father Zossima at this moment simply judges from a look in Dmitri's eyes. The eyes are the windows of the soul.)[18] Trials in this novel encompass so much more than legal theatrics that they include practically everything that happens outside the courtroom, all those crises without a predetermined outcome. The outcome of the courtroom proceedings is a given. Before they begin they are already entitled by the author "A Judicial Error."

Other forms of trial exist, anyway, than legal contest. In *Hamlet* we are given not the prosecution but the pursuit of Claudius, not the ceremony of argument but the encounter of lethal antagonists, not the ritual back-and-forth of courtroom drama but the echo and clash of languages, and not the assessments of psychological "experts" but soundings of one another by the principals themselves. Removed from the kind of play where he would perform a predetermined role of revenge, Hamlet is suspended on the threshold of action and placed in dialogue with himself; while Bakhtin argues that the brothers Karamazov don't serve the plot so much as it serves to place them in threshold situations and provoke their dialogues. Between the "novelized" drama and the "dramatic" novel — both keenly concerned with degrees and kinds of moral complicity — is no surface resemblance but a strong underlying affinity.[19]

The trial of Dmitri is a show in the sense Hamlet has in mind when he objects that shows of grief belie grief itself. As a show the trial is not only a hollow exercise but, as such events tend to be, a public entertainment. There is an element of the lewd about it; in the name of moral decency, the prosecutor both blows up and falsifies the details of Dmitri's mental life in something like the way obscenity floodlights private acts. As in the scene in *Crime and Punishment* where lodgers crowd in to watch Marmeladov die, so in the trial Dostoevsky brings out the base aspects of the craving to see into other lives that the genre of the novel certainly plays on.[20] If Dostoevsky excites our curiosity like few others, it is also true that he warns of curiosity going too far and still inhabits a moral universe with some last threshold not to be crossed. Not even the gawkers at Marmeladov's death will take the final step:

> Meanwhile the door that led in from the inner rooms began to be opened once more by the inquisitive crowd. In the passage an ever denser throng of spectators, residents from the whole staircase, was gathering; none of them, however, stepped over the threshold.[21]

The difference in the character of curiosity in our own culture is instructive. With the mass media there is no "too far." Given to playing things up in the name of the public's right to know, professionally averse to silence, and simply infinitely repetitive, the mass media explode the very concept of the limit. Not only this, but the psychological culture makes a sort of duty of peering into the self's inner chambers. Convinced that "there is a mental system which lies hidden under the manifest system"[22] and more interested in the hidden than in a demonstrated quality like courage, it raises voyeurism to the level of a cultural practice. Something like the indecency of the death-gawkers inhabits the psychological society as a whole. And yet the last modesty protects the therapist's office. Even as they collect the highest material rewards of a secular culture, our psychologists claim the confessional privileges of priests.[23]

But before proceeding to a discussion of "the dark side of the soul" in *The Brothers Karamazov*, let me anticipate an objection. "Dostoevsky has caricatured psychology the way he caricatures other things he doesn't like," I imagine a critic saying. "In *real* therapy the psychologist doesn't mechanically impose a diagnosis on the patient in the manner of the prosecutor — who is really no psychologist at all, just an amateur. Maybe crackpots operated like that in Dostoevsky's time, but now we know better. Real therapy means listening to your patients and working with them toward an understanding, not 'reifying' them or whatever. It is tentative, not dogmatic. Odd that you've scarcely mentioned the key word of Bakhtin's literary theory — 'dialogue.' Therapy is dialogue. It's the unprofessional psychotherapists who don't listen, who force a diagnosis on the patient, like the ones who just know you were a victim of sexual abuse even if you weren't." But the "dialogue" of therapy goes only one way, and in any case bears slight relation to dialogue in Bakhtin's sense of a kind of maximal dissonance. Guided "dialogue" is to the latter as a staged event to a real one. Nor does therapy take place only in the consulting room. Therapy is now on the bookstore shelves, on magazine racks, television, radio, the Internet, even in the classroom — its language as repetitive and mechanical as any ready-made theory degrading to human freedom. As the lingua franca of consumer society, psychology now does on the level of society as a whole what it does on that of the single soul in *The Brothers Karamazov*: it reduces the difficult freedom of moral agents to the facility of diagnostic formulas. Not only is psychology our ready-made language, but, as I have tried to suggest, it goes hand in hand historically both with technological increases in the power of "making" — hence Bentham's scheme to industrialize the production of virtue in a prison where the inmates would be under a kind of x-ray vision — and with the popularization of ideas themselves. The triumph of psychology in our own society is the fruition of the same process that saw Lockean psychology used by Wedgwood to enable the mass production of ceramics and saw psychology itself marketed in a big way with the advent of the modern corporation in the United States.

*

By repute and his own account Dostoevsky portrays the depths of the soul. Why then does he deny being a psychologist? First of all, perhaps, because he does not finally explain his characters. "There can be no doubt," writes the Russian literary historian Lydia Ginzburg, "that in creating his novel of ideas, Dostoevskii departed from classical nineteenth-century psychologism, the basic principle of which was *explanation*, whether explicit or concealed."[24] Free to act in the name of their ideas, his heroes possess an indeterminacy that finally defeats psychological analysis. Who doesn't sense the folly of tracing Raskolnikov's crime to his childhood — about which we know almost nothing, except that he was loved — or of explaining it by his poverty as he himself does at his trial, in a ploy "almost indecent"?[25] Not that the author didn't possess, in common with the classical novelists, an interest in the ways of the mind. But for him perhaps even more than them, the psychological cannot be divorced from the historical or the social, so that Ivan's "everything is permitted" reflects not only his own frame of mind but themes of radical thought, while Smerdyakov's handling of the same doctrine reflects his social position as a despised and denied son.[26] In and of itself, then, psychology, like Rakitin's comprehension of all of Dmitri from a single trait, takes the part for the whole. Simply as a specialization or technique it distorts. (When Lydia Ginzburg speaks of a tradition of "psychological prose," the word bears a meaning so much freer and broader than in our usage that we might be tempted to treat it as a mistranslation.)[27] The use of psychology as a technique for getting hold of another mind or diagnosing its condition — this Dostoevsky questions especially.

That human beings contain capacities for destruction and self-destruction is no discovery of modern psychology; only a society lacking a sense of the past could believe it was. We may fairly question whether our own understanding of the heart of darkness equals that of tragedians and moralists who wrote without benefit of modern psychology. His last and greatest novel being more like a medieval mystery play than a psychomedical case history, Dostoevsky does not deny our capacity for destruction and self-destruction; he does, I think, deny both that a special quasi-medical language holds the key to it and that it can be grasped like an object of knowledge. The latter point is dramatized in the story of Ivan Karamazov's complicity in the murder, particularly in his conversations with one who presumes to x-ray his mind right down to its darkest wishes.

Just after the Grand Inquisitor monologue, Ivan falls into conversation with his half-brother Smerdyakov at the gate of their father's house — characteristically a threshold setting — the meeting between them curiously private and confidential as all their later conferences will be as well. In the course of this conversation Ivan is informed in an indirect if not serpentine way that the stage is set for the murder of the father. No one will be on hand to protect old Karamazov — Smerdyakov himself feels an epileptic fit coming on — and Dmitri, as usual in a passion, has got hold of a signal code that can be used to gain entry into the house. Why does Smerdyakov report these things to Ivan only to advise him to leave town? As we learn, it is to secure Ivan's consent — tacit consent — for the murder. Sensing that Ivan wishes his father dead (which may not take much acuity, seeing that Ivan himself has said as much, albeit not in his presence as far as we know), Smerdyakov sounds him carefully like a doctor gently tapping a knee, awaiting the reflexive response. Or, as we might say, he tests his x-ray understanding of Ivan's mind, which reveals to him both that Ivan wants his father murdered and that he doesn't want to be involved in the act; Smerdyakov tests it and finds it accurate. By following his suggestions, Ivan in effect signifies his consent for the murder, which duly takes place. But how accurate is the x-ray in fact?

The trick of Smerdyakov's success is that he makes no blunt proposition. Never does he say point-blank, "The way is clear for me (or Dmitri) to kill our father. Leave him to his fate." If Smerdyakov had spoken like that, the alarm would have sounded and Ivan never would have given his consent. For the fact is that while Ivan does loathe his father, does stand to gain from his death, and does not want to take an active part in the murder, he also feels obligated to protect him and in fact has once already saved him from Dmitri's rage. As subtle a tactician as Smerdyakov is, his understanding of Ivan's mind is no less reductive and caricaturing than, say, Rakitin's claim to have seen into "the very heart" of Dmitri and "caught the whole man from one trait." Ivan's desire to see his father dead is one trait; it is not the whole man.[28] Smerdyakov of all people ought to understand this, seeing that it is only by tiptoeing around Ivan's moral concerns in order not to startle them that he is able to have his way with Ivan.[29]

The end of the nineteenth century saw a growing interest in hypnotism and the phenomenon of the second self — matters memorably discussed by William James in the *Principles of Psychology*. Inside the self, James concludes, may exist another unknown to the first, a stranger.

In certain persons, at least, the total possible consciousness may be split into parts which coexist but mutually ignore each other, and share the objects of knowledge between them. More remarkable still, they are complementary. Give an object to one of the consciousnesses, and by that fact you remove it from the other or others. Barring a certain common fund of information, like the command of language, etc., what the upper self knows the under self is ignorant of, and vice versa.[30]

The under self can write letters while the upper self is doing something else entirely — hypnotism being the method used to parse the patient into his, or more commonly her, various members and bring out the unknown one or ones. On first glance it appears that Smerdyakov too plays the hypnotist, throwing Ivan into a kind of waking dream wherein he (Smerdyakov) can bypass Ivan's vigilant upper self and address that in Ivan which is willing to assist in the murder, if only to the extent of an act of omission. At times Ivan does seem entranced. But only at times. Repeatedly in this conference Ivan has flashes of clarity, even putting sharp questions to his own "hypnotist." There is no second self in Ivan that has a will of its own and is unknown to him, like an under self that writes letters without the knowledge of the upper self. (Significantly, of all the cast of *The Brothers Karamazov* it is the lightheaded Madame Hohlakov who is most taken with the notion of alternate personalities — she calls the phenomenon "aberration.")[31] If such a rogue self did exist, Ivan would be no more responsible for its doings than for those of a perfect stranger, and the narrative itself would lose its point and force. To some extent Ivan does know of the desires and decisions of his "second" self. It is not a stranger he has never seen or heard but stands on the very threshold of his dwelling, a kind of open secret. Hasn't Ivan spoken to Alyosha — spoken to him awake and aware — about his own desire for the father's death?

So too, the doctrine that "everything is permitted" that Smerdyakov took as his warrant to kill was not a secret thought but a topic of conversation in the Karamazov household. There is a story that Voltaire, entertaining his philosophical friends, dismissed his servants when the talk turned to atheism. "Do you want your throats cut tonight?" he asks the unbelievers.[32] Strong echoes of this piece of apocrypha are heard in *The Brothers Karamazov* in the references to Voltaire and the philosophes, the dinner dialogue on the God question (in the presence of Smerdyakov), the intimations of violence on the day the oppressed rise up against their masters, above all in the murder of the libertine father by his servant son. But this is echoing with a difference. One of those who would use religion to keep the masses in check, Voltaire thinks of it as a management tool, a way to exploit fear and credulity, in short a psychological ploy. In *The Brothers Karamazov* things are parodically reversed, with the servant in the role of the canny psychologist, securing his own position by mental trickery. ("As you went away, it meant you assured me that you wouldn't dare inform against me at the trial, and that you'd overlook my having the three thousand" [p. 763].) The point is, however, that Smerdyakov's psychological soundings of Ivan are just as corrupt as the use of religion as a psychological stratagem and instrument of rule.

If Ivan hadn't felt called on to defend his father (as surely as he also believes "everything is permitted"), he would never have undergone such agonies of self-reproach after the crime. One form taken by this last is the apparition of a maddeningly banal devil — he claims to know what Ivan is "secretly longing for" (p. 784) — who throws his own favorite theories back in his face more or less as Smerdyakov gave him back his own theory that all is lawful for the clever. Taking place on the very threshold of insanity, this most fantastic episode of *The Brothers Karamazov* "decrowns" Ivan by mocking his Promethean sense of self and converting his philosophy to babble.[33] In his struggle to maintain a grip on himself Ivan protests, "You choose out only my worst thoughts, and what's more, the stupid ones" (p. 776), as though the phantom, like Smerdyakov, and for equally malevolent ends, took the part for the whole. And by recognizing that the phantom *is* "the incarnation of myself, but only of one side of me" (p. 775), Ivan repudiates the notion of a second self dwelling apart from him, a perfect stranger. Is the phantom then Ivan's "dark side"? Only if one's idea of the dark side includes complaints about rheumatism and endless palavering:

> "Why am I, of all creatures in the world, doomed to be cursed by all decent people and even to be kicked, for if I put on mortal form I am bound to take such consequences sometimes? I know, of course, there's a secret in it, but they won't tell me the secret of anything, for then perhaps, seeing the meaning of it, I might bawl hosannah, and the indispensable minus would disappear at once, and good sense would reign supreme throughout the whole world. And that, of course, would mean the end of everything, even of magazines and newspapers . . ."[34] (P. 787)

It is as though the phantom brought the indictment of God down to the level of gossip. If this mimic, this play-actor is Ivan's dark side, he is at the same time a mockery of the very idea of the mystery of evil. The profundity of evil is itself a shallow enough commonplace of romanticism, as the phantom reminds Ivan:

"I repeat, moderate your expectations, don't demand of me 'everything great and noble' . . . You are really angry with me for not having appeared to you in a red glow with thunder and lightning, with scorched wings, but having shown myself in such a modest form. . . . Yes, there is that romantic strain in you." (P. 786)

Hannah Arendt did not discover the banality of evil: Dostoevksy did. His devil is less like the implacable enemy of God and more like Adolf Eichmann, looking for sympathy from his Israeli interrogator and lamenting his own hard luck. And Eichmann was no study in abnormality. Paradoxically, it may be his very transparency that makes him seem so opaque, like a pane of glass that blinds us in the light. With Ivan the desire to see his father dead is arguably no more psychologically occult or veiled from himself than the will to defend him.[35] The mystery of his role in the murder may simply be that a man with something of the Grand Inquisitor's sense of standing above the human multitude could have allowed himself to be governed by such petty motives as resentment and greed, and could have cowered behind the moral cover of a perfect alibi not only like Eichmann but like his own image of the masses under the Inquisitor's moral protection.

So far it appears that Dostoevsky rejects psychology on the grounds that it deals in caricature, denies the complexity of moral agency, and, by transforming the other into an object of analysis, demeans the soul. His antipathy to psychology may go beyond even this, however, if we factor in his politics — that is, his hostility to the revolutionary program of tearing down traditional structures and erecting a "scientific" society that in turn creates the conditions for a new man. For the fact is that both the theory of breaking and making habits — forming human beings by bringing the conditions of their production under control — and the reduction of the other to a knowable object were introduced by the tradition of Locke, whose philosophy is also a psychology. Certainly we catch an echo of Locke during Dmitri's trial when the defense lawyer contends that old Karamazov didn't deserve the name of a father because "the father is not merely he who begets the child, but he who begets it and does his duty by it" (p. 903). According to Locke in a discussion of paternal power, "the bare act of begetting" gives a man no power over his child "if all his care ends there and this be all the title he has to the name and authority of a father."[36] Unlike a political monologue, in *The Brothers Karamazov* a thesis rooted in a tradition the author opposes is delivered with great power (too much power for the jury). The defense lawyer speaks in the name of progress and enlightenment, though not revolution. The revolutionaries, rebellious stepchildren of the Enlightenment, identified bourgeois ideas like those under-writing the ideology of progress as obstacles to progress in their own right. If the Locke tradition, as we have seen, put in motion the idea of "making" men, the ideology of revolution places the means of human production in the hands of the state. The efforts of revolutionary regimes to transform citizens from the inside out and produce model workers are like a nationalization of Josiah Wedgwood's campaign to transform traditional laborers into efficient moderns by systematic discipline and conditioning — just as the prison-house society (with its psychiatric "hospitals") expands Bentham's Panopticon to the dimen-sions of the whole. Both Wedgwood and Bentham build their strategies of influ-ence and control on psychological principles, as both also stand in the tradi-tion of Locke.

The ambition of wiping the past clean and reconstructing knowledge from zero makes perhaps its first appearance in the world of thought with Francis Bacon. Bacon dreams of a new world, one where the past leaves no residue and the human mind is "like a fair sheet of paper with no writing on it." Though contemplating the renovation of knowledge, not the political order, Bacon is something like a revolutionary who wants to eradicate the traces of the past. "We must begin anew from the very foundations."[37] But not until an educational method viewing the child as "white Paper, or Wax, to be moulded and fash-ioned as one pleases" was worked out by Locke, who searched the foundations of the political order, did the implications of Bacon's project come to fruition.[38] Locke's method of careful supervision and conditioning, guided at every step by psychological calculation, became the de facto model of later efforts to reform human beings by controlling the causes that make them as they are; as a method it lent itself to wider and wider applications. When the intelligentsia of Dostoevsky's Russia cast itself as the people's pedagogue,[39] did it realize how deeply embedded the pedagogical model was in the bourgeois tradition it despised, and how inseparable from mechanisms of discipline? It was in disci-plinary utopias like the Panopticon designed by men in the Locke tradition of psychology — it was in reformatories, factories, and hospitals intended to pro-duce new men through the application of Locke's principles of engineering on a larger scale — that perhaps the first architectural sketches of the vastly larger prison-utopias of the twentieth century are to be found. "The eighteenth-cen-tury dream has become the twentieth-century nightmare."[40] Grotesquely mag-nified and inverted, Wedgwood's "brave new world" of prosperity, moral health, and "complete obedience"[41] becomes the brave new world of socialism. And fueling the thought of reformers like Wedgwood was the assumption that others can be known right down to their "causes" — an assumption that Dostoevsky denies in the strongest terms. "One of [Dostoevsky's] basic ideas, which he advances in his polemic with the socialists, is precisely the idea that man is not a final and defined quantity upon which firm calculations can be made."[42] But this idea did not originate with socialism. Like the theory and practice of social engineering itself, it goes back to bourgeois reformers inspired by a psychology that pictured human beings as "knowable and manageable."[43] And so Dostoevsky's argument with psychology is really one with his argument with socialism, resting as the latter does on a model of the mind instituted by reformers under the influence of psychological theory — reformers who also reduced thought itself to a medical problem. Trotsky's dream of a new Man "transparent" to himself (as though endowed with x-ray vision into his own being) and fortified by methodical "psychophysical training" derives squarely from the educational tradition rooted in the psychology of the Enlightenment.[44]

If it is a peculiarity of revolutionary rhetoric that, while seeing history as determined, it calls on us to author history with all our energy, the Lockean psychologist David Hartley was one of those who "loudly proclaim[ed] that men's characters are the product of circumstances" even as they strove anxiously "to control and alter circumstances so as to produce the right kind of character."[45] Before revolutionaries came to speak of human beings as the product of impersonal forces, bourgeois reformers sought to produce character as it were with their own hands. As strange as it may seem to trace revolutionary thought to bourgeois precedents (although we do just this whenever we speak of the famous "puritanism" of revolutionaries), it was thinkers in the Locke tradition who first framed and applied the thesis that human beings can be reformed by controlling the conditions that produce them, and who in their engineering zeal introduced measures of control later to be nationalized in the socialist utopia, such as systematic surveillance and the sanitizing of thought. And just as in socialist society, the dictatorship deemed necessary in penitentiaries, factories, schools, and hospitals was projected to be temporary. The reformation of human nature once accomplished, repression would end. Precisely because psychology promised that human beings could be remade under controlled conditions, "the need for discipline would be transitory."[46] Exemplifying this disciplinary project is the Panopticon, that modernistic but unbuilt prison where every condition would be controlled in the interest of reforming the inmate for eventual release — for Bentham too turned his thoughts to crime and punishment. Though we might not think of Bentham as a psychologist (especially in view of Mill's comments on the poverty of his understanding), the Panopticon itself can be considered a device for producing psychological effects with certainty by controlling their causes. Exposed to the view of the inspector, the tenants of the Panopticon would be subjected to x-ray vision and transformed into objects of knowledge much as Dmitri is made to strip during his interrogation and transformed into a specimen of guilt. Bentham, we know, saw the hidden hand of a cabal behind the failure of his plans for the Panopticon. Like Mandeville, who claimed to discern the true motives of men; like the enlightened who saw through the plots all around them and the revolutionaries of France who put conspiracy theory into practice, he himself had x-ray vision.[47]

Also gifted with the power of seeing through deceptions is Kolya Krassotkin, that Napoleon of fourteen in *The Brothers Karamazov*. Already beginning to talk the pedagogy of revolution, Kolya is convinced that "everything is habit with men" (p. 640). Ilyusha needs to be trained, his character formed. Real life will "cure" Alyosha of his delusions (p. 671). As though taking the Locke tradition to a higher level, the charismatic Kolya seems to have some loose idea of an education where habits are broken and reset, backwardness cured, and the learner subjected to the shaping power of a guiding hand. As it happens, his ideas come to him ready-made from Rakitin.

While in prison awaiting trial Dmitri is visited by Rakitin, who once typed him as a sensualist but now has a theory that his crime was caused by the environment — even though he didn't commit it — and furthermore that thought itself is the product of physical mechanisms. As Dmitri paraphrases it (reported speech and ironic echoing being characteristic of the circulation of language in *The Brothers Karamazov*), "Imagine: inside, in the nerves, in the head — that is, these nerves are there in the brain . . . (damn them!) there are sort of little tails, the little tails of those nerves, and as soon as they begin quivering. . . . " Rakitin wants to write up his theory of Dmitri with "a tinge of Socialism" (p. 716). And here too socialism borrows heavily from the funds of a despised parent. For it was an article of belief among bourgeois reformers like Bentham and Wedgwood, inspired by Hartley's psychology, that thought took shape as a physiological necessity under the impress of environmental conditions. Arising through sensation as Locke asserted, bound together by the laws of association, ideas themselves can be controlled in theory like any other mechanical process. Antedating Rakitin's kind of materialism, or that of the theorists he parrots, was the explicit materialism of bourgeois reformers convinced that prisons or factories or schools could serve as actual laboratories of social and moral reform. If minds are the product of environmental conditions, then by the rigorous control of conditions — hence the minute oversight and stringent discipline of Wedgwood's factory or Bentham's prison — minds themselves can be reformed with something like certainty. If physical conditions are moral influences, by the same token thought itself is a medical problem. Locke as we know was a physician, as was Hartley, and men like Wedgwood and Bentham with "sanatory" intentions enlarged his educational program of curing the mind through its habituation to a discipline at once exacting, benevolent, and psychologically informed. In this medicalization of the mind, in all likelihood, lies the source of the view that incorrect thought is a problem to be treated with "therapy" — a view common enough among reformers today.

The theory of curing corrupt habits of thought and reforming humanity by controlling moral causes was not confined to England. In his enthusiasm for Hartley's system of psychology, which traces thought to vibrations conducted by the nerves, the American physician Benjamin Rush proposed to use the principle of association to purge the young nation of prerepublican habits and implant correct ideas in all subjects. With the new science of Hartley at their command, Americans, Rush believed, were capable of destroying for good the vicious habits of thought established in the days of monarchy. "Utopia itself was now attainable." According to Rush, the nation need only be made into a school in which the truth, already known, is inculcated and enforced. In the society now fully enlightened, fully cured of the corruption of the past, "all truths on all subjects would ultimately stand in their correct relation to one another in correspondence with the divine order."[48] The last word already having been spoken, the nation itself would be "finalized." Rush's utopia is another's tomb. Certainly Dostoevsky would have found it so, if Bakhtin's reading of him is at all just. It is Dostoevsky's conviction (writes Bakhtin) that

> nothing conclusive has yet taken place in the world, the ultimate word
> of the world and about the world has not yet been spoken, the world is
> open and free, everything is still in the future and will always be in the
> future.[49]

What could be more completely contrary to this indeterminacy than a national program, underwritten by the science of psychology, to dictate the final truth on all questions? The very mood of radical uncertainty in *The Brothers Karamazov* declares the author's revolt against such a regime, just as the painful and undeniable fact of their own freedom separates the brothers from the imaginary republican who can only think one way (virtuously) because the "associations" in his brain have been soldered to make anything else impossible. If that is what utopia calls for, then no wonder Dostoevsky is identified with the anti-utopian tradition.

Within a decade of Dostoevsky's death the social psychologist (and author of a utopia) Gabriel Tarde foretold the conclusion of history in a kind of Pax Romana. While his blend of scientism and clairvoyance and his sense of possessing the key to everything have analogies in Marxism, Tarde's prophecy is also in the tradition of John Stuart Mill's vision of a pacified society where all are assimilated to all and scientific consensus is so broad and deep that almost nothing remains in dispute. The difference is that while Mill is disturbed by the "inevitable" approach of this sort of steady state,[50] Tarde welcomes the thought of an empire of uniformity that has and is the last word of history. "A rule of general caprice and all-pervasive fashion succeeds to the old usages of past times until the appointed hour comes for the quiescence of people's souls in wants that are alike stable and uniform."[51] As opposed to this ending to the story of history, that of *The Brothers Karamazov* — with Ivan between life and death, Dmitri between prison and escape, Alyosha between the monastery and the world — seems notably lacking in finality itself.

Gifted with insight into the course of history, Tarde is certain of its outcome. "War tends to the hypertrophy of states; — it will go on producing enormous agglomerations until the political unity of the civilised world is finally consummated and universal peace is assured."[52] Exactly this final truth was ironized in Orwell's *Nineteen Eighty-Four*.

CHAPTER 7

George Orwell:
Moral Effort

Famed for his inferno *Nineteen Eighty-Four*, George Orwell, like the central figure of the anti-utopian tradition, Dostoevsky, was a moralist concerned with the expiation of guilt: his own guilt over serving the cause of British imperialism. He tells of his burden in *The Road to Wigan Pier*:

> When I came home [from Burma] on leave in 1927 I was already half determined to throw up my job, and one sniff of English air decided me. I was not going to be a part of that evil despotism. But I wanted much more than merely to escape from my job. For five years I had been part of an oppressive system, and it had left me with a bad conscience. . . . I was conscious of an immense weight of guilt that I had got to expiate.[1]

Rather than seeking professional help, Orwell seems to have cleansed himself by descending into the social depths. Prose for Orwell is the moral record of such events. That Orwell indeed inhabits a moral universe is implied by the near equivalence of "conscience" and "conscious" in the passage just cited. The real thrust of his celebrated essay on prose style, "Politics and the English Language," is accordingly a moral one: Choose your words not just well but conscientiously.

In an essay on the anti-utopian tradition, Gary Saul Morson sets the belief in "ready-made" theories once prevalent in the Russian intelligentsia against a vision alive to concrete particulars and the everyday possibilities of freedom.[2] "Politics and the English Language" is cast in exactly these terms, with the author condemning "prefabricated" language, especially that of the intelligentsia, and recalling writers to everyday reality and the exercise of choice. Among the works favorably cited by Morson is Eugene Zamyatin's *We*, an anti-utopian precursor of *Nineteen Eighty-Four*. Among the examples of prose style held up to infamy by Orwell in "Politics and the English Language" is an excerpt from an "essay on psychology" that, so far as one can make it out, ridicules the shallow consciousness of the average man.[3]

In its first sentences "Politics and the English Language" implies a certain skeptical familiarity with the psychological idiom. Rejecting the theory that the decline of the language is too deeply determined for us to do anything about it by "conscious action," Orwell maintains that those of this opinion are themselves but "half-conscious" — he doesn't say unconscious — of their own postulates:

> Most people who bother with the matter at all would admit that the English language is in a bad way, but it is generally assumed that we cannot by conscious action do anything about it. Our civilisation is decadent, and our language — so the argument runs — must inevitably share in the general collapse. . . . Underneath this lies the half-conscious belief that language is a natural growth and not an instrument which we shape for our own purposes.[4]

While Orwell questions the existence of some all-powerful underlying force on the order of the unconscious (which lies beyond human ken except for those who know all about it, and works irresistibly except in those who tame it), he grants that consciousness is neither complete nor clear. We are somewhere between knowing and not knowing what we are about. Is this not, in the most general terms, the way human beings are portrayed in literature?

Though his advice on composition is intended more for the journalist than the writer of fiction, Orwell himself, like Dostoevsky, was both. In fact, in a certain tradition of satiric irony well known to Orwell — that of Swift, Smollett, and Dickens — the author plays the reporter of facts, so that "journalism" and literary art become one and the same.[5] Anyway, I believe it is because Orwell writes with a deep, rich literary tradition behind him that no one has yet managed to sound like him, or even perhaps write passably good prose, by following his few simple maxims. Maybe his literary ancestry also contributes to his dislike of the kind of psychological prattle quoted in "Politics and the English Language," for modern psychology takes over for its own purposes questions once within the purview of literature. Two centuries ago, before the divorce of "the two cultures" was what it is today, physicians of the mind looked to the works of Johnson, Mandeville, and Swift,[6] the second of these a physician himself, as was Smollett, and the last a strong precursor of Orwell both in his use of the Menippean satire and his elevation of plainness to a literary art.[7] With his interest in the mind of someone like the Grub Street Hack or the modest proposer, Swift might even be reckoned a psychologist of sorts, though on the other hand he would have seen the engineers of the mind who figure in this study as spiders, architects of a cobweb world, weavers of illusion. (By now, Swift has been identified as a psychological case in his own right, one who constructed a world in the image of his own pathology, as has Orwell.)[8] It is evident, anyway, that literary interest in the human mind predates psychology as such. As I will suggest, Locke himself takes over themes of the most heroic of the English poets, Milton — like him an advocate of tolerance, writer on education, defender of the right of rebellion, and discipliner of the passions.[9] If Locke can be regarded as the founder of scientific psychology, then this becomes a field of study by separating itself from literature, which nevertheless remains its shadow and rival. As a man of literature, Orwell might well be averse to the professionalizing of issues formerly in the public domain, and all the more averse to the kind of language that conceals its own vacuity under a parade of science.[10]

"Dare to be a Daniel, / Dare to stand alone."[11] Orwell's motto places him closer, surely, to Milton than Locke, and yet in reading "Politics and the English Language" we meet Locke. Locke's own criticism of abuses of words was in the spirit of the new scientific ideal of plain language:

> There should be little figurative language, especially metaphors, which falsely describe actions and things. There should be no verbal superfluity, but rather an economy of words sufficient to match exactly the phenomena. Words should be the plainest possible, with intelligible, clear, and unequivocal meanings, preferably common words which are closer to material realities. There should be no emphasis upon or interest in the mode of expression for its own sake.[12]

No one who has read "Politics and the English Language" can fail to recognize a bond. Orwell too is wary of metaphor, he too demands economy ("If it is possible to cut a word out, always cut it out"); the stress is negative, on getting rid of, as though it were best to use as little of language as possible.[13] And yet what is the language policy of the Party in *Nineteen Eighty-Four*, if not to whittle language down to the barest minimum in order to diminish the possibilities of thought, dependent as it is on language? (In Swift's Laputa, where poetry is generated by machine as in Oceania, thought is given to cutting words of many syllables as the next best thing to disposing with language altogether.)[14] If in the scientific utopia every citizen is viewed by the state as wax to be "moulded and fashioned as [it] pleases" like the child in Locke's theory of education (but without Locke's provisos, of course),[15] in Oceania something like the scientific ideal of language is nationalized as well, again with inhuman results.

The fact is that Orwell's prose is far too rich to reduce to a set of maxims, and maxims essentially negative at that. Bakhtin was a historian of the prosaic: Orwell's word *bears* the history of the prosaic. Like the modernists in their disgust with the fictions of progress, he too is driven to originality. With the nineteenth-century realists he feels "the moral urgency of seeing with disenchanted clarity."[16] He is Dickens ridiculing the Circumlocution Office; Hazlitt insisting that even in turbulent times one "need not, in the rage of party-spirit, discard the proper attributes of humanity, the common dictates of reason;"[17] Smollett, "bravely, grimly pessimistic," refusing to disavow what his brain tells him is true.[18] In the spirit of Swift taking the experiments of the Royal Society one step beyond sanity in *Gulliver's Travels,* he takes the experiment of socialism one step beyond reality in *Nineteen Eighty-Four.*[19] Orwell is Swift, a deadly ironist and "Tory anarchist" (his own label for both Swift and himself);[20] he is also the reportorial Defoe.[21] He is Milton, a radical infused with the passion of rebellion who nevertheless warns against the construction of "Atlantic and Utopian polities" — Orwell's Atlantic utopia being Oceania.[22] Orwell is Rabelais, repudiating Latin and everything that goes with it in favor of the vernacular and situating prose "here, in this time and space, under this sun."[23] For that matter, he recalls the authors of the fabliau tradition — the profane precursors of realism — as well as the masters of the picaresque; his first work, *Down and Out in Paris and London,* combining fabliau material with a narrative of the road, rediscovers as it were the counter-romantic influences on the modern novel.

If Locke breaks down complex structures into their elements and the Locke tradition seeks first principles (such as pleasure and pain for Bentham) and underlying causes, so much underlies Orwell's prose that it simply defies reduction. And everything touched by his prose, no matter how ordinary, participates in its richness:

> In front of the fire there was almost always a line of damp washing, and in the middle of the room was the big kitchen table at which the family and all the lodgers ate. I never saw this table completely uncovered, but I saw its various wrappings at different times. At the bottom there was a layer of old newspapers stained by Worcester Sauce; above that a sheet of sticky white oilcloth; above that a green serge cloth; above that a coarse linen cloth, never changed and seldom taken off. I used to get

to know individual crumbs by sight and watch their progress up and down the table from day to day.[24]

So evocative is this description that it calls up another who reports the telling detail in a style at once perfectly straight and pungently ironic: Chaucer. In one of Orwell's novels Lionel Trilling picks up "a dim elegiac echo of Defoe and of the early days of the middle-class ascendancy as Orwell's sad young man learns to cherish the small personal gear of life, his own bed and chairs and saucepans."[25] But if in Orwell we encounter the realism of Defoe after the fact, the Wife of Bath is Moll Flanders before the fact. Centering on her own bed, the Wife's speech with all its scurrilous particulars settles in time into the prosaic reportage of Defoe and much later, for Orwell, into realities as stubborn as a table standing out against the lies of politics.

Was Orwell himself aware of every last one of the influences on his way of seeing and saying that are cited here (not that the list is exhaustive)? In all likelihood not. But in no way does this mean that he suffers from blindness, or that the critic, by getting hold of something Orwell didn't realize, could somehow possess his secret like a reporter getting the scoop. Not knowing a genre in its entirety, even if this were possible in the first place, is no bar to working in it and extending its possibilities. Some of the authors of Menippean satire — the genre of *Nineteen Eighty-Four* — apparently had a definite, others a less definite idea of the genre and its history.[26] From a theorist like Bakhtin, moreover, we get a sense of the fathomless riches of the genre itself. As with genre, so with tradition. That we cannot sufficiently know the tradition in which we stand — not because we are trapped in its narrowness but because we are surpassed by its richness and depth — doesn't mean we are blind. I bring this up to put in question, at least provisionally, what I take to be the master myth of modern culture: that we are captives of ignorance awaiting a moment of liberating insight. We are indeed somewhere between knowing and not knowing what we are doing, but this isn't necessarily a handicap. As Bakhtin argues convincingly, not even the great writers, those who tap most deeply into the potential of the genres, can say just what their works mean. For all its topical immediacy *Nineteen Eighty-Four* stands as literature because it is so powerfully informed by the history of the menippea, even back to the *Consolation* of Boethius and its tale of a captive sentenced to death who receives the emancipating word of true philosophy. Orwell may not have even known this work. Should we say he was unconscious of it?

*

At the conclusion of his reflections on nationalism, by which he means a form of political worship so abject that all decency and reason are sacrificed, Orwell offers a corrective. He asks us to look inside ourselves.

> As for the nationalistic loves and hatreds that I have spoken of, they are part of the make-up of most of us, whether we like it or not. Whether it is possible to get rid of them I do not know, but I do believe that it is possible to struggle against them, and that this is essentially a *moral* effort. It is a question first of all of discovering what one really is, what one's own feelings really are, and then of making allowances for the inevitable bias. . . . But this, I repeat, needs a *moral* effort.[27]

At one stroke Orwell distinguishes himself from those who would correct the thoughts of *others* and those who believe moral categories are passé. The psychological culture of today leans decidedly to the second position.

In spite of his belief in moral categories and ordinary standards of evidence, Orwell himself, ironically, slips into the psychological idiom now and then — ironically, because psychology in our time tends to replace moral categories with those of medicine and has come into conflict with ordinary standards of evidence. (Think of what counts as evidence in a Freudian reading of a literary text, or in the recovery of a "repressed memory.") And yet, to double the irony, it is a desire to understand the *abandonment* of common sense and moral standards by the political creeds of his day that inspires Orwell's vague search for psychological causes. Conspiracy theories apparently "answer to some obscure psychological need of our time." Rumors of secret weapons in the hands of the enemy "evidently fulfill some obscure psychological need." The "neurosis" of antisemitism "lies very deep." Something, he writes, "some psychological vitamin, is lacking in modern civilisation, and as a result we are all more or less subject to this lunacy of believing that whole races or nations are mysteriously good or mysteriously evil."[28]

Psychological vitamin? The absurdity of the term seems an admission that political beliefs are not medical matters after all. And they are not. Obscure psychological causes are an unknown something invented to explain belief systems whose more patent attractions — their vast simplicity, for example, or their concentration of evil in an external enemy — are thought too weak to account for their hold over the mind. The existence of such causes is purely conjectural. However great the temptation to claim the authority of science for our own political positions, the beliefs of adversaries, even antisemites, are not produced by ideological microbes that science can identify and kill.[29] Diagnoses of such "diseases" are political, not scientific statements. Orwell himself, digger-up of others' secret motives (such as the fear of emotional pain that inspires the saint's flight from earthly attachments),[30] seems to believe of psychology what he says of politics: that it is a foul but necessary business. Psychology is politics by another name. But what would it really mean to control the conditions under which political beliefs are "produced"? And what distinguishes those really convinced that opponents are sick — their beliefs a function of some psychological deficiency — from the ideologue who defines dissenters as suffering from "neuroses, psychoses, mental derangements, genuinely requiring psychiatric aid," diseases "to be cured, that is, made to disappear, if possible without a trace"?[31] That Orwell himself knew where political psychiatry pointed we can surmise from the great satire, *Nineteen Eighty-Four.*

I cited before an ironic affinity between *Nineteen Eighty-Four* and the *Consolation of Philosophy:* in both a doomed man's mind is prepared for death in private lessons with a mighty pedagogue. The stated intention of Lady Philosophy is to cure, and hence free, the mind of Boethius. Lady Philosophy plays the psychiatrist, saying of the Muses, "They do not liberate the minds of men from disease, but merely accustom them to it. . . . Get out, you Sirens; your sweetness leads to death. Leave him to be cured and made strong by [philosophy]."[32] In the talking cure administered to Winston Smith the psychiatric model is thoroughly ironized. The mind is freed but, according to the official motto, freedom is slavery.

According to Dostoevsky's Grand Inquisitor, slavery is just what people really want. As I have argued, the Inquisitor's claim to pierce to the very core of the human mind is made with such rhetorical force and flair that we are apt to excuse its exaggerations. *Nineteen Eighty-Four* poses its own criticisms of the Inquisitor's line. It is not only that O'Brien himself, in the course of his talking cure, jeers at the idea that he and his brethren dominate the many out of tender concern for their happiness, as the old cardinal claims to do. It is that Winston Smith, despite his attraction to O'Brien and final besotted surrender to Big Brother, possesses no such univocal will to slavery as the mind reader of the human race supposes. Smith is made, not born, a slave; and ironically, it is by playing on his rather formless yearning for liberty itself that the State undoes him.

If Stanley Milgram produced by a kind of manipulation the very data he "discovered," Winston Smith in *Nineteen Eighty-Four* is arrested and tortured for the crime of rebellion that the State itself seems to have worked him into, as it clearly supplies him with the criminal Book. Psychologists in Oceania, we are told, keep busy "studying with extraordinary minuteness the meaning of facial expressions, gestures, and tones of voice, and testing the truth-producing effects of drugs, shock therapy, hypnosis, and physical torture," the very investigation evidently performed on Smith. With the activation of Locke's theory of education, plans were devised to subject workers, paupers, and others to discipline and tutelage, and it is these schemes to reform many under controlled conditions that introduced modes of engineering later adopted for altogether different ends, and on a different scale, in socialist society. As Richard Pipes has argued, those who made the Russian Revolution also accepted the Enlightenment doctrine that human beings themselves can and should be made. Even as they worked from "psychological premises [derived] directly from Locke and Helvétius,"[33] they drove those premises to lengths never attempted and scarcely imagined. So it is that in the socialist paradise of *Nineteen Eighty-Four* we return seemingly impossibly to Locke, with O'Brien now in the role of the benevolent father who cures his wayward son. Locke tells of making a gentleman. O'Brien too is engaged in the making of a person. "We make him one of ourselves before we kill him. . . . We make the brain perfect before we blow it out."[34] Though Oceania is not prosperous, the State does, it appears, have the resources to lavish on ordinary citizens some perverse equivalent of the "constant Attention" Locke prescribes for the sons of the well-born. The care of the Lockean father becomes the solicitude of O'Brien watching over his ward. The father who puts aside his own "Absolute Power" in favor of "a milder Sort of Government" becomes the relenting torturer. Punishments that "reach the Mind" become rats.[35] And if the education of the gentleman is finished when his conduct looks perfectly natural (so that no sign appears of the labor that went into its making), the correction of thought is complete when the process covers its own tracks in accordance with the laws of doublethink. As though by a Swiftian change of scale, techniques of education proposed by Locke are raised in Oceania to the level of the monstrous.

The cure of Winston Smith — his transformation from a soul lost in disaffection to a devotee of Big Brother — satirizes what we might call the public relations of those regimes that play most radically on the hopes and fears and dreams of their citizens. "All twentieth century totalitarian movements have sold themselves to the masses as antidotes to alienation."[36] Some years before alienation became a topic in the consumer society where all have to work out their own psychic salvation, totalitarianism held out a dream of collective salvation — the vision of a citizenry strong because at one. In Winston Smith's reconciliation with Big Brother this closing of divisions is satirically acted out. The mind of O'Brien, agent of his return, seems for its part completely without doubt and division. Unlike the Grand Inquisitor, who lies and dominates out of professed love of humanity, this inquisitor has no story and avows his use of power for its own sake. His mind blank and pitiless, he seems one of those executioners of whom it has been said that they "can no longer be psychologically understood."[37]

In the liberal myth of therapeutic recovery, the healed self overcomes the state of estrangement and division that continues to prevail in the world. According to the "reigning diagnosis" (wrote M. H. Abrams in 1971), "man, who was once well, is now ill, and . . . at the core of the modern malaise lies his fragmentation, dissociation, estrangement, or (in the most highly charged of these parallel terms) 'alienation,' "[38] as though the most private sense of loss had become a society's most general affliction, and a purely psychological antidote its most coveted good. Under the same myth, moral judgment itself becomes a kind of "oldspeak," not just an archaism but an affront to progress and embarrassment of the therapeutic project, relic of a dark past destined to be overcome.

CHAPTER 8

The Voiding of Moral Categories

In the one-dimensional society envisioned by Herbert Marcuse, both dissent and discontent are extinguished and citizens embrace the System almost like a captive bonding with the captor. On this hyperbole is founded Marcuse's proposal to turn universities into hospitals where minds are returned to political health. The one-dimensional society Marcuse wrote of is a fiction, a dystopia masking as history and justifying his own countermeasures. The real one-dimensionality, it seems to me, is that of the psychological culture itself, not in the sense that it has totalitarian power but that it deals in simplification and caricature, especially caricature of a past from which we are now said to be getting free. In the past people lived under a benighted code of morality now being lifted. They walked in darkness, we in light. In one version or another this tale of exodus circulates widely and influentially throughout our society.

Under the force of this caricature of history the very word "morality" falls into disrepute, taking on dark connotations of the punitive and the archaic. Forty years ago Lionel Trilling was struck with the antique sound of the statement that Orwell was "a virtuous man."[1] By now it appears the sentence of history has been passed on the entire moral lexicon. Even Stanley Milgram, professing to show that ordinary Americans are perfectly capable of acting like Adolf Eichmann, disavows moral judgment. Though dismayed at the stylization of language that "guard[s] the person against the full moral implications of his acts," he discusses mindless obedience "with the aim of understanding rather than judging it from a moral standpoint."[2] Milgram's investigation might well be called one-dimensional in that it goes only one way: the subjects' conduct is subjected to a cold critical scrutiny from which the experimenter himself is exempt under his own rules. Foreclosing real analysis and discussion in the name of insight into the full moral implications of human action, the

Milgram experiment dramatizes the estrangement of social science from the moral philosophy in which it originated. It belongs to a culture that would like to consign moral judgment in particular to the past as a historical embarrassment.

"About nothing," wrote Hannah Arendt in her reflections on the Eichmann controversy, "does public opinion everywhere seem in happier agreement than that no one has the right to judge somebody else."[3] If we are all the same deep down, if we all have the same hopes and fears and dreams (as the psychological like to say), then moral distinctions as such may seem a grotesque mistake. I have known some so averse to moral judgment, so bound to the belief that everyone is at core the same, that they maintain Eichmann would have behaved better if only he had received love as a child. Others maintain no one can judge a Nazi precisely because we are all no different deep down.[4] Others in their antipathy to distinctions of any kind claim that all have their own private holocaust, or all are slaves of the corporations, the former confusing personal misfortune with the murder of millions, the latter chattel with a modern citizen. In one sense or another the feeling in the psychological society seems to be that moral distinctions represent a throwback to the past and an offense against modernity. It is forgotten that this line itself is a throwback to the past — to thinkers like Bentham, whose "psychological approach" was intended to supplant "the old moralising vision of man."[5] The fiction of pioneering novelty indexes the public relations success of the therapeutic culture. That morality itself has been made to connote the drone of hypocritical pieties and the lock-up of human expression in a code of rules does so as well.

If freedom of expression is what we want, it may seem this freedom is here. Whether the limits of the permissible are teased as on television or simply exploded as in more advanced forms of expression, it has become so common to show and speak the forbidden — to defy the taboos of "tradition" — that the act itself has become conventional. George Steiner once tracked the increasingly stark depiction of sex in contemporary culture under a dehumanizing imperative of saying all. As he reminds us, in *Madame Bovary* sex is evoked through cadence and allusion, not literal portrayal — to which it can be added that the exoticism and visions of abundance haunting Emma's imagination became elements of department store decor and finally the daily fare of consumer society. From intimations to trumpetings, from the half-light of fantasy to the glare of the marketplace. Nor has reticence simply been laid aside. It has been positively repudiated, as if every breach of the threshold of reserve were an act of liberation, the taking of a Bastille. What makes the publicist Bernays an apt figure of the consumer society is that society's belief that nothing exists that cannot be shown and said to all — publicized. Boasting of its emancipation from the darkness of tradition, the consumer society tends to regard all cautions against saying too much ("But that I am forbid / To tell the secrets of my prison-house, / I could a tale unfold") as so much priestcraft.[6] Just as the ideology of progress told of "the gradual liberation of the forces of innovation and production from the fetters of religious and social inhibition"[7] — a tale so influential its theme of resistless advance was taken over by the critics of capitalism — so the liberation of speech puts an end to the very tale of the past.

Ever since the adoption of a code of "terrible honesty" that would not permit Victorian evasions,[8] the age of the Victorians has borne the special animus of modern caricature. Loaded with the worst connotations of the word "morality," the era itself is made to stand for a stifling oppression and a regime of hypocritical complacency that prove our own emancipation by contrast. In a way, though, the picture of language "freed" as it departs ever more emphatically from the Victorian consensus misleads us. For both the relegation of moral judgment to the status of an archaism and the pursuit of truer forms of expression than the restraints of a bygone age are thought to have allowed exemplify a belief in progress as naive as any that may have been held by the Victorians. After all, if popular culture proclaims that society has just now been liberated from the dark ages of intolerance and inhibition, emergence from the medieval past was itself a leading theme of Victorian discourse. (Walter Houghton's classic *Victorian Frame of Mind* opens on just this point.) Edward Bernays, as we know, fancied himself a sort of American Freud and as a young man campaigned against the sexual code of silence, yet in his very rebellion against Victorianism he clung to its central myth, that of progress.[9] To Bernays, progress meant liberation from archaic attitudes especially, and, in the consumer society he helped build, "liberation from archaic attitudes" becomes a received idea in its own right — one that obscures the costs of its own ascendancy.

The consumer society claims victory over the past, and particularly over the constraints thought to have choked speech. But in saying all we may end up saying less. The celebration of our own power of speech, the vaunting of our freedom from the falsehoods and inhibitions of "back then," not only gratifies a kind of cultural vanity but conceals a reduced capacity for speech itself. That censorship weighed heavily on Victorian culture — the expurgation of Shakespeare, the pressuring of novelists, in the United States the Comstock Act — is indisputable. Nevertheless, and contrary to the popular caricature of the past as one long spell of silence that has just now been broken, men and

women as recently as a hundred years ago possessed an entire lexicon of evaluation that has since dried up. They could say an action was well or ill done,
generous or mean-spirited, courageous or base (or anywhere in between)[10] —
terms that have since taken on a patina of the archaic. In the psychological rendering of the argument of Mill's *Liberty*, where emancipation means breaking
out of the mind-forged manacles that keep us from doing what we want and
becoming what we could be, all "Victorian" terms of evaluation drop away, so
that nothing is said, for example, about conduct that makes one a "fit object of
moral reprobation."[11] In a culture that prides itself on being, like a good psychologist, unshockable, the idea of moral reprobation has become shocking in
its own right. Evidently we no longer possess or even wish to possess the means
of moral discrimination that Mill held in common with the very society he
argued with.

Claiming to be freer for the loss of these distinctions is like claiming to
be freer for the loss of a skill, say the use of the fingers. The thinking seems to
be that since our own boldness of speech is a good thing, whatever it displaced
must have been worthless because one good cannot conflict with another —
a variant of the belief in ordained harmony that Isaiah Berlin has shown to be
one of the most seductive fallacies of political thought. The notion that moral
categories are destined to wither away and be replaced by others, so that it will
never again be necessary to make moral judgments except perhaps in furtive
asides — is this one last version of the utopian fallacy Berlin has exposed?

In one of his essays Berlin muses on the possibility that laws of causation
governing human action may be found. Among the consequences, he reasons,
would be the invalidation of all customary modes of moral evaluation.

> Such expressions as "I should not have done *x*," "How could you have
> chosen *x*?" and so on, indeed the entire language of the criticism and
> assessment of one's own and others' conduct, would undergo a sharp
> transformation. . . . It seems to me that we should be unwise to under-
> estimate the effect of robbing praise, blame, a good many counterfac-
> tual propositions, and the entire network of concepts connected with
> freedom, choice, responsibility, of much of their present function and
> meaning[12] —

unwise because the loss of so intimate a possession and so strong a check would
be simply incalculable (as if voyagers to some new land were to leave behind
not only home and compass but memory). In the consumer society the language of moral evaluation is being undermined primarily by psychology, and

undermined the more effectively in that this sharp transformation is being carried out in the name of good feeling and human emancipation. Today we actually hear "I have a problem with X" instead of "I object to X," as though the latter were too crude and contentious, too charged with criticism and assessment; better the sociable language of neurosis than the scandal of conflict.[13]

The costs exacted on moral argument by the institution of psychology are borne out by a renowned fighter for emancipation who was not scandalized by conflict and did not want to see the language of freedom, choice, and responsibility discarded — Martin Luther King. A passionate moralist, King was also given to the language of psychology (particularly that of the self-realization school, which caught on widely and has never since let go), with the result that his moral pleas rest in good part on a foundation inimical to morality itself. In an early sermon King condemns the abandonment of God in favor of material things, at the same time stressing over and over that this apostasy was perfectly unconscious. That the unconscious nature of America's transgressions, as though the nation had been sleepwalking, absolves it from the moral law whose supremacy is supposed to be the theme of the sermon, seems to escape King entirely.[14] Psychological and moral ways of speaking have in fact grown incompatible. The bill of grievances in the Declaration of Independence is underwritten by the moral psychology of the Scottish Enlightenment.[15] King's attempt to moralize psychology in *his* bill of grievances, the "Letter from Birmingham Jail," fails. Indeed, moral psychology no longer exists.

With its psychodramatic theory of politics and its use of the idioms of self-realization like "repressed emotions" and "chains of conformity," King's most famous writing has even more of a psychological cast than the 1954 sermon, the assumption that psychology equals morality being groundless in both cases.[16] As phrases like "chains of conformity" suggest, King goes along with the psychological revision of John Stuart Mill's argument even though he does not want to accept its consequence — the voiding of moral categories. The consequence has followed nonetheless. That King's language of psychological impairment has since become a cant used by multitudes with no history of the suffering he documents — this in itself illustrates the cancellation of moral meaning by the culture of mental health. The very concept of moral law affirmed in King's "Letter" is vacated by psychology.[17] Where is the evidence that as we learn to talk with ever greater facility about "latent frustrations" and "pent-up resentments," as King calls them, we become more serious about moral law? In a society as psychologically concerned as our own, people might well feel that to ask one burning with frustration and resentment to abide by the moral law is itself unfair. The resentful might argue that their suffering takes precedence over moral law. The language of moral law might just dry up. None of these outcomes would please King to be sure, but all are more likely, I believe, than the prospect of Americans devoting themselves to moral reform under the inspiration of psychology.

"Any law that uplifts human personality is just," writes King. "Any law that degrades human personality is unjust." What follows from these psychological criteria? As is seen today, once the claim that one feels degraded is enough to show injustice, there is not much that cannot be "proven" unjust by those who produce their own wounded feelings as conclusive arguments. Claims of belittlement become acts of power, cries of pain peremptory challenges. Not just *Huckleberry Finn* or the racial signs King objected to but practically anything, including the renowned authors whose names adorn the "Letter from Birmingham Jail," can and will be condemned if damage to one's personhood is the test and the act of objection itself, moreover, is said to be healing and empowering. If in *Brown v. Board of Education* the Supreme Court cited the "authority" of modern "psychological knowledge" in support of school integration,[18] concern for the self-esteem of black students leads just as readily to Afrocentric curricula and all-black dormitories. Evidently psychology really does cut two ways. Evidently too King's psychology, which has since been adopted by so many claiming victim status and disclaiming the old lexicon of freedom, choice, and responsibility, is at odds with his own moral postulates.

Contrary to its author's intention, then, the "Letter from Birmingham Jail" stands as a reminder of the moral costs of psychology's dominance. Indeed, nothing has done more to discredit the very language of morality than psychology. Psychology speaks after all of needs and wants, not courage or cowardice, not duty or dereliction. (And the emptiness left as moral language recedes into the archaic makes more work for psychologists.) The cherished notion of a potential hidden within us and waiting to be actualized — this is especially undercutting, for to say "I am potentially generous" simply makes no sense. Potential generosity is no generosity at all. In all such cases the critical thing is what a person does when tried — what one shows, not what qualities may lie "deep inside." Even the heroic are capable of cowardice; they just don't act like cowards. The cant of human potential dissolves all such distinctions. In one of the peaks of irony in *The Brothers Karamazov* both Grushenka and Dmitri long to realize their felt potential for renewal, to become a new person. This would mean in her case walking away from her responsibility for inflaming the rivalry between father and son, in his from the wreckage that seems to be strewn all around him. How Dostoevsky would respond to the aggressive vacuity of the jargon of human potential now so influential — jargon assuring us that a happier and more productive self lies within waiting to be realized — can only be surmised. But the corrosive effect of psychology goes further yet. Not only does it efface moral issues and unwrite the very language of moral judgment, it intimates that such judgment is a hindrance to human emancipation, even a disease. Only a profound aversion — as to something taboo or diseased — could account for the recoil from moral distinctions throughout the psychological sphere of influence from the Recovery movement to the cult of human potential and its corporate equivalent to the therapeutic Left. Morality indeed has such a bad name on the Left that some feminists insist pornography itself is not a moral but a political issue. Yet the Left interpretation of morality as a mask of power is but a special case of the more general aversion to moral judgment as a shameful reminder of a gothic past. In the Recovery movement, "terms such as 'character,' 'weakness,' and 'individual responsibility' are no longer deemed appropriate,"[19] as though the key words of Victorian culture were themselves subjected to a thoroughly Victorian expurgation. Proclaiming its liberation from Victorian timidity, the psychological culture as a whole practices the kind of avoidance it likes to impute to the Victorians themselves.[20]

The Victorian age indeed represents a crest of "the civilizing process" that tightened standards of propriety and fostered the sort of emotional discipline called for by the modern order. As its historian Norbert Elias tells the story, in fact, the civilizing process seems to terminate in the Victorian period, when the denial and delay of pleasure were preached most strenuously, delicacy was normative, and fiction portrayed what he calls long chains of action.[21] At times it seems Elias leaves out the twentieth century. Yet even in a culture seemingly as far from Victorian as our own, one that bares the body and converts Rousseau's act of telling all into a daily rite of exhibitionism, the muting of expression is possible. When Matthew Arnold ventured to hope that as judgment improves, our harsher passions will "be induced gradually to moderate themselves, to get rid of what in them is excessive and offensive, and to fall into a softer and truer key" (in complete accordance with the civilizing process),[22] could he have imagined that moral judgment itself would come to seem a relic of a harsh past? As the civilizing process heightens embarrassment, so in the broadly therapeutic culture that inherits the program of making and remaking the self, the "crudity" of moral judgment seems to produce something like the recoil once felt at offenses against manners and other barbarisms.[23]

Even as the hunt for "the Secret Springs, Motives and Principles of human Actions" takes a sexual turn,[24] even in the face of a constant voyeuristic probing of the hidden, politeness tames the exercise of moral judgment. Perhaps it is not the rigidity but the very freedom of moral language that the psychological culture, for all its show of emancipation, finds so affronting.

Contrary to its own representations, the ideal of curing hypocrisy and delusion did not originate with the psychological culture. Just that, after all, is one of the traditional ends of satire, an expression of satiric morality. If King's theory of civil disobedience has him holding up a mirror to society and forcing it to recognize itself, the satirist does much the same; and if King hopes to break through our habits of denial (another word whose fortunes have soared since he wrote), Swift satirically defines satire itself as a looking-glass in which viewers behold everyone but themselves. Not only the psychologist but the satirist labors to cure. The satires of Swift, in the words of their author, were "with a moral view designed / To cure the vices of mankind."[25] But to an audience possessed of the therapeutic prejudice against words like "vice" — and if the term "weakness" is too strong, "vice" is that much more so — the freedom of Swift's satires must be unimaginable or else barbaric. Swift draws strength from the satiric tradition going back to Rabelais and Lucian and beyond. While the tradition abounds in types and indeed caricatures, as well as other "finalized" products of the pen, Bakhtin has shown us how richly it also underwrites the work of one who shattered this sort of characterization: Dostoevsky. The moral views taken in the satiric tradition are as far from Comstockery as the tradition itself is diverse. In satire we are reminded of a morality far more free-spoken, various of voice, and even subversive than current caricatures will allow.

That Rabelais, known for celebration of the flesh and the wildest libertinism of the imagination, should also assert a moral ideal is just impossible, according to the starved conception of morality now so widely influential. Nevertheless, near the center of *Gargantua and Pantagruel* is a moral exhortation of the son by the father, which begins thus:

> Most dear Son,
>   Among the gifts, graces, and prerogatives with which the Sovereign Creator, God Almighty, endowed and embellished human nature in the beginning, one seems to me to stand alone, and to excel all others; that is the one by which we can, in this mortal state, acquire a kind of immortality and, in the course of this transitory life, perpetuate our name

and our seed, which we do by lineage sprung from us in lawful marriage.[26]

Far less methodological than Locke's manual, this letter of advice animated by the humanist ideal stands among the most beautiful expressions in literature of paternal love — a theme strong in the Rabelaisian *Ulysses*. (As a testimonial of love it throws a strong light of contrast, too, onto old Karamazov's determination to live for himself alone.) In view of Rabelais's medical interests it's not impossible, either, that he saw the work of his pen as contributing to the "cure" of ignorance and mental decrepitude. "The qualities that morality and religion usually call ribald, obscene, subversive, lewd, and blasphemous have an essential place in literature," writes Northrop Frye, "but often they can achieve expression only through ingenious techniques of displacement."[27] That these qualities appear undisplaced in Rabelais is itself of moral significance as an expression of frankness in the old full sense of the word that includes, in addition to candor, a rejection of everything stinting, mean, and indirect.

There is a lot of Rabelais in Swift in spite of his obliquity and hostility to license: another sign of the diversity of the satiric tradition and the moral ideals that inform it. There is a lot of both Rabelais and Swift in Dickens. According to the lore of the psychological culture, Victorian morality was a system of organized hypocrisy and stifling oppression. Dickens, the best loved of the Victorian novelists, *indicts* hypocrisy and oppression with both satiric energy and moral ardor. If morality according to some is a prop of falsehood and sanction of cruelty, in Dickens such props and sanctions are themselves undercut in the name of morality. In perhaps his most satirical work, *Little Dorrit*, the attack is at its sharpest, taking the form of a kind of anatomical survey of the body politic and exposure of its moral ills. Psychologists administer tests designed to detect "unrealistic self-appraisal," "grandiose aspirations," inability "to see [one's] own limitations," and so on.[28] At one time, of course, these clinical insights were the stuff of the novel. Out of the cluster of traits just named Dickens fashions William Dorrit, patriarch of the Marshalsea Prison and both victim and symbol of a society of impostors. Not only does Dickens baffle the now popular notion of morality as an imprisonment of the spirit, he complicates our reading by making William Dorrit, for all of the corruption and false majesty he shares with the powers of England, a pitiful figure, a Lear. In appropriating the terms of character, in removing them from the public pages of literature into the heavily secured private space of the consulting room, psychology also voids the rich moral content that is always present in enduring

works of fiction, including works that expose the hypocrisies of official morality like *Little Dorrit.*

Dickens's satire on parliamentary babble and official circumlocution in
Little Dorrit flows in turn into Orwell's classic exposé of the corruption of political speech. Swift too resounds in the voice of Orwell. In fact, through *Nineteen
Eighty-Four* Orwell picks up the entire Menippean tradition (which includes
Gulliver's Travels) in the manner of a Dostoevsky tapping deep into an ancient
genre and making it speak to the present. Nor is Orwell with those who think
morality "Oldspeak," a fiction handed down from the past and destined to van-
ish in the society of the future like the illusion it is. His repudiation of this doctrine is attested throughout his work. With its undercurrent of satire Orwell's
prose itself records the richness of his participation in a morally animated tradition, where "morally" bears a meaning antithetical to the portrayal of morality as a gag on the human voice. For the satiric tradition that underwrites
Orwell, endowing the plainness of his speech with such a wealth of resonance
brought to life freedom of speech itself. "Menippus," says a philosopher in
Lucian's underworld who resents the equality of souls, "how about your getting
rid of that independence, frank speaking, cheery resignation, high-mindedness,
and mockery?"[29] As we see in a work like *Homage to Catalonia*, which asserts the
equality of souls, these are precisely the virtues of Orwell himself.

In speaking of Orwell it is hard to avoid yet again converting a moral quality into a psychological one by extolling the sanity of his prose. I want to suggest that the tempered, self-possessed quality of Orwell's writing at its best
actually reflects its possession in memory of the words of others. According to
Locke, memory, the awareness of our own continuance in time, supports personal identity. But there exist nonpsychological modes of memory as well, such
as a culture's conservation of the past — the very sense of tradition that is on
the wane in consumer society, with its animus against the past as such. Informed
as it is by a sense of tradition, Orwell's prose remembers some things he may
not even have read, like the *Consolation of Philosophy*, and some things twice over,
like the work of Smollett which he knew for himself but reacquired through
Dickens. It is the unique assimilation of all these riches of remembrance that
makes for the "personal identity" of Orwell's prose. His readers learn on their
very pulse that not only self but words and works endure through time.

The tradition of satiric realism inherited by Orwell makes up but a part
of "the canon," the loaded term for a body of mostly secular writing that served
no single cause or principle and made a tradition of originality itself. The fullest
expression of the moral power in all senses of the word is to be found in "the

canon." And canonically, the psychologist is the player on the minds of others, the illusionist. Chaucer's Pardoner, Iago, the Prince of Machiavelli, these are psychologists. In *Great Expectations* Magwitch uses psychology when he terrorizes the young Pip, Miss Havisham when she works on his weakness for Estella — and "makes" Estella herself, in a dire parody of education, into a heartless thing. The treacherous Vladimir in Conrad's *Secret Agent*, calculating the way to wake up public opinion to the threat of anarchism — for he too wants to raise consciousness — plays the psychologist. The "psychological moment" is right for a bomb at the Greenwich Observatory, he informs Verloc.[30] And even the seemingly amoral games of the mental technicians presume the existence of a moral framework, if only to depart from. Never does Machiavelli himself deny that murder and perfidy are just that, though he does argue their occasional utility. As much as his love of republican virtue, Machiavelli's criticism of customary hypocrisies expresses a moral intention. It is this kind of contestation of received opinion, surely, that is responsible for the original censorship of so many of the works now loosely spoken of as belonging to "the dominant culture," as though all took part in a single transhistorical conspiracy (the melting of differences again). If we ask what Machiavelli, Milton, Dostoevsky, indeed Freud, as distinct as they are, had in common apart from their skin and sex, the answer can only be they are moralists who tested and contested received ideas and encountered censorship. The canon dramatically illustrates the depth and range of speech lost to a culture that sees moral judgments as relics of a dark past, the equivalent of branding. Ironically, one member of this quartet of strong moralists — he is remembered in Mill's classic essay *On Liberty* — stands at the source of the psychological culture's myth of emancipation.

CHAPTER 9

Final Reflections:
Locke and Milton

Seeing that Locke helped establish the science of the mind by turning the investigation of knowledge into that of the knower, it is fitting that his influence "permeates modern psychology."[1] That the term "self-consciousness" entered English in the year on the title page of the first edition of the *Essay concerning Human Understanding* (1690) is poetically just too, for it is by reflecting on the mind's own processes that Locke ascertains the scope and certainty of human knowledge. In settling what we cannot know, given the limits of our capacities, he offers a tonic against pride, just as in determining what we can know he offers a cure for indolent skepticism. Philosophy performs a therapeutic function. In the words of Isaiah Berlin, Locke

> supposed himself to be practicing the method of Newton; but in fact he far more resembles the physician (that he was) who seeks to cure diseases (in this case delusions about the external world and the mental faculties of men), and as part of this process traces them to their origin and examines their symptoms, and so finds himself compiling something which is partly a textbook of anatomy, partly a manual on methods of healing.[2]

In the face of the Revolution of 1688, and with the memory of civil war still warm, the task of fostering civility by "curing" distempers of thought takes on urgency. If, as Berlin himself has written elsewhere, ideologues of our own day consider incorrect positions symptoms of a diseased brain, this practice makes its entry into modern political thought in the work of a man justly famed for his relative tolerance and undogmatic turn of mind. No doubt Locke's virtues, among them the modesty tempering the boldness of his inquiries, contributed to his influence.

With his counsels of moderation and prescriptions for civility, Locke seeks to defuse high passions like those of the recent Civil War — passions alive in Milton. It is as though Locke said, not "Where id was, let ego be," but "Where Milton was, let me be." But only if he is like Milton can Locke in some sense displace him. And with allowance made for the profound difference in temper between the philosopher of moderation and the poet of fervor, there are, in fact, affinities binding the two.[3] Locke acts the physician to the mind; Milton, explaining his intent of stirring passion in order to purge it, cites the theory of "physic" in the preface to *Samson Agonistes*. In the spirit of Bacon's dismissal of secondhand knowledge as mere cobwebs, both call on each of us, as independent beings, to examine our beliefs. Both have a chastened awareness of the insufficiency of the human intellect and a commensurately firm belief in the importance of inner discipline. Both plead for toleration up to a point. The Puritan practice of self-examination so powerfully in evidence in Milton's poetry — as when the captive Samson searches his soul — becomes in Locke a methodical search of the grounds of knowledge, just as the Puritan attitude of strict humility becomes a philosophical principle. Locke denies the glory of conquest, Milton ironizes the glory of warfare traditional to the epic poem. Locke uses a plain style, as does God, in his own fashion, in *Paradise Lost*. Locke with his wingless words and Milton with his winged ones both challenge received knowledge, superstition, and the corruptions of ornament. If psychology begins with Locke, by the same token it is something like a twin separated at birth — removed from the culture of the sects. In Locke the ethos of an embattled minority, an Israel, is transformed into the foundation of the cosmopolitan culture of the Enlightenment.

While the impress of Lockean philosophy shows itself in the novel, the full force of Milton's literary influence wasn't felt until the resurgence and disappointment of millennial hopes in the age of the French Revolution. Wordsworth, who experienced all this, wrote like Milton in the visionary vein, but, as Basil Willey has pointed out, in his conviction that "there must be no abstractions, no symbols, no myths, to stand between the mind and its true object" he also stands in the Lockean tradition.[4] In the tradition of Locke tracing the formation of ideas, Wordsworth traces the formation of his own poetic identity in *The Prelude*. Through Milton, as it were, it was still possible for a poet to converse with the author of scientific psychology. Wordsworth reminds us in effect of those affinities between Locke the physician of the mind and Milton the poet that have made it possible for a psychological culture to blend the one with the other. So does John Stuart Mill. Brought up in the doctrines of

associationist psychology, Mill found a reviving tonic in the poetry of Wordsworth, and in his most enduring work wrote in the empirical spirit of Locke
even as he echoed the "Areopagitica" of Milton, a work informing *On Liberty* so
decisively it is less a distant influence than an inhabiting presence. If Locke says
in a way, "Where Milton was, there will I stand," Mill gets back to Milton himself, enriching his argument with republican themes (themes hard for a therapeutic culture even to discern, much less enter into) and telling, like Milton,
of a freed people yearning for the sweets of slavery. Behind Mill's doctrine of
the testing of ideas lies the great Puritan narrative of the trial or testing of the
person. As a kind of unwilling disciple of Milton, John Stuart Mill writes in the
now obscure language of literature. His German translator Freud deemed Mill,
we know, one emancipated from common prejudices. For Freud the Puritans,
worshipers of the great Searcher of hearts, were figures of self-command. His
favorite poet was Milton.[5]

The story of the human mind liberated from the toils of illusion — a story
heard across the breadth of modern culture, from the psychoanalytic fable to
its political imitations — reflects the deliverance narrative of the Puritans even
as it does the psychology of Locke. It is Milton's story of the clearing of sight
clouded by custom and habit. Release from "mindless, habitual, mechanical
action . . . the doing of what has been done before because it has been done
before"[6] becomes the release of the neurotic from his repetitions via personal
insight. Most radically, the Revolution of the Saints becomes a Marxist drive
for millennial change led by a few who embrace their role and destiny with
religious zeal, the result perhaps of a "psychic revolution."[7] In America psychic
revolution is depoliticized like the products of Hollywood and Madison
Avenue generally. At work in either case, though, is a dream of redemption
from the inside out that distantly reflects and distorts the narrative vision of
the Puritans. The goal of the Royal Society at its founding, seven years before
the publication of *Paradise Lost,* was to "redeem the minds of Men from obscurity, uncertainty, and bondage."[8] Who can read these words without hearing in
them, in spite of the Society's objections to figurative language, a suppressed
allusion to the story of Exodus or without sensing in them an inspiration of the
program of freeing the mind from myth that has since grown into a master
myth in its own right? To the question of whether Freudianism is myth or science (for example), the presumptive answer must be the first, if only because
the aim of emancipating the mind from bondage to itself arises from a mythopoetic vision of redemption.[9]

The doing of what has been done before because it has been done before is challenged by Milton. The same view of the deadening effects of custom and habit is taken by John Stuart Mill; and the therapeutic culture paraphrases Mill's account. We live a kind of psychomedical transcription of Puritanism. The fighting among sects of Freudians, Jungians, Adlerians, behaviorists, existentialists, and the rest — some claiming a virtually revealed truth — mimics the division of the Puritan movement itself into sects. The hundred flowers of sectarian opinion celebrated by Milton become the hundred flowers of psychology. It is even possible to affirm sex Miltonically. In arguing physician-like that his depictions of sex purge the corrupted mind of its poisons, D. H. Lawrence finds himself using the same argument used by Milton in "Areopagitica": all things are pure to the pure.[10] In its peroration, the defense in the trial of *Lady Chatterley's Lover* in fact placed the book "in the puritan tradition."[11] Lawrence, the experts said, "redeems" our understanding of sex. But what of the teacher who seeks to free students "dominated by automatically absorbed prejudices and expectations"[12] — the wording is itself prejudicial — employing literature as a kind of psychiatric social work? Even in leading students out of the shadows of tradition and into the light of social science, that teacher too acts out the old story of deliverance. Nor is Miltonic instruction confined to the classroom. The poet's practice of breaking through our self-deceptions, of uncovering the devices we use "subconscious[ly] to avoid uncomfortable truths,"[13] has been reduced to a genre in the exposé. The Puritan dream of a new world cleansed of the corruption of the past takes the form of a routine, not to say mindless and mechanical, acclamation of shocks to our habits of response as psychologically wholesome. Embarrassed though modernism is by the backwardness of moral judgment, its own preferred language of therapy tells of the moral drama of liberation — the freeing of a mind enthralled to its own illusions, Milton's great theme.[14] It is an irony of history that a therapeutic culture whose dislikes can be summed up in the word "Puritanism" continues to trade on the story of redemption from bondage introduced into public culture by Puritanism itself.[15]

Also evocative of the Puritans was Martin Luther King. With his powerful rhetoric of deliverance, his citation of Bunyan, his effort to break through society's self-deceptions, and his adoption of the prophetic role which was also Milton's role, King in the "Letter from Birmingham Jail" taps into the very source of our liberation narrative. Tellingly, however, through the whole of this famous letter runs a psychological undertone. "The Negro has many pent-up resentments and latent frustrations, and he must release them." The black child

develops an "unconscious bitterness" toward whites. In the manner of a therapist King brings all this out — brings "to the surface . . . hidden tension." Like
a doctor opening a boil he exposes the disease of racism to the public so that
it can be "cured." By the same token civil disobedience is consciousness-
raising — a method of piercing the psychological armor of society, stinging it
into awareness. Intimated in King's argument is a story once and perhaps still
influential in the classroom, that of a society populated with conformists who
live in numb denial and bigots who persecute in others what they fear in themselves, along with a saving few unafraid to feel and secure enough to cultivate
knowledge of self and tolerance of others. By the decade of King's prominence
this had become a favored myth of psychology both popular and academic.[16]
Nor was it long after King told of clergymen "anaesthetized" to reality and well-
to-do blacks grown "insensitive" to the suffering of others that therapists
appeared in abundance on the public scene seeking to put us in touch with our
feelings as the way to personal and collective salvation. Repressed emotions,
latent frustrations, inner fears, unconscious bitterness: the diction of the "Letter
from Birmingham Jail" is now the lingua franca of a psychological culture that
empties the content of King's argument by applying it to practically everyone
and undercutting the moral categories King still believed in.[17] Just as psychology has engrossed matters once in the public domain of literature, so it has laid
claim to the theme of redemption that inspires the "Letter" and was once the
common possession of the Puritan imagination.

Antedating psychology itself, in fact, is the Puritan practice of intense self-
examination — the searching of the soul to expose one's own deceptions. This
process is both spurred and directed by *Paradise Lost,* and it is because our myth
of deliverance harks back to Puritan sources even as it claims the science of
Locke that the teacher liberating students from "automatically absorbed prejudices and expectations" can be said to offer a weak version of the education
given the reader of Milton's poem. Students, we recall, are first to react "spontaneously" to the literary text and then work through that response in order to
reach a more critical understanding. What is this but a faint tracing of Milton's
method of instructing the reader in *Paradise Lost* — a procedure in which the
reader first responds in error and then becomes the critic of his own mistake?
"It is only by encouraging and then 'breaking' conventional responses and
expectations that Milton can point [the] reader beyond them."[18] Substitute
"teacher" for "Milton" and you have the influential Rosenblatt method. More
or less as the "natural" reading is corrected in *Paradise Lost,* in the Lockean
tradition understanding generally takes the form of sensation followed by

reflection (also a two-phase process), and it is this model, politically adapted, that produces at last the cliché of the critical thinker, the Rosenblatt, who educates others out of ideas they merely receive. But where Milton intends his education for the fit audience of a few, the classroom, by the kind of increase in the level of production we have seen before, now offers therapy for millions. A claim can be reduced to absurdity; psychology seems to have been multiplied to absurdity. So standardized, so set, in fact, is the argument of the psychological reformers that to this day it repeats claims already well in place at the time of the first edition of Rosenblatt's book in 1938. There is a strongly verbatim quality to the emancipation polemic. For practically a century now its terms have been gone more or less unchanged,[19] even as its spokesmen have gone from insurgency to positions of comfort. In the name of liberation from received ideas it enforces the rigidity it constantly inveighs against, as though the Enlightenment program of curing minds and effecting all things possible had resulted at last in the mass production of thought itself.

Such is the dominance of the therapeutic model that the leading American scholar of romanticism noted a quarter century ago, "Theologians, philosophers, economists, sociologists, psychologists, artists, writers, critics, and readers of *Life* magazine and *The Reader's Digest*" all embrace the myth that modern man is sick and awaits a curing reunion with his true self and his world.[20] (That psychology draws power both from romantic myth and from the Enlightenment that the romantics in some ways revolt against may help account for its hold over our culture.) The myth of reunion is a variation on Wordsworth — his own poetry a displacement of Milton's[21] — but where Wordsworth holds forth poetry as a cure of the ill effects of commercial civilization, the promulgation of the healer's myth by a workforce of professionals and publicists means it has been more or less industrialized in its own right. So it is that psychological man as analyzed with such cutting effect by Philip Rieff bears the impress of the industrial system, his indifference and moral facility the very image of "the automaticity and ease with which an infinity of created needs can now be satisfied."[22]

Considering the proliferation of patients in the psychological society — the sheer market for diagnoses of injury and impairment, from learning disorders to sexual abuse by alien beings — it is hard to avoid concluding that this society multiplies psychological wants and needs as it clearly does economic ones; that the distinction between real and imaginary has been dissolved in the one case as in the other. Indeed, if "people generally tend to be only as mentally sick as they can afford to be,"[23] we can say that consumer society enables more people to be ill. Helping services expand like the economy. Since 1950 the number of Americans seeking psychological care has increased perhaps tenfold.[24] New ailments get accredited and come into fashion, like the Multiple Personality Disorder inspired by the spurious *Sybil.*[25] At the height of the Victorian age Fitzjames Stephen speculated that "Progress and science may perhaps enable untold millions to live and die without a care, without a pang, without an anxiety," a prospect he found dismal.[26] Fitzjames Stephen was wrong. Progress and science have enabled millions to multiply anxiety as never before. Psychological needs turn out to have the same vast potential for expansion as those "wants of the mind" that economic theorists once identified as spurs to trade.[27] Evidenced in the spread of groups like Overeaters Anonymous, Sex Addicts Anonymous, Spenders Anonymous, and Smokers Anonymous, moreover, is the same runaway replication so apparent in video shops and bookstores, in fact throughout the world of consumer goods. The Puritan narrative of deliverance is thus reduced to the line that the way to freedom lies in recognition of your enslavement to spending or sex or what have you. How a democracy can base itself on the helplessness of the citizenry is a question the psychological society has not confronted.

Too many laws, too many lawyers, too much litigation, it is sometimes said, denote moral disarray. There is also such a thing as too much psychology, and not only in the sense that each twelve-step program for self-renovation seems to presuppose the futility of the others. In one respect psychology works only too well, not just fraying morality as legalistic wrangling does but discrediting the very language of morality as backward. In this it has certainly outrun the intentions of those who started it on its course of expansion.

Twelve-point programs, self-improvement diagrams, universities turning out the Ph.D.'s who author them — all this is a long way from the tempered Puritanism of Locke, admittedly. But if, as Alasdair MacIntyre argues, the manager bent on getting the most out of you is the therapist in another guise;[28] if consumer society takes production so far as to produce the needs it then "addresses," a concern with techniques of production — human production — is already apparent in Locke. And like Locke converting the "fashioning" of civility from an act of imagination to a method of production, a number of those in this study convert the narrative of deliverance to a technique.[29] Milton writes a poem of temptation: Milgram stages a temptation in the laboratory with the minutest niceties of procedure, at the end correcting the mistakes of his subjects as the poet does the reader, albeit without moral judgment. The epigraph to his autobiography taken from Milton, Edward Bernays — master of the facile — lays out a method for breaking the hold of blind habits, as does Rosenblatt. Their formulas generate a lot of the most oppressively familiar clichés of the mass media and the classroom respectively. And along with the mechanization of language goes the mass production of ideas.

Recognizing the quickening effect of consumer desire, theorists in England at the time Locke was writing began to portray human appetites as "psychological stimulants" to trade.[30] In the consumer society of today psychology itself is trade. Wedgwood strove to reform his workers in order to get the most out of them. Today the promise of getting the most out of oneself is held out by a pop psychology as pervasive as the marketing devices introduced by Wedgwood. Experts in the association of ideas thought to bring children, the poor, society in general under their improving influence. They did not envision a society where everyone is a psychologist. If the Marxist program calls for man "to remake himself 'with his own hands,'"[31] which in practice means the subjection of all to a directorate of a few, consumer society counters both by celebrating its own "revolutionary" advances in electronics and by placing the means of remaking the self, at least in theory, in the hands of everyone. In this respect too the mass-produced ideas of psychology bear comparison with mass-produced goods as such.

Bruno Bettelheim in a late work censured those aspiring psychoanalysts who apply Freudian categories and methods to others but never themselves. They chatter about the unconscious of others sooner than look into their own.[32] While it is true that few go around talking of "My Oedipus Complex" (in the words of a brilliantly entitled story by Frank O'Connor), a great many in the psychological culture stand ready to talk of their own "societal conditioning," their cant no less glib than the kind of psychologizing Bettelheim found intolerable. The vogue of terms like "societal conditioning" — with the implication that with a healthy dose of deconditioning we become truly free — is one of the victories of psychologism. Another is the popularizing of the doctrine that everyone is the same at heart. But if we still subscribe in some way to the ideals of toleration and diversity asserted by both Milton and Locke, perhaps these are better served by recognizing that we are not identical. The claim that we can be predefined in this way — that we can be known as it were presumptively — runs contrary to the critique of dogma in which the toleration argument itself originated. Even assuming, gratuitously, that Eichmann and his victims had the same needs or that Hitler was at heart an abused child in need of love — as some do not shrink from saying[33] — what would this show but the vacuity of the explanatory concept of needs? Not our presumed needs but our words and acts characterize us. A rich sense of human plurality would be more mindful of differences, and at the same time more attentive to moral qualities illumined in speech and action, than psychologism at present permits.

Just as the consumer economy serves our wants and needs with standardized goods, the psychological culture standardizes the portrayal of "behavior" as a function of wants and needs. Strangely, in this context wants and needs turn out to be our least private and distinctive attributes, lending themselves to the most facile description. In truth there is something dehumanizing about this jargon of wants and needs, as though underlying the lowest common denominator of the marketplace were one lower yet. In her last work but one Hannah Arendt remarked on "the monotonous sameness and pervasive ugliness so highly characteristic of the findings of modern psychology, and contrasting so obviously with the enormous variety and richness of overt human conduct."[34] Psychologism renders us alike. "We all have the same hopes and fears and dreams." "We are all Eichmann." The uniformity of human nature was a doctrine of the Enlightenment. Probing "the true motives" of men's hearts,[35] Mandeville finds identical motives everywhere, and the poem prefixed to the *Fable of the Bees* speaks of men accordingly by "thousands," by "millions," by "multitudes." Today in the consumer society which is also the psychological society, the same denominations are used. The modern myth of liberation from the trammels of custom becomes in the consumer society a kind of consumable in its own right, advertised as aggressively as any cola. The project of emancipating the mind from its own deceptions is as old as Plato's *therapeia*. Only recently was it supposed that emancipation could be mass produced.

Notes

Introduction

1. Robert Cushman, *Therapeia: Plato's Conception of Philosophy* (Chapel Hill: University of North Carolina Press, 1958), p. xv.
2. For an excellent reading of the *Consolation* that throws into question the possibility of any final "cure," see F. Anne Payne, *Chaucer and Menippean Satire* (Madison: University of Wisconsin Press, 1981), chap. 3. On positive liberty, see Isaiah Berlin, *Four Essays on Liberty* (Oxford: Oxford University Press, 1969).
3. Cushman, *Therapeia*, p. xxi.
4. Perry Miller and Thomas Johnson, *The Puritans* (New York: American Book Company, 1938), p. 284.
5. Cf. Lionel Trilling, *Sincerity and Authenticity* (Cambridge, Mass: Harvard University Press, 1971), p. 141, where a path is traced from early-modern exposure of the mind's deceptions to the "wide acceptance" of the unconscious today. The course Trilling has in mind is not the same as the one marked out here, although it begins and ends in roughly the same places.
6. Even academic psychology is given to "sudden and frequent reversals of course." Clifford Geertz, "Learning with Bruner," *New York Review of Books*, April 10, 1997, p. 22.
7. *The Missoulian* (Missoula, Mont.), February 12, 1997, p. B6. Blue Cross is now suing.
8. Michael Massing, "How to Win the Tobacco Wars," *New York Review of Books*, July 11, 1996, p. 35.
9. Louise Rosenblatt, *Literature as Exploration* (New York: D. Appleton-Century, 1938), p. 246. This work is still influential.

10. See the exposés of the repressed memory craze by Frederick Crews in the *New York Review of Books*, November 17, 1994 and December 1, 1994.

11. Cited in Robert Fulford, "American Demons of the 1950s," *Queen's Quarterly* 102 (1995): 539. The play is *Tea and Sympathy*.

12. Cited in Michael André Bernstein, *Bitter Carnival: Ressentiment and the Abject Hero* (Princeton, N.J.: Princeton University Press, 1992), p. 169. On the related platitude that the Nazis cannot be judged because "the true enemy is . . . within ourselves," see Harold Rosenberg, *The Case of the Baffled Radical* (Chicago: University of Chicago Press, 1985), p. 133.

13. *New York Times*, August 2, 1995, p. A16.

14. Robert Jay Lifton, *Revolutionary Immortality: Mao Tse-tung and the Chinese Cultural Revolution* (New York: Norton, 1976).

15. Jürgen Habermas, *The Structural Transformation of the Public Sphere: An Inquiry into a Category of Bourgeois Society*, trans. Thomas Burger and Frederick Lawrence (Cambridge, Mass.: MIT Press, 1991).

16. Cited in Ernst Cassirer, *The Philosophy of the Enlightenment*, trans. Fritz Koelln and James Pettegrove (Princeton, N.J.: University Press, 1951), p. 107.

17. Gordon Wood, "Conspiracy and the Paranoid Style: Causality and Deceit in the Eighteenth Century," *William and Mary Quarterly*, 3d ser., 39 (1982): 401–41.

18. John Stuart Mill, *Autobiography* (New York: Library of Liberal Arts, 1957), p. 70.

19. David Spadafora, *The Idea of Progress in Eighteenth-Century Britain* (New Haven, Conn.: Yale University Press, 1990), p. 178.

20. Graham Wallas, *The Great Society: A Psychological Analysis* (New York: Macmillan, 1917), p. 121.

21. Albert Hirschman, *The Passions and the Interests: Political Arguments for Capitalism before Its Triumph* (Princeton, N.J.: Princeton University Press, 1977), p. 42.

22. Isaac Kramnick, *Republicanism and Bourgeois Radicalism: Political Ideology in Late Eighteenth-Century England and America* (Ithaca, N.Y.: Cornell University Press, 1990), chap. 4, esp. pp. 111–12.

23. Joyce Oldham Appleby, *Economic Thought and Ideology in Seventeenth-Century England* (Princeton, N.J.: Princeton University Press, 1978), p. 184.

24. The phrase is actually taken from a duly skeptical evaluation of the new methods by Leon Edel. See Leon Edel, "Notes on the Use of Psychological Tools in Literary Scholarship," *Literature and Psychology* 1, 4 (1951).

25. The quoted phrase is that of the interim committee that advised Truman on the use of the atomic bomb; cited by David McCullough, *Truman* (New York: Simon and Schuster, 1992), p. 391.

26. See *Washington Post Weekly*, November 6–12, 1995, pp. 6–8.

27. Kramnick, *Republicanism and Bourgeois Radicalism*, p. 97.

28. Charles Taylor, *Sources of the Self: The Making of the Modern Identity* (Cambridge, Mass.: Harvard University Press, 1989), p. 171.

29. David Rieff, "Victims, All?" *Harper's* (October 1991): 52.

30. Locke speaks of the child as wax to be molded, reformers in the decades after his death of the pliability of human beings in general. See Spadafora, *Idea of Progress*, p. 145. In turn, when the expansion of a given model toward infinity is reduced to a "scientific" law, as in the social psychology of Gabriel Tarde (which likens the propagation of influences with that of waves and light), the foundation takes shape for those twentieth-century ideologies of worldwide ambition that pretend to the authority of science. In this sense too ideology is psychology in action.

31. Compared to the vast claims of ideology in our era, the psychological paradigm begins on a modest, human scale. The control function of psychology begins, similarly, at home. In the sense that careful analysis "is required for men to secure the fullest control of the conduct of their own understandings," psychology for Locke is certainly a means of control — self-control. See John Dunn in Dunn, J. O. Urmson, and A. J. Ayer, *The British Empiricists* (Oxford: Oxford University Press, 1992), p. 78. Considering that "self" only gradually achieved independence as a word, arising from practices like self-scrutiny (the opposite of self-deception), the term for my very identity may well contain traces of processes of control. Reflexives like "self-knowledge" and "self-deception" burgeoned in the seventeenth century. See Peggy Rosenthal, *Words and Values: Some Leading Words and Where They Lead Us* (New York: Oxford University Press, 1984), pp. 11–12.

32. Erich Kahler, *The Inward Turn of Narrative*, trans. Richard Winston and Clara Winston (Princeton, N.J.: Princeton University Press, 1973), p. 21.

33. Spadafora, *Idea of Progress*, p. 177.

34. Mary McCarthy, foreword to *Madame Bovary*, trans. Mildred Marmur (New York, NAL Penguin, 1964), p. xvii.

35. On *bovarysme*, see Stephen Heath, *Madame Bovary* (Cambridge, U.K.: Cambridge University Press, 1992), p. 140. I think a richer question than whether pornography causes the subjection of women is what responsibility is borne by psychology, with its special concern for woman and her

"problems." No such debate is heard. In fact, and in the teeth of her own criticism of scientific knowledge, the leading crusader against pornography, Catharine MacKinnon, cites the findings of experimental psychology as demonstrative. On this point, see J. M. Coetzee, *Giving Offense: Essays on Censorship* (Chicago: University of Chicago Press, 1996), p. 245.

36. George Steiner, *On Difficulty and Other Essays* (New York: Oxford University Press, 1978), p. 129.

37. Hannah Arendt, *Eichmann in Jerusalem: A Report on the Banality of Evil* (New York: Penguin, 1977), p. 284.

38. On privacy and its violation, see Rochelle Gurstein, *The Repeal of Reticence: A History of America's Cultural and Legal Struggles over Free Speech, Obscenity, Sexual Liberation, and Modern Art* (New York: Hill and Wang, 1996).

39. On *Sybil*, see Mikkel Borch-Jacobsen, "Sybil — The Making of a Disease: An Interview with Dr. Herbert Spiegel," *New York Review of Books*, April 24, 1997, p. 63.

40. Similarly, as Christopher Lasch has remarked, the psychology that advises the aging to let go of their old self and take up something new models the self on disposable consumer goods. "This is a recipe not for growth but for planned obsolescence." See *The Culture of Narcissism: American Life in an Age of Diminishing Expectations* (New York: Warner, 1979), p. 362.

41. The worker's need for therapy was discovered a half century ago. Elton Mayo, professor of industrial research at Harvard, emphasized the need for private listening sessions where the worker could have grievances heard without comment or emotion, "under the seal of professional confidence" — in other words, in psychoanalytic style. In one of these sessions a woman "discovered for herself that her dislike of a certain supervisor was based upon a fancied resemblance to a detested stepfather." Thus Freud enters the workplace. See Elton Mayo, *The Social Problems of an Industrial Civilization* (Cambridge, Mass.: Harvard University Press, 1945), pp. 73, 78.

42. See Robert Jay Lifton, *Thought Reform and the Psychology of Totalism: A Study of "Brainwashing" in China* (New York: Norton, 1963), p. 27: "In the cell you work in order to recognize your crimes. . . . They make you understand your crimes are very heavy. . . . In the cell, twelve hours a day, you talk and talk — you have to take part — you must discuss yourself, criticize, inspect yourself, denounce your thought. Little by little you start to admit something, and look to yourself only using the 'people's judgment.'"

43. George Orwell, *As I Please,* vol. 3 of *The Collected Essays, Journalism, and Letters of George Orwell* (New York: Harcourt Brace Jovanovich, 1968), p. 242. The view is that of an author Orwell discusses.

44. Or that the psychological injury caused by a boss's unwelcome kisses is responsible for all that went wrong in one's life from that point forward, as a number of Robert Packwood's accusers claimed of their own. See Julia Reed, "The Case of the Kissing Senator," *New York Review of Books,* February 1, 1996, p. 27.

45. Rosenblatt, *Literature as Exploration,* pp. 134, 183.

46. Arthur Miller, *Collected Plays* (New York: Viking, 1957), p. 11.

47. Miller himself came to have some doubts about the psychological orthodoxy; see *Collected Plays,* pp. 53–54. The refusal to recognize what one actually knows is now commonly called denial. The ennobling results of the popularization of this term can be seen on television.

48. Albert Hirschman, *The Rhetoric of Reaction: Perversity, Futility, Jeopardy* (Cambridge, Mass.: Harvard University Press, 1991).

49. James Boswell, *The Life of Samuel Johnson* (New York: Alfred A. Knopf, 1992), p. 346. Characteristically, however, he also asserted — in writing — that "we cannot dive into the hearts of men; but their actions are open to observation" (p. 973).

50. "In the conscious field, as experienced by human beings, the presentation is organized with its simplifications, its background, foreground, abstractions, distortions, enhancements, and suppressions according to the interests which James says are the products of consciousness." Craig Eisendrath, *The Unifying Moment: The Psychological Philosophy of William James and Alfred North Whitehead* (Cambridge, Mass.: Harvard University Press, 1971), p. 105. How novelistic this "presentation" is — how much like sheer narration. James also possesses something of a novelist's sense of what might have been but was not; on which see Gary Saul Morson, *Narrative and Freedom: The Shadows of Time* (New Haven, Conn.: Yale University Press, 1994), and Eisendrath, *Unifying Moment,* pp. 131, 216. Joyce of course breaks with nineteenth-century practice, but perhaps it is by interiorizing the qualities of voiced speech that Joyce gives the inner speech of the Blooms the illusion of presence.

51. Kahler, *Inward Turn,* p. 20. On the influence of Locke's thought on the novel, see Ian Watt, *The Rise of the Novel: Studies in Defoe, Richardson, and Fielding* (Berkeley: University of California Press, 1957), chap. 1.

52. If Freud practices "the hermeneutics of suspicion," *Northanger Abbey* is a cutting criticism of the interpretive license that results when suspicion takes possession of the mind.

53. In an effort to demedicalize our understanding of Freud, however, Bruno Bettelheim likens him admiringly to an astrologer and a midwife. See Bruno Bettelheim, *Freud and Man's Soul* (New York: Vintage, 1984), pp. 36, 67.

54. Walter J. Ong, S.J., "Swift on the Mind: The Myth of Asepsis," *Modern Language Quarterly* 15 (1954): 208–21.

55. Stanley Fish, *Surprised by Sin: The Reader in Paradise Lost* (Berkeley: University of California Press, 1971).

56. Alan Elms, "Social Psychology and Social Relevance," cited in *Experimentation with Human Beings*, ed. Jay Katz (New York: Russell Sage Foundation, 1972), p. 405.

57. Bernard Mandeville, *The Fable of the Bees* (London: Penguin, 1970), p. 29. Mandeville was himself a close reader of Locke's work on education; see J. A. Passmore, "The Malleability of Man in Eighteenth-Century Thought," in *Aspects of the Eighteenth Century*, ed. Earl Wasserman (Baltimore: Johns Hopkins University Press, 1965), p. 31.

58. Preface to the "Lyrical Ballads," in *The Great Critics: An Anthology of Literary Criticism*, ed. James Smith and Edd Parks (New York: Norton, 1932), p. 508.

59. Technical terms in *Hamlet* derive from astronomy, military tactics, and the law, among other fields.

60. Rosenblatt, *Literature as Exploration*, chap. 6.

61. Milgram hints at the connection between psychology and the division of functions when he observes that only with the division of labor does obedience become a psychological problem. Stanley Milgram, *Obedience to Authority: An Experimental View* (New York: Harper and Row, 1974), p. 11.

62. The Winter–Spring 1994 issue of *Salmagundi* examines "The New Puritanism."

63. "The guts of modern brains": Jonathan Swift, *The Battle of the Books*, in *A Tale of a Tub and Other Works* (Oxford: Oxford University Press, 1986), p. 113. On Swift's investigation of the brain and its relation to Locke's philosophy, see Ronald Paulson, *The Fictions of Satire* (Baltimore: Johns Hopkins University Press, 1967), pp. 149–50.

64. Tobias Smollett, *Humphry Clinker* (London: Penguin, 1967), p. 52.

65. On the exhibition of ill health as a point of pride in Paris at this time, see Rebecca Spang, "Rousseau in the Restaurant," *Common Knowledge* 5, 1 (1996), 95–97.

66. Laurence Sterne, *The Life and Opinions of Tristram Shandy, Gentleman* (New York: Odyssey Press, 1940), p. 9. Sterne is reported to have said that "those who knew the philosopher [Locke] well enough to recognize his presence and his influence would find them or sense them on every page, in every line." Cited in Dorothy Van Ghent, *The English Novel: Form and Function* (New York: Harper and Row, 1953), p. 89. See also Ernest Tuveson, "Locke and Sterne," in *Reason and the Imagination: Studies in the History of Ideas, 1600–1800*, ed. J. A. Mazzeo (New York: Columbia University Press, 1962), pp. 255–77.

67. Taylor, *Sources of the Self*, p. 159.

68. See the spoof of Locke's ideal of simplified language — the purgation of obscurity and ornament — in Sterne, *Tristram Shandy*, vol. 3, chap. 31, concluding, "For by the word *Nose*, throughout all this long chapter of noses, and in every other part of my work, where the word *Nose* occurs, — I declare, by that word I mean a Nose, and nothing more, or less."

69. One measure of the internal turn of narrative is the distance between the Wife's wholly public and Molly Bloom's interior monologue.

70. So too, we are reminded by the text itself that the care and cure of the soul were not always a "science" in the hands of specialists. Note the satire of jargon in Fyodor Dostoevsky, *The Brothers Karamazov*, trans. Constance Garnett (New York: Vintage, 1955), p. 717: "Mitya hurriedly pulled out a piece of paper from his pocket and read: 'In order to determine this question, it is above all essential to put one's personality in contradiction to one's reality.' Do you understand that?" The author of this gabble is Rakitin, facile analyst of Dmitri's soul.

71. In his *Diary of a Writer*, Dostoevsky pleads the case of a woman who threw her stepchild out of a window without knowing why (and without denying her guilt). Considering her a victim of temporary insanity, he points out to his critics that psychiatric experts at the trial were more or less of the same opinion. He does not, however, base his opinion on theirs. Above all, he never presumes to explain the action of Kornilova, which remains as unaccounted for and as mysterious to himself and us after his analysis as before. Even when using the language of pathology, Dostoevsky never really diagnoses Kornilova.

72. Kramnick, *Republican and Bourgeois Radicalism*, p. 95.

73. M. H. Abrams, *Natural Supernaturalism: Tradition and Revolution in Romantic Literature* (New York: Norton, 1973), p. 334.

74. The next chapter touches on Wordsworth's repudiation of this scheme.

Chapter 1

1. Gordon Wood, "Conspiracy and the Paranoid Style: Causality and Deceit in the Eighteenth Century," *William and Mary Quarterly*, 3rd ser., 39 (1982): 401, 402.

2. The last section of Locke's handbook on education reminds the reader that no two children are alike. John Locke, *Some Thoughts concerning Education*, ed. John W. Yolton and Jean S. Yolton (Oxford: Clarendon Press, 1989), para. 217. Subsequent references are given in my text by paragraph.

3. On Locke's removal of original sin, see J. A. Passmore, "The Malleability of Man in Eighteenth-Century Thought," in *Aspects of the Eighteenth Century*, ed. Earl Wasserman (Baltimore: Johns Hopkins University Press, 1965).

4. Isaiah Berlin, *Four Essays on Liberty* (Oxford: Oxford University Press, 1969), p. 24.

5. Michel Foucault, *Discipline and Punish: The Birth of the Prison*, trans. Alan Sheridan (New York: Vintage, 1979), pp. 104f.

6. Montesquieu as cited in Albert Hirschman, *The Passions and the Interests: Political Arguments for Capitalism before Its Triumph* (Princeton, N.J.: Princeton University Press, 1977), p. 60.

7. *Some Thoughts concerning Education* was reprinted several times during Locke's life and then throughout the eighteenth century.

8. Alexandre Beljame, *Le Public et les hommes de lettres en Angleterre au dix-huitième siècle, 1660–1744*; trans. E. O. Lorimer; cited by Donald Bond, ed., *The Spectator*, vol. 1 (Oxford: Clarendon Press, 1965), p. lxxxviii.

9. *The Spectator*, no. 532.

10. Michael Ignatieff, *A Just Measure of Pain: The Penitentiary in the Industrial Revolution, 1750–1850* (New York: Pantheon, 1978), p. 72.

11. Hannah Arendt, *The Human Condition* (Chicago: University of Chicago Press, 1958), p. 254.

12. Dugald Stewart, cited in Peter Gay, *The Enlightenment: An Interpretation*, vol. 2, *The Science of Freedom* (New York: Alfred A. Knopf, 1969), p. 168.

13. Bernard Mandeville, *The Fable of the Bees* (Harmondsworth: Penguin, 1989), p. 87.

14. Sterne, *Tristram Shandy*, vol. 5, chap. 7. Locke is cited in this chapter.

15. Michael Meranze, *Laboratories of Virtue: Punishment, Revolution, and Authority in Philadelphia, 1760–1835* (Chapel Hill: University of North Carolina Press, 1996), pp. 120–26.

16. Like the devising of checks and balances, the training of such intellectual force on a single point suggests the activity of *homo faber,* man the tool-user.

17. Marilyn Butler, *Romantics, Rebels, and Reactionaries: English Literature and Its Background, 1760–1830* (Oxford: Oxford University Press, 1981), p. 159.

18. David Erdman, "Coleridge, Wordsworth, and the Wedgwood Fund," *Bulletin of the New York Public Library* 60 (1956): 425–43, 487–507.

19. David Spadafora, *The Idea of Progress in Eighteenth-Century Britain* (New Haven, Conn.: Yale University Press, 1990), chap. 4.

20. David Hartley, *Observations on Man, His Frame, His Duty, and His Expectations* (1749; Gainesville, Fla.: Scholars' Facsimiles and Reprints, 1966), 2: 453.

21. See Isaac Kramnick, *Republicanism and Bourgeois Radicalism: Political Ideology in Late Eighteenth-Century England and America* (Ithaca, N.Y.: Cornell University Press, 1990), chap. 3. Percival cited on p. 93. On the Enlightenment ideal of the physician to a sick society, see also Gay, *Science of Freedom,* pp. 12–17.

22. Butler, *Romantics, Rebels, and Reactionaries,* p. 30.

23. With its fateful incident of the unwound clock, and its general play with time, *Tristram Shandy* might be read as a parody of the mechanization of time. Sterne himself was a disciple of Locke, if a wayward one.

24. Neil McKendrick, "Josiah Wedgwood and Factory Discipline," *The Historical Journal* 4, 1 (1961): 32.

25. Alasdair MacIntyre, *After Virtue: A Study in Moral Theory* (Notre Dame, Ind.: University of Notre Dame Press, 1981), p. 29.

26. McKendrick, "Wedgwood and Factory Discipline," 34–35.

27. This context brings out sharply the meaning of Blake's couplet, "Tools were made & Born were hands / Every Farmer Understands" ("Auguries of Innocence").

28. McKendrick, "Wedgwood and Factory Discipline," 35.

29. Cited in McKendrick, "Wedgwood and Factory Discipline," 41.

30. Arendt, *Human Condition,* p. 188 and n.

31. Cited in Spadafora, *Idea of Progress,* p. 178.

32. See Emile Coué and J. Louis Orton, *Conscious Autosuggestion* (New York: D. Appleton-Century, 1924), p. 3: "In the case of the elevated plank, if you cannot walk along it, that is because you think you cannot. Steeplejacks succeed because they think they can."

33. In his dream of leaving both the holders of power and the powerless no place to hide, Bentham bears comparison with Rousseau, whose thought, through all its twists, pursues the aim of clearing away whatever conceals heart from heart. See Jean Starobinski, *Jean-Jacques Rousseau: Transparency and*

Obstruction, trans. Arthur Goldhammer (Chicago: University of Chicago Press, 1988). Rousseau's "transparency," Bentham's prison of glass.

34. Locke, *The Conduct of the Understanding*, sec. 1.

35. Roy Porter, *The Enlightenment* (London: Macmillan, 1990), p. 67.

36. The best study of the Panopticon is Janet Semple, *Bentham's Prison: A Study of the Panopticon Penitentiary* (Oxford: Clarendon Press, 1993).

37. Arendt, *Human Condition*, p. 73.

38. Jeremy Bentham, *Works*, ed. John Bowring (Edinburgh, 1843), 4: 40.

39. The connection between psychology and technique is also borne out, albeit in a different way, by the "solution" to the "problem" of narration, and even more by the manipulation of the reader, in that novel of psychology, *Clarissa*. Here it is the reader who occupies the all-seeing position, spying on everyone, most deliciously of course on the heroine. When Dorothy Van Ghent speaks of the "publicity tactics" of *Clarissa*, her language may remind us not only of the invention of tactics of publicity by Wedgwood (who as we know kept watch over his workers) but the mechanical reproduction of images and ideas in our own psychological culture. See Dorothy Van Ghent, *The English Novel: Form and Function* (New York: Harper and Row, 1953), p. 50.

40. Semple, *Bentham's Prison*, p. 213.

41. Bentham, *Works*, 8: 436n.

42. Foucault, *Discipline and Punish*, p. 169.

43. John Stuart Mill, *On Liberty*, ed. David Spitz (New York: Norton, 1975), p. 65n.

44. Ibid., p. 68.

45. MacIntyre, *After Virtue*, p. 99.

46. Philip Rieff, *The Triumph of the Therapeutic: Uses of Faith after Freud* (New York: Harper and Row, 1966), p. 68.

47. Mill, *On Liberty*, p. 10.

48. It must be said, too, that Mill did much to accredit the consumer society that, by turning the loss of vitality into a psychological condition, robs his argument of its depth. On the depth of Mill's argument, see Stewart Justman, *The Hidden Text of Mill's "Liberty"* (Savage, Md.: Rowman and Littlefield, 1991).

49. Alexis de Tocqueville, *Democracy in America*, trans. Henry Reeve; rev. Francis Bowen and Phillips Bradley (New York: Vintage, 1945), 2: 141.

50. The "subconscious" is less bewildering, forbidding, and archaic than the "unconscious," hence better suited to popularization. On the coming of the therapeutic culture, see T. J. Jackson Lears, "From Salvation to Self-Realization: Advertising and the Therapeutic Roots of the Consumer

Culture, 1880–1930," in *The Culture of Consumption: Critical Essays in American History, 1880–1980*, ed. Richard Wrightman Fox and T. J. Jackson Lears (New York: Pantheon, 1983). In the emerging consumer society of turn-of-the-century America the very liabilities of leisure — the sensed loss of vital energy — contributed to the search for psychological remedies. On psychoanalysis and leisure see Kenneth Burke, *The Philosophy of Literary Form: Studies in Symbolic Action* (Berkeley: University of California Press, 1973), pp. 263–64: "The especially elaborate process of diagnosis involved in Freudian analysis even to this day makes it more available to those suffering from the ills of preoccupation and leisure than to those suffering from the ills of occupation and employment (with people generally tending to be only as mentally sick as they can afford to be). This state of affairs makes it all the more likely that the typical psychoanalytic patient would have primarily private sexual motivations behind his difficulties. (Did not Henry James say that sex is something about which we think a great deal when we are not thinking about anything else?)"

51. Cited in Craig Eisendrath, *The Unifying Moment: The Psychological Philosophy of William James and Alfred North Whitehead* (Cambridge, Mass.: Harvard University Press, 1971), p. 213. Among other correspondences it should be noted that both men passed through a crisis of paralysis. To the psychologically knowing, that Mill's depression broke when he read Marmontel's account of his father's death can only signify his wish for the death of *his* father; and that Mill did not see the obvious shows the darkness in which even a man of brilliance walked before the dawn of psychology.

52. Mill, *On Liberty*, p. 6.

53. Gabriel Tarde, *The Laws of Imitation*, trans. Elsie Crews Parson (1890; New York: Henry Holt), pp. ix, 295, 84, 358.

54. Hannah Arendt, *Totalitarianism*, pt. 3 of *The Origins of Totalitarianism* (New York: Harcourt, Brace, and World, 1968), chap. 4.

55. The arguments of the anti-Victorians are being reproduced to this day. See Rochelle Gurstein, " 'Puritanism' as Epithet: Common Standards and the Fate of Reticence," *Salmagundi* 101–2 (1994): 95–117.

56. Lionel Trilling, *The Liberal Imagination* (New York: Viking, 1950), p. 227.

57. Freud claimed to own the key to the mind. "Psychoanalysis has put [the Oedipal complex] beyond the reach of doubt and has taught us to recognize in [it] the key to every neurosis." Sigmund Freud, "Dostoevsky and Parricide," in *The Standard Edition of the Complete Psychological Works of Sigmund Freud*, trans. James Strachey, 24 vols. (London: Hogarth Press, 1953–74), 21: 184.

58. On the consumer economy and the origins of "hysteria," see J. G. A. Pocock, *Virtue, Commerce, and History: Essays on Political Thought and History, Chiefly in the Eighteenth Century* (Cambridge: Cambridge University Press, 1985), pp. 112–14.

59. No less an enemy of capitalism than Lenin wanted to appropriate the new science of efficiency underwriting the psychology of management. On Lenin and "Taylorism," see Sudhir Kakar, *Frederick Taylor: A Study in Personality and Innovation* (Cambridge, Mass.: MIT Press, 1970), pp. 2–3.

60. Timothy McVeigh, convicted for the bombing of the Federal Building in Oklahoma City, is reported to have said that the real measure of a terrorist event is its psychological impact.

61. Excerpts from the Unabomber's manifesto, beginning with an account of the "widespread psychological suffering" inflicted by industrial society (including "inferiority feelings" and all the rest), appear in the *New York Times*, August 2, 1995, p. A16.

62. Henry Kissinger as cited in Thomas Franck and Edward Weisband, *Word Politics: Verbal Strategy among the Superpowers* (New York: Oxford University Press, 1972), p. 141.

Chapter 2

1. Ann Douglas, *Terrible Honesty: Mongrel Manhattan in the 1920s* (New York: Farrar, Straus, and Giroux, 1995), p. 27.

2. Erving Goffman, *The Presentation of Self in Everyday Life* (Garden City, N.Y.: Doubleday, 1959), p. 4.

3. James Joyce, *Ulysses* (New York: Vintage, 1961), p. 490. Plural Voting was a proposal of John Stuart Mill, in whose tradition Bernays cast himself. Concert Entertainments become Shakespeare in the Park, which Bernays helped get started — and so on.

4. Leonard Doob as cited in Edward Bernays, *Biography of an Idea: Memoirs of Public Relations Counsel Edward L. Bernays* (New York: Simon and Schuster, 1965), p. 459. With its glorification of the light bulb, the event offers a kind of unwitting parody of public festivals of enlightenment in revolutionary France, with Bernays in the role of the prop designer of the republic, David.

5. Jürgen Habermas, *The Structural Transformation of the Public Sphere: An Inquiry into a Category of Bourgeois Society*, trans. Thomas Burger and Frederick Lawrence (Cambridge, Mass.: MIT Press, 1991), p. 193. Public relations techniques,

writes Habermas, are widely used in the "diagnosis" of the public realm, his choice of words bringing out the psychomedical fiction that served Bernays so well.

6. Kenneth Burke, *The Philosophy of Literary Form: Studies in Symbolic Action* (Berkeley: University of California Press, 1973), pp. 132–37.

7. With her star quality, Verena Tarrant in *The Bostonians* is to bring publicity to the cause of women's rights. That Verena Tarrant is the daughter of a "mesmeric healer" suggests how dubious the arts of publicity remained to some, even (or especially) in their most enlightened form.

8. Isaac Kramnick, *Republicanism and Bourgeois Radicalism: Political Ideology in Late Eighteenth-Century England and America* (Ithaca, N.Y.: Cornell University Press, 1990), p. 97.

9. Louise Rosenblatt, *Literature as Exploration* (New York: D. Appleton-Century, 1938), pp. 150–51. On the immensity of Rosenblatt's influence, see the introduction by Wayne Booth to the 1995 edition of *Literature as Exploration* published by the Modern Language Association. The imprimatur of the MLA is itself a mark of the author's influence.

10. With her statement that "in recent years . . . it has been increasingly recognized that the newspaper, the radio, the moving picture, and the literary work often take their place beside other social agencies in the important task of molding the individual" (p. 223), Rosenblatt takes her place beside Bernays.

11. Edward Bernays, "Manipulating Public Opinion: The Why and the How," *American Journal of Sociology* 33 (1928): 958–71.

12. Douglas, *Terrible Honesty*, p. 5.

13. Richard Pipes, *The Russian Revolution* (New York: Alfred A. Knopf, 1990), p. 133.

14. John Money, *Experience and Identity: Birmingham and the West Midlands, 1760–1800* (Montreal: McGill-Queen's University Press, 1977), chap. 2.

15. Josiah Wedgwood, cited in ibid., p. 25.

16. Anthony Burton, *Josiah Wedgwood* (New York: Stein and Day, 1976), p. 161.

17. Josiah Wedgwood, cited in Robin Reilly, *Josiah Wedgwood, 1730–1795* (London: Macmillan, 1992), p. 206.

18. David Erdman, "Coleridge, Wordsworth, and the Wedgwood Fund," *Bulletin of the New York Public Library* 60 (1956): 432.

19. Kramnick, *Republicanism and Bourgeois Radicalism*, p. 97.

20. Hannah Arendt, *Totalitarianism*, pt. 3 of *The Origins of Totalitarianism* (New York: Harcourt, Brace, and World, 1968), p. 139.

21. Theodor Adorno, "Freudian Theory and the Pattern of Fascist Propaganda," in *The Essential Frankfurt School Reader,* ed. Andrew Arato and Eike Gebhardt (New York: Urizen Books, 1978), p. 136.

22. The paternalistic project came to life in the efforts of reformers in Bernays's early years to make the state itself a surrogate parent. Many of these social engineers, writes Christopher Lasch, well understood "the importance of public relations." See Christopher Lasch, *Haven in a Heartless World: The Family Besieged* (New York: Basic, 1977), p. 15. An ironic application of in loco parentis is the use of the classroom to liberate students from beliefs "unconsciously" acquired at home, as in the loosely psychoanalytic method of Rosenblatt. From "in place of the parent" to the displacement of the parent is only a half turn.

23. Benjamin Franklin, *Autobiography,* in *Writings,* ed. J. A. Leo Lemay (New York: Library of America, 1987), p. 1405.

24. The doctrine of deference plays a critical role in the thought of J. S. Mill. "No government by a democracy or a numerous aristocracy, either in its political acts or in the opinions, qualities, and tone of mind which it fosters, ever did or could rise above mediocrity, except in so far as the sovereign Many have let themselves be guided (which in their best times they always have done) by the counsels and influence of a more highly gifted and instructed One or Few." See John Stuart Mill, *On Liberty,* ed. David Spitz (New York: Norton, 1975), pp. 62–63. In contrast to a multitude under the heel of a tyrant (or a Carlylean hero), the people act freely; in contrast to a multitude intolerant of its own benefactors, it acts intelligently. For Mill the doctrine of deference passed down by the republican tradition is the answer to a riddle, a solution to what would otherwise be an intolerable conflict between his allegiance to popular sovereignty and his belief that all good things come from original minds. The many choose to defer to a wise few.

25. Bernays, *Memoirs,* p. 345.

26. Shelley Fisher Fishkin, *From Fact to Fiction: Journalism and Imaginative Writing in America* (Oxford: Oxford University Press, 1985), p. 170. Cf. Bernays, *Propaganda* (1928; Port Washington: Kennikat, 1972), p. 151: "It was not that many years ago that newspaper editors resented what they called 'the use of the news columns for propaganda purposes.' Some editors would even kill a good story if they imagined its publication might benefit any one. This point of view is now largely abandoned."

27. Cited in N. McKendrick, "Josiah Wedgwood: An Eighteenth-Century Entrepreneur in Salesmanship and Marketing Techniques," *Economic History Review*, 2d ser., 12 (1960): 424.

28. At one point Bernays himself mocks this doctrine as a fantasy born of the excesses of the twenties (*Memoirs*, p. 419).

29. Bernays, *Propaganda*, pp. 9–10.

30. Rochelle Gurstein, *The Repeal of Reticence: A History of America's Cultural and Legal Struggles over Free Speech, Obscenity, Sexual Liberation, and Modern Art* (New York: Hill and Wang, 1996), e.g., p. 70. The utopianism of the progressives and their belief in the malleability of the psyche are both reminiscent of Bentham.

31. Bernays, "Manipulating Public Opinion," 960; Edward Bernays, *The Later Years: Public Relations Insights, 1956–86* (Rhinebeck: H and M, 1986), p. 151. The recently voguish notion of "pulling your own strings" suggests not so much a repudiation of this kind of trickery as a buying into it. Some idea of what it might really mean to pull your own strings is given by professional athletes who talk about the tactics they use to work themselves up to the requisite pitch. On "pulling your own strings," see Peggy Rosenthal, *Words and Values: Some Leading Words and Where They Lead Us* (New York: Oxford University Press, 1984), p. 41.

32. Helvétius, cited in Robin Evans, *The Fabrication of Virtue: English Prison Architecture, 1750–1840* (Cambridge: Cambridge University Press, 1982), p. 214.

33. Bernays, "Manipulating Public Opinion," 960.

34. On Lindbergh, see Leo Braudy, *The Frenzy of Renown: Fame and Its History* (New York: Oxford University Press, 1986), pp. 19–25.

35. In an interview with Bernays, Bill Moyers points to his successes and says, "That's not influence, that's power." Replies Bernays, "I never thought of it as power." See "The Image-Makers," part of the television series *A Walk through the Twentieth Century*.

36. Jean-Jacques Rousseau, *Emile*, trans. Allan Bloom (New York: Basic, 1979), p. 387.

37. Introduction to ibid., p. 11.

38. Bernays's wife was his unofficial business partner.

39. See Bernays's interview with Bill Moyers. On recent publicity operations by Philip Morris, including its patronage of the arts and contribution to liberal causes, see Michael Massing, "How to Win the Tobacco War," *New York Review of Books*, July 11, 1996, p. 33.

40. Bernays, *Memoirs*, p. 387. On the incorporation of women into the tobacco market, see Carole Shammas, "Changes in English and Anglo-American Consumption from 1550 to 1800," in *Consumption and the World of Goods*, ed. John Brewer and Roy Porter (London: Routledge, 1993), p. 181.

41. Margaret Mead, "Research with Human Beings: A Model Derived from Anthropological Field Practice," *Daedalus* (Spring 1969): 376n.

42. John Locke, *Some Thoughts concerning Education*, ed. John W. Yolton and Jean S. Yolton (Oxford: Clarendon Press, 1989), para. 155. As we know, Addison, writing in the service of Lockean ideas, did cajole the public into reading.

43. Bernays, "Manipulating Public Opinion," 967.

44. Douglas, *Terrible Honesty*, p. 108f.

45. Edward Bernays, *Crystallizing Public Opinion* (New York: Boni and Liveright, 1923), p. 173.

46. Bernays, "Manipulating Public Opinion," 959.

47. Bernays, *Memoirs*, p. 91.

48. Lasch, *Haven in a Heartless World*, p. 15.

49. Michael Ignatieff, *A Just Measure of Pain: The Penitentiary in the Industrial Revolution, 1750–1850* (New York: Pantheon, 1978), p. 60.

50. On the deceits of doctors, see Sissela Bok, *Lying: Moral Choice in Public and Private Life* (New York: Vintage, 1978), chap. 15. In Kenneth Burke's island of Psychoanalysia the great article of public faith and rhetoric is the "curative value" of a massive electoral victory. Winning with a big enough majority will cure the island's troubles. Burke, *Philosophy of Literary Form*, p. 133.

51. Bernays makes this point both in his *Memoirs*, p. 387, and in his interview with Moyers.

52. John Flynn, "Edward L. Bernays: The Science of Ballyhoo," *Atlantic Monthly* (May 1932): 563.

53. George Steiner, *On Difficulty and Other Essays* (Oxford: Oxford University Press, 1978), p. 93.

54. Bernays, *Memoirs*, p. 658.

55. Carl Schorske, "Freud's Egyptian Dig," *New York Review of Books*, May 27, 1993.

56. For what it's worth, the central section of a notable study of Mill is entitled "The Biography of an Idea." See Gertrude Himmelfarb, *On Liberty and Liberalism: The Case of John Stuart Mill* (New York: Alfred A. Knopf, 1974), pt. 2.

57. Letter to Martha Bernays, November 15, 1883, in Ernest Jones, *The Life and Work of Sigmund Freud* (New York: Basic, 1953), pp. 175–76.

58. Bernays, *Memoirs*, p. 396.

59. Frederick Crews, *New York Review of Books*, February 3, 1994, p. 41.

60. Lionel Trilling, *Freud and the Crisis of Our Culture* (Boston: Beacon, 1955), p. 29. Fame, we might say, pertains to the ancients, celebrity to the moderns.

61. Freud, cited in Bernays, *Memoirs*, pp. 264–65.

62. *The Engineering of Consent,* ed. Edward Bernays (Norman: University of Oklahoma Press, 1955), p. 7.

63. On the dream of a frictionless society, see Janet Semple, *Bentham's Prison: A Study of the Panopticon Penitentiary* (Oxford: Clarendon Press, 1993), p. 323.

64. Bruno Bettelheim, *Freud and Man's Soul* (New York: Vintage, 1984), p. 40.

65. Sigmund Freud, *The Standard Edition of the Complete Psychological Works of Sigmund Freud,* trans. James Strachey, 24 vols. (London: Hogarth Press, 1953–74), 20: 9.

66. Bernays, *Memoirs,* pp. 269–70.

67. Trilling, *Freud and the Crisis of Our Culture,* p. 49. In Trilling's own manner of address as a critic, psychology reaches an entente with literacy and high civility that has since broken down.

68. The case against Freud is powerfully made by Adolf Grünbaum, *Is Psychoanalysis a Pseudo-Science?* (typescript, 1977).

69. Bernays, "Manipulating Public Opinion," 967.

70. Bernays, *Later Years,* p. 121.

71. Bernays, *Crystallizing Public Opinion,* p. 150.

72. *Washington Post Weekly,* July 13–19, 1992, p. 36.

73. Hannah Arendt, *Crises of the Republic* (New York: Harcourt Brace Jovanovich, 1972), p. 35.

74. Stanley Karnow, *Vietnam: A History* (New York: Viking, 1983), p. 547.

75. Bernays, "Manipulating Public Opinion," 970; cf. *Memoirs,* p. 169; *Propaganda,* p. 51.

76. Cf. Mary McCarthy, *Vietnam* (New York: Harcourt, Brace, and World, 1967), pp. 3, 41.

77. Bernays, "Manipulating Public Opinion," 970.

78. Bernays, *Crystallizing Public Opinion,* p. 173.

79. JUSPAO figures in McCarthy's *Vietnam.*

80. Theodore Draper, *New York Review of Books,* May 11, 1995, p. 7.

81. These are excerpts from a Joint U.S. Public Affairs Office Field Memorandum, "Lessons Learned from Evaluation of Allied PsyOp Media in Viet Nam," dated December 13, 1967. The document is included in Harry Latimer, *U.S. Psychological Operations in Vietnam* (Providence, R.I.: Brown University, 1973).

82. On Goebbels's theory and practice, see Leonard Doob, "Goebbels's Principles of Propaganda," in *Public Opinion and Propaganda*, ed. Daniel Katz, Dorwin Cartwright, Samuel Eldersveld, and Alfred McClung Lee (New York: Dryden Press, 1954). The Bernays method centers on the use of "created circumstance." Goebbels staged funerals, book burnings, and the Night of Broken Glass, as well as such media events as the visit of Finnish children to Germany for health reasons. See also H. R. Trevor-Roper, "Hitler's Impresario," *New York Review of Books*, June 1, 1978.

83. Habermas, *Structural Transformation of the Public Sphere*, p. 194.

84. Cf. McCarthy, *Vietnam*, p. 39: "At lunch in his house, the local JUSPAO official expressed hurt and bewilderment over a *New York Times* story about Phu Cuong. The reporter had interviewed several refugees and printed what they told him; he quoted one woman as saying that she wished she were dead. . . . 'He ought to have given a cross-section,' the man said in injured tones. 'It creates the wrong picture of the camp.' 'If only one woman out of five wished she were dead, you're lucky,' I said. But he was not persuaded. The story was unfair, he repeated. He actually wanted to think that the évacués in the camp were *happy*."

85. Bernays, *Engineering of Consent*, p. 24; "Lessons Learned" in Latimer, *U.S. Psychological Operations in Vietnam*.

86. McCarthy, *Vietnam*, p. 77.

87. General William Westmoreland as quoted in the *New York Times Magazine*, August 10, 1997, p. 33.

Chapter 3

1. Stanley Milgram, *Obedience to Authority: An Experimental View* (New York: Harper and Row, 1974), p. 18.

2. In all cases it seems the subjects are paid at the start, which may strengthen the sense that they owe it to Milgram to see the ordeal through. The eye-catcher in Milgram's advertisement for subjects is "WE WILL PAY YOU $4.00 FOR THE ONE HOUR OF YOUR TIME" (ibid., p. 15).

3. Ibid., p. 43.

4. Stanley Milgram, "Some Conditions of Obedience and Disobedience to Authority," *Human Relations* 18 (1965): 68.

5. John Locke, *Some Thoughts concerning Education*, ed. John W. Yolton and Jean S. Yolton (Oxford: Clarendon Press, 1989), para. 87.

6. Milgram, *Obedience to Authority*, p. 24.

7. Lionel Trilling, *The Liberal Imagination* (New York: Viking, 1950), p. 226.

8. Consider also the double standard of those revolutionaries in France who declaimed against politics even as they seized the political stage and repudiated all the conventions of representation even as they professed to represent the Nation. See Lynn Hunt, *Politics, Culture, and Class in the French Revolution* (Berkeley: University of California Press, 1984), chap. 1.

9. Edward Bernays, "Manipulating Public Opinion: The Why and the How," *American Journal of Sociology* 33 (1928): 961–62.

10. Hannah Arendt, *The Human Condition* (Chicago: University of Chicago Press, 1958), p. 45.

11. Sissela Bok, *Lying: Moral Choice in Public and Private Life* (New York: Vintage, 1978), p. 194.

12. Hannah Arendt, *Between Past and Future: Eight Exercises in Political Thought* (New York: Penguin 1978), p. 209.

13. John Flynn, "Edward L. Bernays: The Science of Ballyhoo," *Atlantic Monthly* (May 1932): 563. Wedgwood for his part was a canny psychologist. In elevating his tea sets to the status of cultural objects and endowing them with an aspect of art, he seems to appeal to buyers uneasy with the impermanence of consumer goods and the follies of fashion itself.

14. See, e.g., the cases cited by William James, *The Principles of Psychology* (New York: Henry Holt, 1890), vol. 1, chaps. 8–10.

15. Milgram, *Obedience to Authority*, p. 54.

16. Michael Bilton and Kevin Sim, *Four Hours in My Lai* (New York: Viking, 1992), pp. 101, 129. A number of men refused to take part in the debauchery. Milgram interprets My Lai, improbably, as a confirmation of his obedience thesis.

17. That within the voice of the narrator of "The Yellow Wallpaper" is another voice, defiant and subversively ironic, does not make this a story about "multiple personalities." The story asks from its readers not diagnostic acumen (we can leave that to the husband) but an ear for the intonation of words and a sense of the woman's position. There is nothing all that hidden about the second voice, either. It is all but overt.

18. Milgram, *Obedience to Authority*, pp. 73–76.

19. Milgram dismissed moral objections to his experiment. See Stanley Milgram, "Issues in the Study of Obedience: A Reply to Baumrind," *American Psychologist* 19 (1964): 848–52. As though lacking a sense — the sense of irony, perhaps — the author maintains that subjects were treated respectfully.

20. M. M. Bakhtin, *The Dialogic Imagination: Four Essays*, ed. Michael Holquist, trans. Caryl Emerson and Michael Holquist (Austin: University of Texas Press, 1981).

21. Milgram, *Obedience to Authority*, p. 123.

22. *Orwell's "Nineteen Eighty-Four": Text, Sources, Criticism*, ed. Irving Howe (New York: Harcourt Brace Jovanovich, 1982), p. 169.

23. Arendt, *Human Condition*, p. 295.

24. Milgram reminds us that the full intensity of the lab situation, especially the artistry of the "victim's" screams, cannot be reproduced on the printed page (p. 23) — much as the performance of a play brings the script to life.

25. Panoptic language is used by Milgram himself. The subject in the experiment "is controlled by many forces in the situation beyond his awareness" but not that of the experimenter. "The participant, and he alone, has experienced the predicament, but he cannot place it in the perspective that comes only from an overview" (Milgram, *Obedience to Authority*, pp. 44–45).

26. *Orwell's "Nineteen Eighty-Four,"* p. 304.

27. Milgram, *Obedience to Authority*, p. 199.

Chapter 4

1. T. W. Adorno, Else Frenkel-Brunswik, Daniel Levinson, and R. Nevitt Sanford, *The Authoritarian Personality* (New York: Norton, 1969).

2. Peter Gay, *The Enlightenment: An Interpretation*, vol. 2, *The Science of Freedom* (New York: Alfred A. Knopf, 1969), p. 16.

3. On the costuming of political positions in the garb of science, see Frederick Crews, *Skeptical Engagements* (New York: Oxford University Press, 1986), chap. 1.

4. Albert Hirschman, *The Rhetoric of Reaction: Perversity, Futility, Jeopardy* (Cambridge, Mass.: Harvard University Press, 1991), p. 155.

5. John Stuart Mill, *On Liberty*, ed. David Spitz (New York: Norton, 1975), p. 6.

6. Herbert Marcuse, *One-Dimensional Man: Studies in the Ideology of Advanced Industrial Society* (Boston: Beacon, 1964), p. 62.

7. William Cobbett, cited in Joseph Hamburger, *Intellectuals in Politics: John Stuart Mill and the Philosophic Radicals* (New Haven, Conn.: Yale University Press, 1965), p. 65n.

8. Herbert Marcuse, "Repressive Tolerance," in Robert Paul Wolff, Barrington Moore Jr., and Herbert Marcuse, *A Critique of Pure Tolerance* (Boston: Beacon,

1965). "Repressive Tolerance" being a short piece of writing, I have foregone page references.

9. Louise Rosenblatt, *Literature as Exploration* (New York: D. Appleton-Century, 1938), p. 180.

10. Ibid., p. 327.

11. Gary Saul Morson and Caryl Emerson, *Mikhail Bakhtin: Creation of a Prosaics* (Stanford, Calif.: Stanford University Press, 1990), p. 109.

12. Adolf Grünbaum, "Psychological Explanations for the Rejection or Acceptance of Scientific Theories," *Humanities in Society* 1 (1978): 293–304.

13. Gordon Wood, "Conspiracy and the Paranoid Style: Causality and Deceit in the Eighteenth Century," *William and Mary Quarterly*, 3d ser., 39 (1982): 417; and "Classical Republicanism and the American Revolution," *Chicago-Kent Law Review* 66 (1990): 29.

14. J. A. Passmore, "The Malleability of Man in Eighteenth-Century Thought," in *Aspects of the Eighteenth Century*, ed. Earl Wasserman (Baltimore: Johns Hopkins University Press, 1965), p. 39. Emphasis in the original.

15. Marcuse, "Repressive Tolerance."

16. *The Age of Enlightenment: The Eighteenth-Century Philosophers*, ed. Isaiah Berlin (New York: Mentor, 1956), p. 31.

17. John Locke, *Some Thoughts concerning Education*, ed. John W. Yolton and Jean S. Yolton (Oxford: Clarendon Press, 1989), para. 64.

18. David Spadafora, *The Idea of Progress in Eighteenth-Century Britain* (New Haven, Conn.: Yale University Press, 1990), p. 174.

19. Janet Semple, *Bentham's Prison: A Study of the Panopticon Penitentiary* (Oxford: Clarendon Press, 1993), p. 301.

20. Margaret Mead, "Research with Human Beings: A Model Derived from Anthropological Field Practice," *Daedalus* (Spring 1969): 369.

21. Alasdair MacIntyre, *Herbert Marcuse: An Exposition and a Polemic* (New York: Viking, 1970), p. 105.

22. Cf. the discussion of Skinner in William Barrett, *The Illusion of Technique: A Search for Meaning in a Technological Civilization* (Garden City, N.Y.: Doubleday, 1978), esp. pp. 311–12.

23. Stanley Fish, *Surprised by Sin: The Reader in Paradise Lost* (Berkeley: University of California Press, 1971), pp. 212–13.

24. In *The Brothers Karamazov*, to be discussed later, Dmitri has his movements tracked, his clothing stripped, and his mind in effect x-rayed. This may be superficial compared to the treatment Marcuse has in mind for the masses. With its tales of conversion, *The Brothers Karamazov* also reminds us that

literature concerned itself with identity change — with "altered consciousness" — before radical psychology did.

25. Basil Willey, "On Wordsworth and the Locke Tradition," in *English Romantic Poets: Modern Essays in Criticism* (London: Oxford University Press, 1960), pp. 84–94.

26. Donald D'Elia, "Benjamin Rush, David Hartley, and the Revolutionary Uses of Psychology," *Proceedings of the American Philosophical Society* 114 (1970): 109–18.

27. Ibid., 115.

28. Locke, *Some thoughts Concerning Education*, para. 217.

Chapter 5

1. Cf. Tzvetan Todorov, *Genres in Discourse*, trans. Catherine Porter (Cambridge: Cambridge University Press, 1990), p. 103. Riddled with gaps, *Heart of Darkness* explodes the connected-link structure of the Victorian plot.

2. Erich Kahler, *The Inward Turn of Narrative*, trans. Richard Winston and Clara Winston (Princeton, N.J.: Princeton University Press, 1973), p. 168.

3. Joseph Conrad, *Heart of Darkness*, ed. Robert Kimbrough (New York: Norton, 1971), p. 11. All further page numbers will be included in the text.

4. Hans Aarsleff, *From Locke to Saussure: Essays on the Study of Language and Intellectual History* (Minneapolis: University of Minnesota Press, 1982), p. 375. On the political twist given today to the theory that "only my own 'I' can know how I feel, look, and experience the world," see Caryl Emerson, "Keeping the Self Intact during the Culture Wars: A Centennial Essay for Mikhail Bakhtin," *New Literary History* 27 (1996): 110.

5. William James, *The Principles of Psychology* (New York: Henry Holt, 1890), 1:226. On James and Locke, see Craig Eisendrath, *The Psychological Philosophy of William James and Alfred North Whitehead* (Cambridge, Mass.: Harvard University Press, 1971), p. 33.

6. Todorov, *Genres in Discourse*, p. 105.

7. Richard Arneson, "Marlow's Skepticism in *Heart of Darkness*," *Ethics* 94 (1984): 424.

8. Hannah Arendt, *Totalitarianism*, vol. 3 of *The Origins of Totalitarianism* (New York: Harcourt, Brace, and World, 1968), p. 174.

9. J. Hillis Miller, "*Heart of Darkness* Revisited," reprinted in *Heart of Darkness*, ed. Ross Murfin (Boston: St. Martin's, 1996).

10. Even this claim can be used to muddle the moral question, as when champions of the Vietnam War — America's encounter with the jungle — argued that no one who hadn't experienced the atrocity of the war was qualified to oppose it.

11. Thanks go to my colleague and teacher Robert Johnstone for referring me to Conrad's "The Tale." On the hermeneutics of suspicion and double guile, see Paul Ricoeur, *Freud and Philosophy: An Essay on Interpretation* (New Haven, Conn.: Yale University Press, 1970), pp. 26–36.

12. Characters are viewed from such a height of *contemptus mundi* in this work that differences among mortals tend to recede anyway.

13. John Locke, cited by Charles Taylor, *Sources of the Self: The Making of the Modern Identity* (Cambridge, Mass.: Harvard University Press, 1989), p. 170.

14. Cited in "A Critical History of *Heart of Darkness*" in *Heart of Darkness*, ed. Murfin, p. 99.

15. Joseph Conrad, *The Secret Agent* (Garden City, N.Y.: Doubleday, 1953), p. 196.

16. Rosalind Williams, *Dream Worlds: Mass Consumption in Late Nineteenth-Century France* (Berkeley: University of California Press, 1982), pp. 61, 73. The exoticism of the Paris exposition lives on in the image of the camel, that ship of the desert, on the cigarette pack of that name.

Chapter 6

1. Fyodor Dostoevsky, *The Brothers Karamazov*, trans. Constance Garnett (New York: Viking, 1955), p. 549. Subsequent page references appear in the text.

2. Michel Foucault, *Discipline and Punish: The Birth of the Prison*, trans. Alan Sheridan (New York: Vintage, 1979).

3. The author himself has been subjected to a kind of diagnosis no less pat. Even in the admitted absence of anything like "a clinical record" of Dostoevsky's life, William Phillips, e.g., felt warranted in tracing his pathologies back to early childhood. "This would account for his ambiguous relations with women. . . . His unconscious was perpetually torn. . . . Here is the source of his absurdity, his paranoia, his criminal instincts." William Phillips, "Dostoevsky's Underground Man," *Partisan Review* (November–December 1946): 560–61. The positivity of the critic's reductions rises in the absence of evidence. Freud for his part figured out Dostoevsky so well that he was able to offer "the formula for Dostoevsky." According to Freud, the

exposé of psychology in the trial actually signifies that the trial, and not psychology, is a mockery. See Sigmund Freud, "Dostoevsky and Parricide," in *The Standard Edition of the Complete Psychological Works of Sigmund Freud*, trans. James Strachey, vol. 21 (London: Hogarth Press, 1961).

4. Citing "the most skilful doctors," the prosecutor also offers a diagnosis of the epileptic Smerdyakov that curiously anticipates Freud's reading of Dostoevsky himself (Dostoevsky, *The Brothers Karamazov*, p. 860).

5. See the advertisement for the Dial Press edition of *The Short Novels of Dostoevksy* in *Partisan Review* (Winter 1946).

6. George Steiner, *On Difficulty and Other Essays* (New York: Oxford University Press, 1978), p. 133.

7. Fyodor Dostoevsky, *Crime and Punishment*, trans. David McDuff (New York: Penguin, 1991), pp. 74–77. Cf. Miss Wade in Dickens's *Little Dorrit*, the "self-tormentor" who claims to see through pretenses with x-ray clarity and discern the native ugliness of everyone's heart. Next to Dostoevsky's self-tormentors, though, there is something a little pat about Miss Wade, as though she were just the contrary of female benevolence.

8. Dostoevsky, *Crime and Punishment*, p. 282.

9. In tormenting him with the thought that his guilt gives him away, like the horns of a cuckold visible to all the world, Porfiry is actually provoking Raskolnikov to reveal himself.

10. The author's attitude toward psychology cuts two ways itself, in the sense of being dialectical. When Dostoevsky himself, in *Diary of a Writer*, construes the action of a woman who threw her stepchild out of a window without knowing why as a flash of insanity, he never really diagnoses the woman at all; for all his allusions to pathology, her deed remains as unexplained as ever, and her case as Dostoevsky relates it more a parable of moral regeneration than a medical history.

11. Mikhail Bakhtin, *Problems of Dostoevsky's Poetics*, ed. and trans. Caryl Emerson (Minneapolis: University of Minnesota Press, 1984), p. 58. With its habit of typing and its way of exposing its victims, satire runs afoul of Bakhtin's principle, although the richness and humor of the tradition excuse the offense. There is a richly humorous satiric element in *The Brothers Karamazov* itself. In any case, no satirist takes the project of "curing" delusion and folly as literally as the psychologist or the psychologically inspired reformer.

12. Gerald Bruns, *Inventions: Writing, Textuality, and Understanding in Literary History* (New Haven, Conn.: Yale University Press, 1982), p. 122.

13. Karl Mannheim, *Ideology and Utopia*, trans. Louis Wirth and Edward Shils (New York: Harcourt, Brace, and World, 1936), p. 262.

14. A finalized character lives a script, identifying with an already written role like the romantic mentioned in the opening sentences of *The Brothers Karamazov* who cultivates such a complete identity with Ophelia that she drowns herself, attaining "finality" indeed. Suicide would write a sort of false ending to the story of the romantic Dmitri, who likes to think his life too is scripted.

15. Dostoevsky, cited in Bakhtin, *Problems of Dostoevksy's Poetics*, p. 60.

16. Bakhtin, *Problems of Dostoevksy's Poetics*, p. 61. In his last essays Irving Howe, who felt a special affinity with the Russian tradition, muses on characters who escape or exceed the designs of their authors. See Irving Howe, *A Critic's Notebook* (New York: Harcourt, Brace, 1994).

17. The paradigm of "the moment of crisis" is the conversion experience. It is the contention of Harold Rosenberg in "Character Change and the Drama," *The Symposium* 3 (1932): 364–67, that conversions in *The Brothers Karamazov* only incidentally fit the descriptions of such experiences in the psychological literature — that despite some naturalistic touches, psychology applies no more to conversions in *The Brothers Karamazov* than to the transformation of Jacob in the Book of Genesis.

18. He sees the same look in Dmitri's eyes as in the faces of others who later suffered. In other words, he reasons from experience. "Once or twice in my life I've seen such a look in a man's face . . . reflecting as it were his future fate, and that fate, alas, came to pass" (Dostoevsky, *The Brothers Karamazov*, p. 339).

19. Bakhtin's way of thinking invites us to view the trial of Dmitri as a kind of novelized or parodic drama, complete with scenes, spectators, brightly lit action, protagonist, antagonist — parodic not only because the wrong man is in the dock but because the sensationally public nature of the event makes it a mockery.

20. "I could wish," says Sterne's sentimental traveler with the sort of moralized prurience that distinguishes the work, "to spy the nakedness of [women's] hearts, and through the different disguises of custom, climates, and religion, find out what is good in them." Laurence Sterne, *A Sentimental Journey* (Oxford: Oxford University Press, 1984), p. 84. Today's psychological society, so eager to see into the heart, practically advertises its own prurience.

21. Dostoevsky, *Crime and Punishment*, pp. 230–31.

22. Lionel Trilling, *Sincerity and Authenticity* (Cambridge, Mass.: Harvard University Press, 1971), p. 141.

23. On the observance of the threshold, see Geoffrey Sampson, *Liberty and Language* (Oxford: Oxford University Press, 1979), p. 182: "In the days before breakdown of marriage was a legal ground for divorce, private detectives spent many hours gathering evidence by hanging round hotel corridors noting who went through which bedroom door with whom, and how much time elapsed before they came out again. Provided that they were genuine detectives rather than blackmailers they did not attempt to get direct evidence about what was actually happening behind the closed doors." On the baring of another as a public entertainment, consider the "public exposure of [Mario's] timid and deluded passion and rapture" at the hands of Cipolla in Thomas Mann's "Mario and the Magician." Part mountebank, part Mussolini, Cipolla is the psychologist in his most indecent guise.

24. Lydia Ginzburg, *On Psychological Prose*, trans. and ed. Judith Rosengrant (Princeton, N.J.: Princeton University Press, 1991), p. 259.

25. Dostoevsky, *Crime and Punishment*, p. 614.

26. Not that his position really "explains" Smerdyakov. It was a critic of a psychological turn who traced Smerdyakov back to a Dickens character — the demonic Blandois in *Little Dorrit* — who beggars every attempt to "explain" him. "We have been forced to believe that there really are people who seem entirely wicked, and almost unaccountably so; the social causes of their badness lie so far back that they can scarcely be reached, and in any case causation pales into irrelevance before the effects of their action; our effort to 'understand' them becomes a mere form of thought." Lionel Trilling, "Little Dorrit," *Kenyon Review* 15 (1953): 583.

27. See the review of Ginzburg's *On Psychological Prose* by Joseph Frank in the *New York Review of Books*, December 1, 1994; Frank brings out the inseparability of psychological issues from broader ones in the Russian novel.

28. Cf. Bakhtin, *Problems of Dostoevsky's Poetics*, pp. 258–60.

29. It is to counteract the work of Smerdyakov that Alyosha reads Ivan's mind after the murder: "You have accused yourself and have confessed to yourself that you are the murderer and no one else. But you didn't do it; you are mistaken: you are not the murderer. Do you hear? It was not you! God has sent me to tell you so" (Dostoevsky, *The Brothers Karamazov*, p. 732). Clearly, however, Ivan is not free of responsibility for the murder.

30. William James, *The Principles of Psychology* (New York: Henry Holt, 1890), 1:206.

31. "Well, you see, a man may be sitting perfectly sane and suddenly have an aberration. He may be conscious and know what he is doing and yet be in a

state of aberration. And there's no doubt that Dmitri Fyodorovitch was suffering from aberration" (Dostoevsky, *The Brothers Karamazov*, p. 702).

32. Cited in Peter Gay, *The Enlightenment: An Interpretation*, vol. 2: *The Science of Freedom* (New York: Alfred A. Knopf, 1969), p. 526.

33. On "decrowning," see Bakhtin, *Problems of Dostoevsky's Poetics*, p. 124.

34. As if parodying Ivan's own theory of the innocent child whose suffering is necessary to preserve God's order, the phantom claims to be the sufferer who holds everything together.

35. "Be sure, I should always defend him. But in my wishes I reserve myself full latitude in this case" (Dostoevsky, *The Brothers Karamazov*, p. 170).

36. John Locke, *The Second Treatise of Government* (Indianapolis: Liberal Arts Press, 1952), p. 36. Contending against patriarchalism, appealing to rational religion, and emphasizing the acquisition of moral habits in childhood, the defense lawyer has strong affinities with the Locke tradition. Although the cool discussion of changelings and confusions of nature in the *Essay* is far from the charged dramatization of these themes in the foul and malignant figure of Smerdyakov, the defense lawyer reads Smerdyakov well. On Smerdyakov, see Gary Saul Morson, "Verbal Pollution in *The Brothers Karamazov*," in *Modern Critical Interpretations: The Brothers Karamazov*, ed. Harold Bloom (New York: Chelsea House, 1988). Perhaps ironically, Locke like Dostoevsky worried that the ground would go out from under morality with the loss of faith in God. This is one of the themes of John Dunn's portrait of Locke in *The British Empiricists* (Oxford: Oxford University Press, 1992).

37. *The English Philosophers from Bacon to Mill*, ed. Edwin Burtt (New York: Modern Library, 1939), pp. 18, 33.

38. John Locke, *Some Thoughts concerning Education*, ed. John W. Yolton and Jean S. Yolton (Oxford: Clarendon Press, 1989), para. 217.

39. Gary Saul Morson, "Prosaic Bakhtin: *Landmarks*, Anti-Intelligentsialism, and the Russian Counter-Tradition," *Common Knowledge* 2, 1 (1993): 63. On the Maoist version of "the irresistible moral power of pedagogy," see *The Analects of Confucius*, ed. and trans. Simon Leys (New York: Norton, 1997), p. 132. Ironically, Confucius, the source of the Chinese pedagogical tradition, considered that "one should not teach the same thing to different people" (p. 115), which ought to rule out blanketing millions with propaganda.

40. J. A. Passmore, "The Malleability of Man in Eighteenth-Century Thought," in *Aspects of the Eighteenth Century*, ed. Earl Wasserman (Baltimore: Johns Hopkins University Press, 1965), p. 46.

41. Neil McKendrick, "Josiah Wedgwood and Factory Discipline," *Historical Journal* 4, 1 (1961): 51.

42. Bakhtin, *Problems of Dostoevsky's Poetics*, p. 59.

43. Isaac Kramnick, *Republicanism and Bourgeois Radicalism: Political Ideology in Late Eighteenth-Century England and America* (Ithaca, N.Y.: Cornell University Press, 1990), p. 95.

44. Richard Pipes, *The Russian Revolution* (New York: Alfred A. Knopf, 1990), p. 137. In tracing revolutionary doctrine to Enlightenment theories of pedagogy, Pipes highlights Locke and Helvétius, the latter an important influence on Bentham.

45. Basil Willey, *The Eighteenth Century Background* (New York: Columbia University Press, 1941), p. 152.

46. Kramnick, *Republicanism and Bourgeois Radicalism*, p. 98.

47. Endowed with x-ray vision, Bentham can see in others what they cannot see in themselves. "How, it may be asked, is it possible that the motive by which a man is actuated can be secret to himself? Nothing, actually, is easier; nothing is more frequent. Indeed the rare case is, not that of a man's not knowing, but that of his knowing it. It is the same with the anatomy of the human mind as with the anatomy and physiology of the human body: the rare case is, not that of a man's being unconversant with it, but that of his being conversant with it." Jeremy Bentham, *Handbook of Political Fallacies* (New York: Apollo, 1971), p. 235. Bentham is an anatomist of the human mind. Behind the Marxist practice of unveiling hidden motives lies bourgeois precedent.

48. Donald D'Elia, "Benjamin Rush, David Hartley, and the Revolutionary Uses of Psychology," *Proceedings of the American Philosophical Society* 114 (1970): 113.

49. Bakhtin, *Problems of Dostoevsky's Poetics*, p. 166.

50. John Stuart Mill, *On Liberty*, ed. David Spitz (New York: Norton, 1975), p. 43.

51. Gabriel Tarde, *The Laws of Imitation*, trans. Elsie Crews Parson (1890; New York: Henry Holt, 1903), p. 329.

52. Ibid., p. 187.

Chapter 7

1. George Orwell, *The Road to Wigan Pier* (New York: Harcourt Brace Jovanovich, 1958), pp. 147–48.

2. Gary Saul Morson, "Prosaic Bakhtin: *Landmarks*, Anti-Intelligentsialism, and the Russian Counter-Tradition," *Common Knowledge* 2, 1 (1993): 35–74.

3. This bit of gabble reads in part, "On the one side, we have the free personality: by definition it is not neurotic, for it has neither conflict nor dream. . . . But *on the other side*, the social bond itself is nothing but the mutual reflection of these self-secure integrities. Is this not the very picture of a small academic? Where is there a place in this hall of mirrors for either personality or fraternity?" See "Politics and the English Language," in *In Front of Your Nose*, vol. 4 of *The Collected Essays, Journalism, and Letters of George Orwell*, ed. Sonia Orwell and Ian Angus (New York: Harcourt Brace Jovanovich, 1968), pp. 128–29. It happens that Eileen Shaughnessy, later Orwell, was doing graduate work in psychology when she met Orwell.

4. Orwell, "Politics and the English Language," p. 127.

5. On Smollett's technique of mock objectivity, see Donald Bruce, *Radical Dr. Smollett* (Boston: Houghton Mifflin, 1965), chap. 12. On Dickens's, see M. M. Bakhtin, *The Dialogic Imagination*, trans. Caryl Emerson and Michael Holquist (Austin: University of Texas Press, 1981), pp. 303–40. On Joyce's tie with Swift and mastery of the art of report, see Hugh Kenner, *Joyce's Voices* (Berkeley: University of California Press, 1978). Joyce was among Orwell's favorite writers.

6. *The Ferment of Knowledge: Studies in the Historiography of Eighteenth-Century Science*, ed. G. S. Rousseau and Roy Porter (Cambridge: Cambridge University Press, 1980), p. 174. A good dose of Shakespeare, writes Johnson, will cure the delirium that lesser authors raise in the brain.

7. Some borrowing may have gone the other way. Pope's "ruling passion" reflects the medical thinking of his day, yet he writes as a moralist in a public medium, not a scientist, and if "ruling passion" is jargon it is jargon of the most elegant kind, a long way from the "self-secure integrities" of the essayist quoted in "Politics and the English Language." *Tristram Shandy* reflects contemporary mind-body theories but also stands in the Rabelaisian tradition of the public square of such interest to Bakhtin.

8. On the psychologizing of Swift and Orwell, see, e.g., Alvin Kernan, *The Plot of Satire* (New Haven, Conn.: Yale University Press, 1965), pp. 53–56. Kernan himself goes only part way with psychological reductions.

9. Cf. Stuart Hampshire writing in the *New York Review of Books*, January 30, 1992, p. 12: Orwell "responded to that idea of the free and independent Englishman which had been debated among the Protestant sects under the Commonwealth. . . . This was a Puritan philosophy in the strict sense."

10. Add to this the ironic handling of specialist or professional jargons in the tradition encompassing all the English writers named here — the tradition of Chaucer, whose *Canterbury Tales* features mock praise of professionals like the lawyer and the physician, each with his own art and terms of art.

11. Orwell, "The Prevention of Literature," *In Front of Your Nose*, p. 60.

12. Richard Foster Jones, "Science and Language in England of the Mid-Seventeenth Century," in *The Seventeenth Century: Studies in the History of English Thought and Literature from Bacon to Pope* (Stanford, Calif.: Stanford University Press, 1951), p. 157.

13. Cf. Stewart Justman, "Orwell's Plain Style," *University of Toronto Quarterly* 53 (1983–84): 195–203.

14. To Orwell, Laputa is a brilliant premonition of totalitarianism, the highlight of *Gulliver's Travels*. See Orwell, *In Front of Your Nose*, pp. 213–14.

15. John Locke, *Some Thoughts concerning Education*, ed. John W. Yolton and Jean S. Yolton (Oxford: Clarendon Press, 1989), para. 217.

16. George Levine, *The Realistic Imagination: English Fiction from Frankenstein to Lady Chatterley* (Chicago: University of Chicago Press, 1982), p. 22.

17. William Hazlitt, *Selected Writings* (Oxford: Oxford University Press, 1991), p. 33.

18. Bruce, *Radical Dr. Smollett*, p. 209.

19. On Swift's technique of "one step further," see Erich Kahler, *The Inward Turn of Narrative*, trans. Richard Winston and Clara Winston (Princeton, N.J.: Princeton University Press, 1973), p. 125n. On Orwell's use of the same, see Irving Howe in *Orwell's Nineteen Eighty-Four: Text, Sources, Criticism*, ed. Howe (New York: Harcourt Brace Jovanovich, 1982), p. 309.

20. Orwell, *In Front of Your Nose*, p. 216; Hampshire, *New York Review of Books*, January 30, 1992, p. 12.

21. He is even Addison, who proposes that men of good will pledge "that we do in our conscience believe two and two make four. . . . We do also firmly declare, that it is our resolution as long as we live to call black black, and white white." *Spectator*, no. 126.

22. John Milton, "Areopagitica," in *Complete Prose Works of John Milton* (New Haven, Conn.: Yale University Press, 1959), 2: 526. In *Paradise Lost* the plain style belongs to God, the ornate to Satan. On Milton's belief that a vitiation of speech signifies the fall of the polity (a belief that Orwell too holds in his more modern way), see Northrop Frye, *The Return of Eden* (Toronto: University of Toronto Press, 1965), p. 117.

23. Bakhtin, *Dialogic Imagination*, p. 194. Cf. Orwell's remarks in "Politics and the English Language" on the use of Latinisms.

24. Orwell, *Road to Wigan Pier*, p. 7.

25. Lionel Trilling, introduction to *Homage to Catalonia* (New York: Harcourt Brace Jovanovich, 1932), p. xv. Trilling refers to *Keep the Aspidistra Flying*.

26. Gary Saul Morson and Caryl Emerson, *Mikhail Bakhtin: Creation of a Prosaics* (Stanford, Calif.: Stanford University Press, 1990), p. 462.

27. Orwell, "Notes on Nationalism," in *As I Please*, vol. 3 of *The Collected Essays, Journalism, and Letters of George Orwell*, ed. Orwell and Angus, p. 380. Emphasis in the original.

28. Orwell, *As I Please*, pp. 82, 91, 153, 340. Is the habit of demonizing other races and nations really peculiarly modern?

29. Ironically, one of the strongest descriptions of the work of ideological microbes is by Dostoevsky. See Dostoevsky, *Crime and Punishment*, trans. David McDuff (Penguin: New York, 1991), pp. 627–28: "In his illness he had dreamt that the entire world had fallen victim to some strange, unheard of and unprecedented plague that was spreading from the depths of Asia into Europe. Everyone was to perish, apart from a chosen few, a very few. Some new kind of trichinae had appeared, microscopic creatures that lodged themselves in people's bodies. But these creatures were spirits, gifted with will and intelligence. People who absorbed them into their systems instantly became rabid and insane. But never, never had people considered themselves so intelligent and in unswerving possession of the truth as did those who became infected. . . . In this place and that people would gather into groups, agree on something together, swear to stick together — but would instantly begin doing something completely different from what had been proposed, start blaming one another, fighting and murdering. Fires began, a famine broke out. Everyone and everything perished. The plague grew worse. . . . " Cf. Dickens's account of the epidemic of speculation in bk. 2, chap. 13 of *Little Dorrit*. On the use of the disease metaphor in *The Idiot*, see Harold Rosenberg, *Act and the Actor: Making the Self* (Chicago: University of Chicago Press, 1983), chap. 5.

30. Orwell, "Reflections on Gandhi," in *In Front of Your Nose*, p. 467. Orwell possessed no knowledge of Gandhi's psyche. The man credited with the emancipation of India from British rule is reduced to an abject coward who hid from life.

31. Isaiah Berlin, *Four Essays on Liberty* (Oxford: Oxford University Press, 1969), p. 25.

32. Boethius, *The Consolation of Philosophy*, trans. Richard Green (Indianapolis: Library of Liberal Arts, 1962), pp. 4–5.

33. Richard Pipes, *The Russian Revolution* (New York: Alfred A. Knopf, 1990), p. 136.

34. Orwell, *Nineteen Eighty-Four*, ed. Howe, pp. 129, 169. On the use of stun technology as a means of psychological conquest, see William F. Schulz, "Cruel and Unusual Punishment," *New York Review of Books*, April 24, 1997, p. 51.

35. Locke, *Some Thoughts concerning Education*, paras. 39, 43, 78.

36. Harold Rosenberg, *Act and the Actor: Making the Self* (Chicago: University of Chicago Press, 1983), p. 203.

37. Hannah Arendt, *Totalitarianism,* pt. 3 of *The Origins of Totalitarianism* (New York: Harcourt, Brace, and World, 1968), p. 139.

38. M. H. Abrams, *Natural Supernaturalism: Tradition and Revolution in Romantic Literature* (New York: Norton, 1971), p. 145.

Chapter 8

1. Lionel Trilling, introduction to *Homage to Catalonia* (New York: Harcourt Brace Jovanovich, 1952), p. viii.

2. Stanley Milgram, *Obedience to Authority: An Experimental View* (New York: Harper and Row, 1974), pp. xi, 187. Under this show of abstention Milgram actually indulged in a good deal of reprobation; see the review of *Obedience to Authority* by Steven Marcus, *New York Times Book Review*, January 13, 1974. Banished, morality reappears as name-calling. Since the Milgram experiment, "ethical" guidelines governing the use of human subjects in the laboratory have been tightened. There are many who will talk ethics but are "not comfortable" with the word "morality."

3. Hannah Arendt, *Eichmann in Jerusalem: A Report on the Banality of Evil* (New York: Penguin, 1977), p. 296. Arendt was about to begin a work entitled *Judging* when she died.

4. An argument subjected to deserved contempt by Harold Rosenberg, *The Case of the Baffled Radical* (Chicago: University of Chicago Press, 1985), pp. 122–33.

5. Roy Porter, *The Enlightenment* (London: Macmillan, 1990), p. 19. As one minor example of the clash between psychological and moral categories, see the argument of Richard Hovey, "Dr. Samuel Johnson, Psychiatrist," *Modern Language Quarterly* 15 (1954): 321–25, to the effect that the real interest of

Rasselas is "psychological, not moral." Contending that Johnson describes his own melancholia under cover of fiction, and this in a way that brilliantly anticipates Freudian findings, the essay pieces together shreds of evidence and mere presumptions into the image of a hidden truth. Johnson was a moralist, not a psychiatrist.

6. It is interesting that the story of Psyche — whence "psychology" — itself turns upon a prohibition on looking. See the tale of Cupid and Psyche in *The Golden Ass*.

7. Lee Patterson, *Chaucer and the Subject of History* (Madison: University of Wisconsin Press, 1991), p. 325.

8. Ann Douglas, *Terrible Honesty: Mongrel Manhattan in the 1920s* (New York: Farrar, Straus and Giroux, 1995).

9. Feminists who insist that an issue like pornography is not moral but political, yet use the tonalities of the antivice crusade of a century ago, similarly repudiate Victorianism even as they claim its civilizing mission.

10. Even Raskolnikov, a rebel against herd morality, accepts this lexicon. Legally speaking, Ivan Karamazov possesses a perfect out for the murder of his father: a valid alibi. This is too base a line for him to take, however.

11. John Stuart Mill, *On Liberty*, ed. David Spitz (New York: Norton, 1975), p. 73.

12. Isaiah Berlin, " 'From Hope and Fear Set Free,' " in his *Concepts and Categories* (Harmondsworth: Penguin, 1981), pp. 188–89.

13. On the genesis of the belief that my objection is my problem, see Charles Taylor, *Sources of the Self: The Making of the Modern Identity* (Cambridge, Mass.: Harvard University Press, 1989), p. 164. Taylor's discussion of an Enlightenment ethic that cannot avow its own moral sources may help account for the seeming paradox of a liberation from Victorian constraints that nevertheless blocks out an entire region of language.

14. "The materialism in America has been an unconscious thing. Since the rise of the Industrial Revolution in England, and then the invention of all of our gadgets and contrivances and all of the things and modern conveniences — we *unconsciously* left God behind. We didn't mean to do it. We just became so involved, in getting our big bank accounts that we unconsciously forgot about God — we didn't mean to do it." And so on. *The Papers of Martin Luther King, Jr.*, vol. 2: *Rediscovering Precious Values* (Berkeley: University of California Press, 1994), p. 254: sermon at Second Baptist Church, Detroit, February 28, 1954; emphasis in the original. Why does King speak of "unconscious" forgetting when forgetting alone would suffice? Normally, after all, we just

forget our keys; we don't "unconsciously" forget them. The word unconscious conveys an obscure notion that forgotten knowledge remains in the mind waiting to be recovered like lost material in psychoanalysis; in a sense, it modernizes the theory, as old as Plato, that we retain some kinship with true being even in our estrangement from it.

15. On Jefferson and the Scottish Enlightenment, see Garry Wills, *Inventing America: Jefferson's Declaration of Independence* (Garden City, N.Y.: Doubleday, 1978).

16. My text of the "Letter from Birmingham Jail" appears in Martin Luther King Jr., *Why We Can't Wait* (New York: Harper and Row, 1964). I omit page references for this short work.

17. There is nothing self-evident or even likely about the proposition that the way to justice lies through psychology. One can listen to psychologists all day on television and radio without hearing a word about justice.

18. 347 U.S. 483.

19. David Rieff, "Victims, All?" *Harper's* (October 1991): 49.

20. In recognition of "the findings of behaviorial sciences . . . about how the human psyche works," the Catholic Church a generation ago began to liberalize annulment. Considered by some a "therapeutic" experience, annulment produces a sort of complete expurgation of the record, which now reads as though the failed marriage never existed. See the *Washington Post Weekly*, April 28, 1997, p. 10.

21. Norbert Elias, *Power and Civility*, trans. Edmund Jephcott (New York: Pantheon, 1982), p. 240. Volume 1 of *The Civilizing Process* is *The History of Manners*.

22. Matthew Arnold, "The Function of Criticism at the Present Time," in *Poetry and Criticism of Matthew Arnold*, ed. A. Dwight Culler (Boston: Houghton Mifflin, 1961), p. 250.

23. The triumph of political correctness would come not so much when every classroom had its monitor as when people felt the same quick sting of shame at making an improper statement as at making a public scene or committing any of the other infractions Elias records in his history of manners.

24. John Adams, as cited in Gordon S. Wood, "Conspiracy and the Paranoid Style: Causality and Deceit in the Eighteenth Century," *William and Mary Quarterly*, 3d ser., 39 (1982): 422.

25. Jonathan Swift, "Verses on the Death of Dr. Swift," ll. 313–14.

26. Rabelais, *The Histories of Gargantua and Pantagruel*, trans. J. M. Cohen (Baltimore: Penguin, 1965), p. 193.

27. Northrop Frye, *Anatomy of Criticism* (New York: Atheneum, 1967), p. 156.
28. John Graham, *MMPI-2: Assessing Personality and Psychopathology* (New York: Oxford University Press, 1990), p. 82.
29. "Dialogues of the Dead," in *Selected Satires of Lucian*, ed. and trans. Lionel Casson (New York: Norton, 1968), p. 201.
30. Joseph Conrad, *The Secret Agent* (Garden City, N.Y.: Doubleday, 1953), p. 37.

Chapter 9

1. Charles Taylor, *Sources of the Self: The Making of the Modern Identity* (Cambridge, Mass.: Harvard University Press, 1989), p. 174.
2. Isaiah Berlin, *The Age of Enlightenment: The Eighteenth-Century Philosophers* (New York: Mentor, 1956), pp. 31–32.
3. The overlap between Milton and Locke may suggest how it is that eighteenth-century Whigs were able to claim Milton and how colonial Americans could be both classical republicans and disciples of Locke. Dr. Johnson couples Milton and Locke in an interesting way. "Education in England has been in danger of being hurt by two of its greatest men, Milton and Locke. Milton's plan is impracticable, and I suppose has never been tried. Locke's, I fancy has been tried often enough, but is very imperfect. . . . It gives too little to literature." James Boswell, *Life of Samuel Johnson* (New York: Alfred A. Knopf, 1992), p. 878.
4. Basil Willey, "On Wordsworth and the Locke Tradition," in *English Romantic Poets: Modern Essays in Criticism*, ed. M. H. Abrams (London: Oxford University Press, 1960), p. 85.
5. On Puritanism and the search below consciousness, see Perry Miller and Thomas Johnson, *The Puritans* (New York: American Book Company, 1938), p. 284: "A large quantity of Puritan sermons were devoted . . . to exposing not merely the conscious duplicity of evil men, but the abysmal tricks which the subconscious can play upon the best of men." The human propensity for self-deception is the "self-deluding sight" of Marvell's "Eyes and Tears," which might be read alongside Milton's sonnet on his blindness. Given the psychological turn of Puritan thought, F. R. Leavis's acclamation of George Eliot as a great psychologist in the Puritan tradition seems fitting. See F. R. Leavis, *The Great Tradition* (New York: New York University Press, 1969), p. 14.
6. Northrop Frye, *The Return of Eden* (Toronto: University of Toronto Press, 1965), p. 96.

7. On "psychic revolution" and the religion of revolution, see Frank Kermode, *History and Value* (Oxford: Clarendon Press, 1989), p. 39. On Auden's figure of the Healer, "a kind of psychiatric saint or redeemer," see F. W. Dupee, "The English Literary Left" (1938), reprinted in *A Partisan Century: Political Writings from Partisan Review*, ed. Edith Kurzweil (New York: Columbia University Press, 1996), pp. 20–30.

8. Thomas Sprat, *History of the Royal Society*, ed. Jackson I. Cope and Harold Whitmore Jones (St. Louis: Washington University Studies, 1958), p. 58. In political terms, redemption from confusion and error means for Sprat, in contrast to Milton, the return to monarchy. For all that, the Puritan character of the Royal Society's program as Sprat states it is marked: "And lastly, they have begun to establish these Reformations in Philosophy, not so much, by any solemnity of Laws, or ostentation of Ceremonies; as by solid Practice, and examples: not, by a glorious Pomp of words; but by the silent, effectual, and unanswerable Arguments of real Productions" (p. 62). The bond between Locke's philosophy and that of the Royal Society is close; in fact, Locke takes up Sprat's suggestion that the "Reformation of [the education of youth] ought to be seriously examin'd by prudent Men" (p. 59).

9. Similarly, Bacon's vision of the purification of science, and the emancipation of minds from thralldom to error, is itself strongly informed by mythopoetic sources. See Michael McCanles, *Dialectical Criticism and Renaissance Literature* (Berkeley: University of California Press, 1975), chap. 1. Milton was an admirer of Bacon.

10. See the discussion of Lawrence in J. M. Coetzee, *Giving Offense: Essays on Censorship* (Chicago: University of Chicago Press, 1996), chap. 3. Do not Adam and Eve enjoy the mysteries of connubial love in a state of innocence?

11. *The Trial of Lady Chatterley: Regina v. Penguin Books Limited*, ed. C. H. Rolph (Harmondsworth, Middlesex: Penguin, 1961), p. 205.

12. Louise Rosenblatt, *Literature as Exploration* (New York: D. Appleton-Century, 1938), p. 190.

13. Stanley Fish, *Surprised by Sin: The Reader in Paradise Lost* (Berkeley: University of California Press, 1971), pp. 212–13.

14. Milton in turn dramatizes the working-through of emotion in the sonnet on his blindness, which ends with the calm of patience, and in *Samson Agonistes*, ending with "all passion spent."

15. See Michael Walzer, *Exodus and Revolution* (New York: Basic, 1985).

16. The text of the "Letter from Birmingham Jail" appears in Martin Luther King Jr., *Why We Can't Wait* (New York: Harper and Row, 1964). In the entry on

"Self-Realization" in vol. 10 of the *International Encyclopedia of Psychiatry, Psychology, Psychoanalysis, and Neurology,* the theories of self of a number of then-renowned psychologists are summarized as follows: "Man is basically constructive, accepting, creative, spontaneous, open to experience, self-aware, and self-realizing. It is parental, societal, and cultural controls, through manipulation of rewards and threats of punishment, which inhibit the otherwise natural development of self-expression and self-actualization." We catch an allusion to this myth, incompatible though it is with Protestant theology, in King's use in the "Letter" of resonant terms like "constructive" and "creative," his reference to "repressed emotions" and "chains of conformity" and citizens lacking awareness of themselves, his anecdote of the child whose mind begins to distort under the force of segregation. For King, it appears, civil rights is a branch of psychology.

17. "Les malheureux sont la puissance de la terre." King strove to make of the misery of oppression a political power. Today a broader, as it were more liberal notion of misery, the misery of wounded self-esteem, finds expression in a vacuous jargon of "empowerment."

18. Fish, *Surprised by Sin,* p. 31.

19. See Rochelle Gurstein, *The Repeal of Reticence: A History of America's Cultural and Legal Struggles over Free Speech, Obscenity, Sexual Liberation, and Modern Art* (New York: Hill and Wang, 1996).

20. M. H. Abrams, *Natural Supernaturalism: Tradition and Revolution in Romantic Literature* (New York: Norton, 1971), p. 145.

21. Thus the "power to chasten and subdue" ascribed by Wordsworth to Nature in "Tintern Abbey" belongs in Milton to God. I have mentioned Milton's sonnet on his blindness. Consider how the poet is chastened and subdued in the sestet.

22. Philip Rieff, *The Triumph of the Therapeutic: Uses of Faith after Freud* (New York: Harper and Row, 1966), p. 239.

23. Kenneth Burke, *The Philosophy of Literary Form* (Berkeley: University of California Press, 1973), p. 263.

24. *Washington Post Weekly,* June 10–16, 1996, p. 5. Even academic psychology proliferates. The American Psychological Association now has forty-nine divisions. Sheer overspending on "psychological services" may force some cutbacks (making the services themselves that much more precious), but it is overinvestment in the psychological *model* that needs correction.

25. It has been learned that "Sybil," the queen of the multiple personality craze, was fictionalized into an MP in order to "make a sellable book." See Mikkel

Borch-Jacobsen, "Sybil — the Making of a Disease: An Interview with Dr. Herbert Spiegel," *New York Review of Books*, April 24, 1997, p. 63. An equally tawdry example of psychology for the marketplace is Joe McGinniss's *Fatal Vision*. The book sold; whether its psychological thesis is valid is another question.

26. Cited in William James, "What Makes a Life Significant?" in *Essays on Morals and Faith* (Cleveland: World, 1962), p. 309.

27. Joyce Appleby, *Economic Thought and Ideology in Seventeenth-Century England* (Princeton, N.J.: Princeton University Press, 1978), p. 169. Quoted is Nicholas Barbon, writing in 1690, the year of Locke's *Essay*.

28. Alasdair MacIntyre, *After Virtue: A Study in Moral Theory* (Notre Dame, Ind.: University of Notre Dame Press, 1981), p. 29. On the introduction into corporate culture of the quackery of self-realization, see the *Washington Post Weekly*, July 8–14, 1996, pp. 19–20.

29. Even King's method of civil disobedience, as set out in the "Letter from Birmingham Jail," has steps.

30. Appleby, *Economic Thought and Ideology*, p. 171.

31. Richard Pipes, *The Russian Revolution* (New York: Alfred A. Knopf, 1990), p. 138.

32. Bruno Bettelheim, *Freud and Man's Soul* (New York: Vintage, 1984), pp. 6–7.

33. John Bradshaw, as cited in David Rieff, "Victims, All?" *Harper's* (October 1991): 53.

34. Hannah Arendt, *The Life of the Mind*, vol. 1, *Thinking* (New York: Harcourt Brace Jovanovich, 1978), p. 35. Dostoevsky's *Underground Man* knows that "even his most 'personal' longings are only commonplace quotations from Rousseau, Byron, Pushkin, Lermontov, etc., etc." Michael André Bernstein, *Bitter Carnival: Ressentiment and the Abject Hero* (Princeton, N.J: Princeton University Press, 1992), p. 105. How much more abject to find one's most personal longings spelled out in some eighth carbon copy of Rousseau, now become a guide to emotional healing.

35. Bernard Mandeville, *The Fable of the Bees* (New York: Penguin, 1989), p. 244.

Index